Tutoring Matters

Tutoring Matters

*Everything You Always Wanted
to Know about How to Tutor*

SECOND EDITION

**Tiffani Chin, Jerome Rabow,
and Jeimee Estrada**

TEMPLE UNIVERSITY PRESS
Philadelphia

TEMPLE UNIVERSITY PRESS
Philadelphia, Pennsylvania 19122
www.temple.edu/tempress

Library of Congress Cataloging-in-Publication Data

Chin, Tiffani.
    Tutoring matters : everything you always wanted to know about how
to tutor / Tiffani Chin, Jerome Rabow, and Jeimee Estrada. — 2nd ed.
        p. cm.
    Rev. ed. of: Tutoring matters / Jerome Rabow, Tiffani Chin,
Nima Fahimian. 1999.
    Includes bibliographical references.
    ISBN 978-1-4399-0740-5 (cloth : alk. paper)
    ISBN 978-1-4399-0741-2 (pbk. : alk. paper)
    ISBN 978-1-4399-0742-9 (e-book)
    1. Tutors and tutoring—United States—Handbooks, manuals, etc.
I. Rabow, Jerome. II. Estrada, Jeimee, 1986– III. Rabow, Jerome.
Tutoring matters. IV. Title.

LC41.R33 2011
371.39'4—dc22   2011002812

♾ The paper used in this publication meets the requirements of the
American National Standard for Information Sciences—Permanence
of Paper for Printed Library Materials, ANSI Z39.48-1992

Printed in the United States of America

2 4 6 8 9 7 5 3 1

Contents

Preface to the Second Edition and Acknowledgments

TIFFANI CHIN

When we wrote the first edition of *Tutoring Matters,* I had no idea how profoundly tutoring would end up shaping my career and my life. Throughout high school, college, and graduate school, tutoring was something that I did and enjoyed, but it was rarely a central part of my life. I got my first tutoring gig, as an SAT tutor, when I was a junior in high school. At the time, I was just amazed that I could receive a raise of more than two dollars an hour above what I had been making in retail, just because I had good SAT scores. In college, tutoring was community service: a way to see the city of Los Angeles and to help a group of amazing young children who needed academic support. In grad school, tutoring became, once again, a way to make money. And, through private tutoring, I entered and learned about a whole new world: the privileged and exclusive world of private-school admissions in Los Angeles. During that time, I continued to do community service, the most compelling of which was with young parolees, on early release from lockup, in South Los Angeles. These smart, articulate young men, with little to no education, were striking in their potential and in the fact that many would never step out of the lives that they had—even given their intelligence and the fact that we wanted to help them.

Overall, I enjoyed tutoring, I learned a ton from my tutoring experiences, and I felt that I had a knack for it (the kids seemed to do well, in any case). I almost always had some kind of tutoring going on, and I toyed with the idea of teaching, but I never followed through. By the time I did the fieldwork for my dissertation, I knew that I was interested in kids—although I still thought I was more interested in the academic side than in actually teaching. But the four years I spent in a fourth-grade classroom under the amazing tutelage and mentorship of career teacher Sue Shultz showed me that teaching is truly one of the highest callings we can follow. And from Ms. Shultz and her students, I learned that many students need a "team" to succeed in school. That team includes the student, the teacher, the parents, and any "others"—from teaching assistants to tutors to older siblings—who can help that student progress.

As I moved from my dissertation to my post-doc, studying students in elementary and middle schools, I learned that the school side of the "team" was often quite good. Although teachers could not always reach and help every child, they tried—and most students seemed to receive relatively good educations during the school day. But many kids struggled tremendously when they left school: They couldn't do their homework, their parents worked long hours and weren't home, their parents or caregivers didn't speak English and couldn't help with homework, or their parents just didn't know how (or did not feel confident enough) to help with homework. It seemed obvious to me that many of these students needed a tutor on their team to help them become successful—and to reach the academic potential that they already had.

And that is where the public school system helped me once again. When I talked with my friend and advisor, Meredith Phillips, a scholar who researches educational equity and cares fiercely about raising achievement, she didn't downplay my concerns. She didn't push me to just focus on publishing my dissertation. Together we created EdBoost—a nonprofit learning center dedicated to improving educational equity by providing educational services (especially tutoring) to low- and moderate-income families. After a few years of offering free classes over the summer, we opened the doors to our learning center in 2004.

And so, I write this new introduction while sitting in my office in EdBoost. I tutor every day and have dedicated my career to providing high-quality tutoring to students. I supervise about thirty college-student tutors a year, and we serve at least two hundred fifty students a year in our learning center (more if you count the SAT-preparation classes and college-counseling programs we run throughout the Los Angeles area). So this book and the notion that everyone can tutor (but that everyone who tutors should try to tutor the absolute best that they can!) have become very dear to me.

I hope that this second edition provides practical tips and insights that the first edition lacked. For these additions, I am deeply indebted to EdBoost's amazing students (I learn something new from them every day) and our incredible, dedicated tutoring staff—thank you all for the care and effort that you put into working with our students (thanks especially to Sunny Tamrakar, Emi Rourke, Erin Moore, Genevieve Richards, Nina Abonal, and Brittany Ramos, exceptional tutors who have really helped make EdBoost the place that it is)! The more I watch our staff tutor, the more I have hope that truly amazing young people in America can make a difference and help the next generation be even better. I also thank all of you, our readers, and I hope that this book inspires you to work with and to help as many students as you can.

Last, but certainly not least, thank you to my wonderful husband, Todd, for all his support, no matter how many hours I spend at EdBoost and how much work I bring home. And, to my sweet baby, Quinn, I sincerely hope that you'll one day know the joy that comes from teaching— and learning from—others.

JEROME RABOW

Twelve years have passed since the publication of the first edition of *Tutoring Matters*. As the finishing touches on this second edition are being completed, I wish I could report that the gap in education between those who attend schools that provide them with a sense of possibility and hope and those who are exposed to the savage inequalities of racism, sexism, classism, and homophobia has diminished greatly. It has not. A sprinkling of dedicated teachers and principals, a curriculum aimed at inclusiveness, and an inspiring superintendent continue to be exceptions rather than the everyday practices of schools and school systems. No national will has developed to ensure that all our children know and feel that schooling, learning, and committed teachers are their rights as citizens. The idea that excellence in education is the most essential foundation of a more equitable, more just America has no national commitment.

Tutoring Matters is a modest offering in this storm of unfairness. Although "life is unfair," much of the unfairness has to do with the injustices created by the ways that schools teach. *Tutoring Matters* will help tutors appreciate and learn how an honest, supportive, compassionate, committed relationship can make a difference in the life of another.

Because learning can "lead" to imagination and hope, to pride and confidence, you, the tutor, can be rewarded in ways that perhaps you may never have experienced before. Discovering that your dedication, compassion, understanding, patience, and support of your tutee can instill hope, confidence, and excitement is awe-inspiring. Discovering that *you* can make a difference in the lives of others is empowering. With this understanding and awareness, we hope that you see that it is now your responsibility to ensure that more of these processes occur in schools, families, communities, and our country.

A key individual who facilitated this new edition is Jeimee Estrada, who after taking my class in public education organized a seminar with her sorority sisters from Lambda Theta Alpha Latin Sorority, Inc. This class, which was known as the Promotora program, tutored older Latina women and was a satisfying and enriching class for myself and the participants. Jeimee became a facilitator for a number of other classes and saw ways of improving the first edition of *Tutoring Matters* by going over notes that we had collected and reviewing every word of the manuscript. Jeimee is pursuing a career in public policy devoted to education. I am personally grateful for her past presence in my classes and in my life.

Two other students, who have since graduated and were extremely helpful and diligent in the reediting of this second edition, are Shannon Mercogliano and Katya Rodriguez. Shannon is dedicated to combating the inequity between dominants and subordinates through action and information. Katya is embarking on a two-year commitment in the Peace Corps; after this endeavor, she will be pursuing a career in public policy, with a focus on international relations.

My class in the Honors College at UCLA, "Dominants and Subordinates in Public Education," continues to be a source of inspiration and hope. These outstanding students—many of whom came to understand their privilege, while others overcame their pain to develop compassion and understanding—shared their time with tutees, fellow students, and their facilitators. The facilitators for this Honors Class have included Azin Ahmadi, Jeimee Estrada, Donna Rahimian, and Pauline Yeghnazar. They contributed enormously to the development of students and the success of the class. Each of them brings a unique vision to the students. The students in my most recent Honors Classes deserve recognition. In the fall of 2009, the students were Azin Ahmadi, Maeva Asare, Bryson Banks, Jun Dizon, Allyse Engelder, Michael Gallin, Jr., Michael Ghalchi, Oghomwen Igiesuorobo, Tamlyn Lee, Noah Lehman, Ginger

McCartney, Tessa McClellan, Shannon Mercogliano, Shawn Moshrefi, Daniel Moss, Amanda Murillo, Priscilla Peffer, Brittany Ryan, Daniela Sanchez, Colin Valencia, Sabena Vaswani, Laura Watson, Melanie Woods, Haijing Zhang, and Xiaoyan Zhang. In the spring of 2009, the members of this class included Sarah Barker, Bianca Bazil, Subir Bhatia, Shaye Blegen, Heather Boberg, Teresa Cho, Leonardo Cortes, Michael Dreim, Sade Elhawary, Kevin Fukuyama, Angelica Galang, Jaime Garza, Christine Gibson, Lauren Goldman, Sabrina Gutierrez, Ester Jeong, Colin King, Minji Kwon, Ruth Lawanson, Marissa Lee, Tiffany McCormack, Nicolas Molina, Socorro Morales, Emily Perez, Samuel Rosenblum, Harry Sa, Mitchel Seaman, Martha Silva, Ashley Sizemore-Smale, Mohammad Tehrani, Anniesha Thomas, Chase Turay, and Mary Yeh.

This second edition is dedicated to the children of the world who receive less in education than they deserve. It is also dedicated to Matthew and Zachary Rabow and Lucie and Liliana Berman, the four grandchildren whom Roslyn Rabow and I share. Although I have met many wonderful teachers who model the finest qualities of a deep educator, Jill Weston deserves special acknowledgment. Finally, there is my special teacher, Roslyn Rabow, who continues to provide me with endless lessons about human relationships and hope.

JEIMEE ESTRADA

I had the good fortune to become involved with this new edition of *Tutoring Matters* as a result of a course I took from Jerry Rabow and a research assistantship with him. The class was one of the most engaging experiences I have had in higher education. I read the first edition of this book in that class, and I was drawn to it, along with other research in education—specifically research on how underprivileged students move through our education system. Tutoring, as many who will read this manual already know or will come to see, is meaningful in so many ways and is particularly important for students who have fallen behind or who learn a little differently.

I have been especially drawn to the tutoring process and have pursued a deeper understanding of it because of my own experiences in education. I am a first-generation college—and now master's level—graduate. As President Barack Obama says in his book *The Audacity of Hope,* "I am a prisoner of my own biography" (2006: 10). Coming from an underprivileged background, where my family and I fought for educational opportunities that weren't readily available to us, I have developed a keen understanding of the value of individuals in advancing a student's educational career. At an early age, I learned that tutoring (and mentoring) is one very powerful avenue through which those who have less can achieve more and those who have more can share the benefits of their privilege.

During my work on this book with Jerry and Tiffani, I participated in the founding of a tutoring program for non-English-speaking, adult Latina women in downtown Los Angeles. With my Lambda Theta Alpha sorority sisters at UCLA, we developed lessons, fund-raised, and traveled downtown with one goal—helping the women learn basic English communication skills for work, for daily activities such as banking and grocery shopping, and even for understanding their kids a little better. Jerry and I developed a class to supervise our tutoring sessions and document our tutees' progress. It was through these experiences—and through study of the works of Paulo Freire, Sylvia Ashton-Warner, John Dewey, James W. Loewen, and Herbert Kohl—that I learned so much about the process of tutoring. The class met weekly, and we discovered that we could impact the lives of human beings in special ways *that were more rewarding to us* than to them. I also spent time searching notes from the tutoring experiences of other UCLA students for examples that would demonstrate the principles outlined in this book and would provide real-world examples of the problems tutors face when they deal with differences in race, gender, sexual orientation, social class, and age. With the help of many students (Janet Ruiz, Destiny Almogue, Ashley Sizemore, Alan Secretov, Jami Hewitt, and others), I collected and learned from hundreds of tutoring experiences for this book.

My own experiences and understanding of the educational system led me to go on to complete a master's degree in public policy at USC and a fellowship with Education Pioneers. I have since moved to Sacramento to become involved in policy decision making in K–12 education with the California Legislative Analyst's Office. On a more personal note, my family, sorority sisters, and fiancé have all been wonderfully inspiring and supporting of my passion for equity in education. I cannot thank them enough for their love.

I hope that this book can make a difference in the lives of those who read it and those who receive the benefits of their tutoring. I dedicate this book to all the students who are at risk of falling through the many cracks in our education system—may your own perseverance and intervention from caring individuals result in your success.

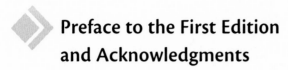

Preface to the First Edition and Acknowledgments

WE WOULD EACH like to begin by describing how we came to write this manual and by thanking the people who made it possible.

JERRY RABOW

This manual probably began some thirty years ago when I was shocked to discover what was going on with my children in one of the "better" public schools in Los Angeles. As a new professor in my first teaching position at UCLA and the father of two young boys, I deliberately settled close enough to a public school with a reputation for excellence.

I took it for granted that "excellence" was just that, a series of good teachers, academically high standards, and the most advanced technology for learning. But what I discovered in this "excellent" public school was something else entirely, which is illuminated by three pivotal incidents.

The first incident occurred when my youngest child told us that he was required to lie down on his mat so that he and all the other children could "benefit" from rest period. At that point I began to wonder about the professed standard of excellence. How could teachers or administrators assume that all children wanted and needed rest at the same time? Was this really for the children's benefit? This was the beginning of my understanding of the horrors of public education in the United States. Schools tend to standardize all. The rules are unmistakable: you fit in, and you conform.

I found the second event, a few years later, even more disturbing. My older son was participating in the required run around the track and was sent home for wearing boxer shorts. He was told that since his boxer shorts were hanging one inch below his gym shorts, he was being sexually provocative. He was also told that we, his parents, must purchase jockey shorts. I could not accept this. I went to the school with my son and argued with a gym teacher who wore short sleeves and no tie—an outfit he would have been sent home for when I was growing up. We were told by the principal and the gym teacher that the boxer shorts were too provocative to young women in this "excellent" junior high school. Neither the principal nor the teacher was able to respond favorably to my comments about shifts in norms and etiquette or about individual taste and freedom of choice. My son took his demerit. The banality and stupidity of rules based on such standards was impressed upon me. But even more disturbing was the attitude that came across loud and clear: there will be no questioning the rules. The rules are for your own good. We know what is best for you. The idea that children might know what is good for them is unthinkable.

The third incident took place when my son stayed home because of a religious holiday. The teacher gave an important exam on this holiday and would not allow any make-ups to the ten children who stayed at home. The punishment for religious beliefs was the final blow to my faith in public education. I realized that something must be fundamentally wrong with public education in this country. Schools seemed to cultivate conformity and obedience, destroy passion and initiative, and have little respect for difference.

It was then that I began my process of self-education. I was determined to teach my students that there were better ways to teach and learn. I elected to teach a sociology class in my department, and with the advantage of never having studied the sociology of education, I could start fresh with my own self-education, and I did. In the sixties, a set of critics/writers were deeply critical of public education, and I read them assiduously. Herb Kohl, Jonathan Kozol, Neil Postman, John Holt, Paolo Freire, and Sylvia Ashton-Warner documented the horrors of public education and illuminated ways in which children should be taught. These readings led me to some of the classic thinkers in the field, such as John Dewey, A. S. Neill, Plato, and Aristotle. Reading and my teaching led me to collaborate with a colleague and a graduate student to write *Cracks in the Classroom Wall* (Robischon, Rabow, and Schmidt

1975). The book was historical and critical but did not offer much in the way of tangible direction for students desirous of enacting change.

By this time I was requesting that my students tutor as part of their educational experience and bring their tutoring problems to my classroom for discussion. Although satisfying and educational, these mini-lessons and lectures proved to be limited in scope. Out of my dissatisfaction, the idea for this book started to take hold. Some ten years ago I began telling students to take notes when they tutored. Before these notes could be transformed into a tutoring manual, four more events had to transpire.

The first event involved a young student, Nima Fahimian, who took an honors course with me entitled "Freud, Fairy Tales, and Feminism," then a class in education, where he took up the tutoring process that I required of all my students. His confrontation with a tutee who seemed unwilling to learn presented him with a challenge, and the challenge provided him with a direction. His interest in and dedication to public-school children continued for four years in conjunction with his UCLA education and courses in his pre-med major. His effort to help me collect notes and work with tutors by organizing their tutoring schedules and matching tutees' hours and needs with tutors' hours and needs made the tutoring venture less chaotic and more focused.

Coinciding with Nima's efforts came strong support from the UCLA Office of Instructional Development, the second major event that led to the development of this tutoring manual. This office, under the leadership of Parvin Kassaie, assigned Cynthia Chavez to work with me. Together they helped to bring about a coherent tutoring venture.

A third event had to do with the publishing of an excellent book, *Writing Ethnographic Field Notes* (1995), by Robert Emerson, Rachel Fretz, and Linda Shaw. This book encouraged students to develop an awareness beyond the content of their note taking. We brought the authors' ideas to class, looked at various tutoring incidents in light of their categories, and found the students thinking more critically about what they were doing.

A fourth event was the arrival of Tiffani Chin, the second author of this manual, in graduate school at UCLA in the Sociology Department in 1996. She was a grader for my undergraduate class in education. Her grasp of the tutoring issues, sensitivity to students and their note-taking process, and passion about education made the final contribution toward making this book a reality. We now had field notes galore, two very involved and concerned students, and myself. Out of this combination would come a tutoring manual.

Although I am concerned about many aspects of U.S. life, I am especially concerned about the way we teach and educate our children. I hope this manual will contribute to a better education for all, one that encourages and supports the development of deep interests, passions, freedom of choice, freedom of expression, and all other human potentialities.

By now a number of tutees have grown and have entered adulthood. Ingrid and Amanda Castro, tutees who came to America speaking not a word of English, have gone on to college. They call me every year to thank me for what their tutors gave them. May all tutors have such an experience.

This manual is dedicated to all children, but especially to Matthew and Zachary Rabow and Lucie Carolina Berman, the grandchildren that Roslyn Rabow and I share and who enrich my life—only a part of what I am so lucky to have with Roslyn.

TIFFANI CHIN

I've been tutoring for the past seven years. In two instances, it's been my job, working with upper-middle-class students on homework and test prep. The other two times I've tutored, I've been a volunteer working with inner-city elementary and high school students in Los Angeles. Although tutoring gets easier with every experience, I'm always left with unanswered questions. I can say with no hesitation that I've never entered a tutoring situation without wondering, "Aren't they going to show me what to do?"

My most recent foray into tutoring has involved working with a group of high-school-aged guys, recently on parole from L.A. County lockup. I remember sitting in the warehouse that had become our tutoring center and asking the coordinator to come up with writing topics for me to give the students. I had been tutoring for years and was in the middle of writing this manual. Still, I was certain that I couldn't come up with writing prompts that would be compelling to minority teenage boys whose experiences on the streets, in gangs, and in jail had set their lives spinning in vastly different directions from my protected, middle-class, academic existence. What if they thought I was stupid? What if I offended them? What if I made them angry? What if I just flat out bored them?

But in the end, I not only came up with my own writing topics, I did it because I came to understand, and in some ways befriend, this group of guys I previously would have feared. They taught me simple knowledge, such as slang terms for drugs and crimes and how to read graffiti tags. But I also learned something about why a kid would become a Crip and what it's like for one gang member to pick a fight with a crosstown rival. I will never again listen in the same way to a newscaster or a politician or a policeman talk about gangs. Working with those kids taught me a lot about a group of people whom everyone talks about but who rarely get a chance to speak for themselves.

And that's one of the best parts of tutoring. You gain insights into people and situations you would never have been exposed to otherwise. Whether it's gang life or just the everyday life of a second-grade boy, it opens up a whole new world. It's also a way to get your hands dirty, to really do something. I like to be able to voice my opinion in social and political debates, and I feel that my tutoring gives me a greater right to do it. Tutoring has been my way of putting my effort where my mouth is.

I began graduate school, the path to spending my life in sociology, because I wanted to study social issues and problems. I tutor because I want to play a role in solving them. In writing this manual, I'm thrilled to be able to play a part in empowering others to do the same.

I would like to thank Jerry and Nima for allowing me into their project. I want to thank all of my tutees, past and present, for it is their work with me that lies behind all the insights I have lent to this book. Thanks also to Bob Emerson, who has taught me many of the skills and techniques that went into the creation of this manual. Most of all, I want to thank my family, especially my mom, who have supported me in everything I've ever wanted to do.

To all future tutors—I wish you luck, and the joy that tutoring has given me.

NIMA FAHIMIAN

The motivation behind writing this tutoring manual was cultivated by my own frustrations and struggles in educating children. What seemed a relatively simple task in 1993 soon became a challenge that only my patience and understanding of the significance of my role as a tutor could overcome. Having tutored university students throughout my college career, I felt confident about taking the opportunity to tutor children at Mar Vista Family Center in Culver City—a nonprofit, community-based organization involved in educating and counseling immigrant, poor, and minority families. I soon realized that my extensive university-level knowledge in a multitude of academic areas was not enough to tutor the two second graders assigned to me.

Shocked by this first experience, I employed every theory and view I had read in Peter McLaren, Mike Rose, Sylvia Ashton-Warner, Paulo Freire, and others discussed in Professor Jerome Rabow's education courses, in which students' field experiences were heavily emphasized. I was fortunate to have Professor Rabow's approach to education and his philosophy of experiential learning as my guiding principles. I then learned from experience and from my tutees how to put my knowledge and skills to work. Soon I realized that my education was a tool, subject to modifications and transformation through real-life experiences, and I suspect this is what Professor Rabow wanted me to learn.

By contributing to this tutoring manual, my hope is that some of you will develop strong feelings about education in this country. As George Dennison mentions in his book, *The Lives of Children,* we do not need genius to bring life into education. What we need are leaders with strong vision who respect children and their right to freedom of choice. We need leaders who can realize children's energy and are willing to promote their curiosity and willingness to explore what is genuinely exhilarating to them.

I thank Professor Rabow for his guidance and friendship. I also appreciate the great work and expertise of Tiffani Chin that helped produce this manual. The hard work and generosity of all the sociology students and tutors who contributed their notes throughout the years must be recognized, although there are too many to mention by name here. I thank my father and mother, Dr. Parviz and Mina Fahimian, for all their support and effort to understand me and let me grow. Most of all, I acknowledge the great work of Ms. Sarah Z. Ter-Minasyan in establishing the "Saturday Tutorial Program" and thank her for her most valuable friendship.

Tutoring for me has been a journey that presented many unexpected challenges and learning experiences, while allowing me to touch individuals whom I would never otherwise have met or found something in common with. Tutoring is a lot like medicine: I am amazed every day when I discover a connection between what I did as an undergraduate and what I do now as a medical student, and I'm sure the same connection will manifest itself when I become a physician.

I hope you enjoy this book and allow yourselves to learn from your tutees and colleagues.

THE THREE OF US would like to thank and acknowledge Antonette Baretto, Annie Markowitz, and Jenny Wong, who facilitated the completion of this manual. Many thanks also to Bobbe Needham for her thoughtful, considered, and sensitive work on the manuscript.

We also want to recognize and appreciate the tutors who have worked with tutees and contributed their field notes, interest, and imagination to this manual, and the teachers and administrators who welcomed them into their classrooms and tutoring centers over the past few years. We thank the many concerned teachers and administrators who worked with us to provide the tutoring sites, especially Lucia Diaz, Risa Getchman, Morgan P. Hatch, Jr., Gloria Martinez, and Sharmen C. Taylor. We also acknowledge the hard work of Cynthia Chavez, who along with Nima Fahimian was the first tutoring coordinator. They were supported from the office of Parvin Kassaie, Field Studies, UCLA. Excellent coordination was continued by Makhameh Maggie Kharrazi, Tiffany Hamilton, Seina Takamatsu, and Roger (Sung Gon) Kim.

We thank all the students from the "Sociology of Education" course who shared their time with tutees and whose experiences with those tutees enriched the class and everyone else's tutoring experiences. We have tried here to personally acknowledge the tutors who specifically contributed to this manual—any omissions are the fault of incomplete records. Thanks to Janet Abronson, Jacob Ahdoot, Adelaida Alfiler, Chantelle Ameli, Elizabeth Antunez, Allison Appleby, John Aquino, Laura Aquino, Anita Avalos, Kecia Ayabe, Eliazer Ayala, Bobby Babai, Esmeralda Barajas, Thomas Barnes, Mary Barr, Jovy-Marie Bayani, Vivian Benitez, Kimberly Berg, Nina Bermudez, Marie Botello, Ashley Braband, Nikki Brinton, Bernadette Bullock, Kim Broadbeck, Eleyna Byington, Darren Capeloto, Tarek Captan, Jennifer Carmel, John Catetti, Lori Chang, Jessica Chavez, Lisa Chinn, Ahra Cho, Hee-Jin Choi, Rose Chung, Deatra Clinton, Veronica Contreras, Maha Dakhil, Marianne de Francia, Lakan de Leon, Yusef Daulatzai, Laurel Davis, Zalika Davis, Dianne Dizon, Andrea Duncan, Trisha Elegino (TRE), Ernso Ermo, Donna Estacio, Wendy Estevez, Tina Farris, Jennifer Fields, Anthony

Fong, Rafael Gaeta, Juana Garcia, Jessica Gawitt, Brenda Generazio, Guelsy Gomez, Maricela Gomez, Minerva Gomez, Marianne Gomis, Paulina Gonzalez, Sara Gonzales, Andre Grissette, Antonia Guerrero, Elena Guerrero, Araceli Gutierrez, Rene Haloossim, Simon Hamlin, Tiffany Hamilton, Vanessa Hartstrom, Sandra Harvey, Michael Haskell, Justine Henry, Belinda Hernandez, Marisela Hernandez, Jasmine Hines, Aiyana Holm, LaShell Holton, Joyce Hu, Suzanna Huesca, Trang Hugnh, Teresa Hui, Kimberley Ingram, Milaine Isaac, Jennifer Jung, Jennifer Kane, Ani Karayan, Hanie Kim, Jessica Kim, Joy Kim, Roger Kim, Young-Ki Kim, Gloria King, Patra Kittichanthira, Elizabeth Kyriacou, Claire Lagao, Christine LeBard, Teresa Lanz, Edna Lopez, Oralia Lua, Elsa Luna, Howana Lundy, Shawn Mai, Sandra Margulies, Scott Markham, Colleen Martich, Lisa Martinelli, Denise Martinez, Thelma Martinez, Brady Matoian, Rebecca McConnell, Kendra Melendez, Joshua Mendelsohn, Deborah Mendoza, Tesz Millan, Jennifer Mickey, Erika Miller, Sylvia Miravet, Scott Mitchell, Christina Montanez, Billie Monzon, Natasha Moradi, Cheryl Morris, Maya Muneno, Christian Munguia, LeBaron Myers, Kevin Nakahara, Nazanin Nassir, Nga Nguy, Justine Nguyen, Christina Nunez, Ijeoma Odu, Eddie Palm, Pamela Park, Leah Pate, Hope Penkala, Rachelle Pensanti, Kelly Petriccione, Darcy Purdy, Natalie Rayes, Lucia Reyes, Vashira Rhodes, Tammy Richardson, Maisha Riddlesprigger, Teresa Robles, Yanitza Rodriguez, Jonathan Rosales, Roselma Samala, Edith Sanchez, Michael Schwartz, Donovan Seno, Angela Seo, Kana Shahabi, Angel Sim, Paula Smith, Joseph Simbillo, Natalie Soohoo, Linda Steele, Branda Stewart, Jocelyn Su, Jenny Sugimura, Brian Suitzer, Kevin Sved, Nicole Swan, Margaret Swift, Nancy Takahashi, Seina Takamatsu, Paulino Tamayo, Polly Tattersall, Tricia Taylor, Jacki Tenerelli, Tara Topper, Karla Torres, Olga Torres, Sigrin Torres, Dinh Tran, Huy Tran, Aarin Ulrich, Joanne Valencia, Priscilla Veres, Yvette Villalobos, Brian Waldman, Chelsea Walsh, Jocelyn Wang, Lisa Ward, Alicia Way, Ben Weitz, Ryan Welsh, Grace Wen, Terri Wong, Amy Wood, Katrin Yadgari, Allison Yen, Mitsue Yokota, Duk Yoon, Joy Yoshikawa, Kevin Yuen, and Margarita Zepeda.

Finally, we wish to acknowledge the contributions that all of our tutees have made, both to the education of UCLA students and to this book. As a way of returning part of what they have given us, a portion of all royalties from this book will be given to the UCLA Field Studies Program for its continuing support of experiential education.

Tutoring Matters

Introduction

E TUTOR, and receive tutoring, all the time. When a classmate or colleague shows us how to do a difficult homework problem or to use a new piece of office equipment, we have been tutored. When we help a younger relative sound out a word or teach a parent or grandparent to program a new cell phone, we are doing a bit of tutoring ourselves. Every one-on-one teaching moment is a kind of tutoring, and most of us "tutor" naturally and easily all the time.

However, entering into more "official" tutoring—whether it involves signing up for a class with a community-service requirement or committing to helping students once or twice a week at a local school or community center—can be daunting. It is easy to put off tutoring ("I'll go sign up next week when I have a little more time.") or to argue that we would not be good at it ("I don't know how to teach math!"). But as easy as it is to make excuses, it is just as easy to tutor someone. And, more importantly, tutors can be essential components to students' academic success.

Tutoring, by its very nature, is individualized—and that is what makes it such a great complement to classroom teaching (and, for some students, an absolutely necessary supplement to classroom learning). Unlike teachers, who often have to follow a set curriculum, tutors get to teach exactly what students need to know at that moment, and they can tailor those lessons so they fit the needs, interests, and abilities of each particular student. Tutors also build individual relationships with their students—and they can do so quickly, because each tutoring experience includes just them: two people sitting at a table together, trying to learn. Because tutoring is so personalized, it has the potential to make big impacts quickly.

By virtue of being responsible for a room of twenty to thirty students, teachers must teach to some specific part of the class. Do they teach to the struggling students (leaving the advanced students bored and not living up to their potential)? Do they teach to the advanced students (leaving the struggling students to fall farther behind each year)? Do they teach to the middle, inevitably leaving some kids bored and others bewildered? Out of necessity, every teacher makes a choice, but that choice always leaves some students who need outside help.

Outside help can come in a variety of forms. Some students who require extra help will have parents who can provide additional help and practice at home. Others are lucky enough to have teachers, siblings, relatives, or neighbors who can help them when they get confused in class. Still others attend neighborhood centers or afterschool programs where they can get help (and that help often comes from volunteer tutors!). But, for these students, their ability to master the school year's material and then to move on to master the next year's material depends on getting help outside the classroom. When students do not get that outside help, they start each school year farther and farther behind their classmates. They come to school each September knowing that the work will be too hard. Each year, they slip closer to the point where it will be impossible for them to catch up. Many of these students will, one day, just slip away and stop going to school.

The act of tutoring is the act of saying to someone else, "Let me help you learn." And, most of the time, the material you will be teaching is material that you are comfortable with. Almost every adult can help a small child practice reading (read together, talk about new words, ask questions, make sure that the student "gets" the funny parts of the story), counting (so many children do not understand the patterns in numbers and just need someone to count with them), or basic math (the number of middle and high school students who struggle with pre-algebra and algebra because they do not know their times tables is staggering!). Almost every competent English speaker can help someone practice English just by talking, explaining, and being patient. Some tutoring is specialized. Not everyone can help with AP Calculus or SAT prep. But a lot of tutoring just comes down to having the courage to be confident in the skills that you have and being willing to try to pass those skills on.

Over the past decade, the United States has undergone continuous education reform, with very little discernible impact on student learning and skills. Over the next decades, we will no doubt continue to change academic standards, to reconstitute "failing schools," and to devise new learning programs that should raise student performance. These long-term goals are noble—and, if they work, these reforms will change the face of our country. But, they are long-term goals that will come too late for many students, even if they do work.

Every individual who is reading this book can make an immediate and visible difference in at least one student's life. Helping a second grader become a fluent reader will open the doors of literature, science, history, and even math word problems to that child for a lifetime. Helping a third grader master times tables means that math will be less onerous and less tedious for that child for as long as he or she is in school, making it more likely that the student will stay in school, go to college, and succeed in a rewarding career. And helping an adult learn to speak English or learn to read will change the scope of that person's job prospects (and ability to navigate and enjoy life) forever. Although tutoring is simple, and often easy, it is powerful. And, with this book, we very much hope to ease people's fears about tutoring, to help them see how other people manage some of the difficulties involved in tutoring, and to provide some practical tips to make tutoring more effective.

Because tutoring sessions are so personalized and individual, it is impossible to tell someone "how to tutor." Every student, tutor, and tutoring session is different—and one of the best "rules" you can bring to a tutoring session is to be flexible and willing to change your ideas and strategies every time you begin to tutor. However, there are ways to make tutoring easier, less scary and stressful, and more effective. *Tutoring Matters* aims to show you those strategies and guidelines and help you navigate your tutoring experience.

This book draws on two sources of information. The main principles of the book (and the quotes that demonstrate those principles) come from hundreds of undergraduates' experiences tutoring in Los Angeles. As members of an education class with a community-service requirement, these students worked with students in a wide range of settings (from schools, to community centers, to ESL programs) and reported their experiences in field notes. From those field notes, we gleaned reports of successes and failures, and we put together a set of general guidelines for beginning tutoring, building relationships with students, teaching academic material, dealing with "differences" between tutors and tutees, dealing with other adults in the tutoring setting, and saying good-bye to tutees. We include a wide range of field notes in each chapter, because we believe that the best way to learn how to tutor is to be a "fly on the wall" in other people's tutoring sessions. We hope that the field notes that we have included can transport you to a variety of tutoring sessions and let you learn from the successes and the mistakes that other tutors have made. (Note: The names of tutors and students have been changed to protect their confidentiality.)

Finally, in this edition, we have scattered tip boxes throughout the chapters. We have pulled these tips from the experiences of the authors as well as the tutors at EdBoost Learning Center, a nonprofit tutoring center in Los Angeles, where undergraduate and graduate students tutor more than two hundred students each year in grades kindergarten through twelve. We have designed these boxes to give you more practical tips on how to work with students. Over the years, readers have been grateful for the help and courage that they gained from *Tutoring Matters,* but they have felt a little lost regarding exactly *how* to introduce themselves to a shy student or exactly *how* to figure out which book is the right book to read with a struggling reader. We hope that the tip boxes included in this edition provide some concrete advice that can make tutoring smoother and more fun for everyone involved.

Everyone who tutors knows that some days are good and some days are bad. Sometimes, you leave a tutoring session feeling like a superhero. Other times, tutoring sessions end in tears (for the student, usually, but sometimes for the tutor as well). But most of the time, tutoring is a simple thing: It involves helping someone learn something that you already know. It means taking skills and information that you possess and making them simpler, less scary, or just more relevant to a student's life. Tutoring also means being a cheerleader and pushing students to work harder, to try harder, and to learn better. And, for many tutors, tutoring also becomes a way to push themselves to become better communicators, better listeners, more patient, more kind, more understanding of others, and more understanding of the world.

Pushing past the excuses and taking the plunge to sign up to tutor will be one of the best and most rewarding decisions you have ever made. You will not only enrich the lives of your students but find that your students enrich your life as well. We sincerely hope that *Tutoring Matters* gives you the knowledge, support, and courage to start tutoring today.

1 ▶ Attitudes, Anxieties, and Expectations

FEAR AND ANXIETY are natural emotions we often feel in our daily encounters and interactions with others. New situations, such as tutoring, in which people start out as strangers, frequently heighten these feelings of insecurity. Furthermore, tutoring is not just any new situation. The great challenges, expectations, and social complications it brings increase normal fears and anxieties. When reflecting upon their first days of tutoring, most tutors describe feelings similar to those that the following new tutor reported:

> I was extremely nervous, since I was not very sure if the kids would like me. I felt a great deal of pressure, since I had never tutored in my life. I thought I could not offer the children anything, because I was questioning my abilities to teach. In addition, would the teacher like me? Would I get along with her? Then, scared and intimidated by the size and the beauty of the school, I did not know if I should turn back and run or walk into the supervisor's office with confidence and integrity.

Even if such anxious feelings subside after the first day, as the setting becomes somewhat familiar and the tutor-tutee relationship gets underway, new fears arise throughout the tutoring experience. Fear, anxiety, and insecurity are intrinsic to tutoring. Intricate situations and emotionally taxing incidents can make tutors feel helpless and even threaten the educational progress of tutees. As complicated and discouraging as such feelings may be, your knowledge and application of certain attitudes and practices will equip you with basic methods of dealing with first-day concerns and ongoing problems.

Many tutors share the same fears and anxieties, and we have found that implementing certain attitudes and practices can ease most of those concerns. New tutors often worry about connecting with their tutees: Will my student like me? Will I like my new student? Will I be able to fit in and to relate to a student who is very different from me in terms of gender, age, race, ethnicity, religion, or socioeconomic status? Will I be able to teach everything that needs to be taught? Will I succeed as a tutor?

Such questions are common and reasonable for anyone entering a new or unfamiliar tutoring situation, but they need not be paralyzing. In spite of your fears and anxieties, rewarding experiences will emerge once you have connected with your tutee. When your tutees realize that you tutor because you care and that you are genuinely interested in them and in having a strong tutor-tutee bond, tutoring becomes an experience filled with moments of pleasure, satisfaction, and joy. Eventually, your fears and anxieties recede. Tutors often come out of their tutoring relationships with a deeper sense of satisfaction than they had expected. Reactions often include such sentiments as, "I got so much more than I offered," "He'll never know how much he affected me," and "I found this experience to be the most important thing I've ever done."

We have found that most successful tutoring partnerships spring from a common underlying concept: acceptance. It is the most basic and essential foundation for a strong, successful tutoring relationship and thus the basis for the attitudes and practices we discuss later in this chapter. The first step in acceptance is adopting a certain set of attitudes. These attitudes ease tutors' fears and shape tutors into better and more open teachers. The essential attitudes for tutoring, all flowing from tutor acceptance, involve giving up expectations, displaying enthusiasm and interest, and feeling empathy. These attitudes lay the foundation for a number of effective tutoring practices. We have found that three general practices are very useful in creating a comfortable and successful tutoring relationship: being patient, being observant and asking questions, and understanding students on their own level.

NORMAL FEARS AND ANXIETIES

The good news is that most tutors overcome their initial fears and anxieties about tutoring. Knowing what to expect and knowing that most of your fellow tutors have felt the same concerns may alleviate your anxieties. Tutoring is not easy; it will constantly confront you with your own weaknesses and failings. Facing those weaknesses can be difficult. For someone who has just committed to helping others, it can be devastating. But because almost every tutor experiences these feelings, almost every successful tutor has overcome them.

Will the Students Like Me?

Many new tutors worry about whether their students will like them. Will the tutee accept the tutor as a friend and a role model? As a female tutor reflected on her experience, she expressed a general concern of many tutors: "Although I do like children, I do not know that I am very approachable, for some reason. Maybe it is because I do not have much contact with children in my daily activities. I suppose I am not quite used to being around them nor know how to treat them, or, at least, do not have much experience in doing so."

Like this tutor, many tutors worry that they will not be compatible with children in general or with their specific tutees. Besides worrying about how kids will react to their personalities, tutors worry about how tutees will see them and what first impressions they may form. Tutors are often afraid that they will not look like the type of person the tutee will want to work with.

Most tutors wake up on the morning of their first day of tutoring anxious about what to wear, how to do their hair, and how they look overall. One male tutor wrote, "Maybe I would be looked up to as a big brother, or maybe because of my six foot three inch stature they would be afraid of me."

Will I Like My Students?

Tangential to the previous concern is the question of whether you will like the students you are supposed to tutor. What if a child is obnoxious or completely unmotivated? What if a tutee does not want to be there or deliberately asks things that you cannot answer and makes tutoring difficult?

Whenever you are assigned to spend a lot of time with someone whom you do not know, it is natural to wonder whether you will get along. And obviously, if you have been assigned to help someone, it is normal to wonder whether you will really want to once you get to know the person.

Will I Be Able to Fit in with and Understand Kids Who Are Different?

In tutoring, differences between tutors and tutees are a very big concern, especially because tutors and tutees often come from different backgrounds. Although many tutors want to work through these differences, the life differences separating many tutors and tutees scare some tutors away. Is it possible for an upper-middle-class white university student or business executive to form a close relationship with a young African American student from the inner city? Can a female tutor from a sheltered background ever hope to relate to a street-tough gang member? It is easy to wonder. And because people often interact with a rather homogeneous group of people in their everyday lives, many people find the notion of tutoring "other" types of people intimidating.

Even tutors who are confident that they can form relationships with students from different backgrounds sometimes worry that they will not be appropriate role models for students who may have to face radically different life experiences than they have ever known. This fear occurred to one white female student at a nonprofit community-outreach program in Los Angeles that works to empower minority children (mostly African American students, with some Latino students):

> At the beginning, it was very difficult. I had many fears and wondered how I could possibly make an impact on anyone's life. I kept questioning why these minority children would look up to an upper-middle-class white person who is almost their own age. In addition, I also questioned how I would fit into the environment and become involved in the things the children and the program are taking part in. What do I know about the South Los Angeles community anyway? I mean, I am an outsider here. How do I become an insider, and am I even supposed to?

Regardless of their backgrounds, many tutors fear that they will not be able to relate to students who are "different." In the following example, a

Latina tutor worried about not being able to connect with an African American tutee because of their different racial backgrounds:

> I have always tutored students of Latino descent, and I will openly admit it has become my comfort zone, one that I haven't breached until today. Immediately I began to think back into my comfort zone and contemplated starting my own tutoring program for Latino, immigrant children in downtown Los Angeles rather than participating in the program I was currently in. As much as I hate to admit it, I was doing this because I was scared of getting an African American tutee. Not because I'm racist; rather because I was scared of being too different from him or her, and my biggest fear was not being able to overcome our cultural differences. It's just that because of his or her experiences and hardships being completely different from my own, I was scared that I wouldn't be right for my tutee.

Will I Be Able to Teach the Students?

In addition to wondering whether forming a relationship is possible, many tutors worry about their teaching competence. In fact, even when tutors find that they are immediately accepted and put at ease by the students they have been assigned to tutor, the issue of how well they will teach still lingers, as in the following example. This female tutor was welcomed into the fourth-grade classroom to which she was assigned, yet she was still nervous about being an effective teacher:

> A perceptive boy named Roger from the front of the room yelled out, "Hey, are you one of the tutors from UCLA?" When I confirmed Roger's question with a nod, smiles spread throughout the room. Two girls seated near me shyly asked, "Can we work with you today?" This was my first experience in the classroom, and it felt wonderful. I was really nervous, because I felt the children looked up to me and expected me to know all of the answers, since I was a big college student. I was also nervous, because I was afraid that the children wouldn't be interested in working, but only talking. I wasn't sure how I would be able to focus their attention or motivate them to learn.

Maybe you have never taught before. Maybe you are shaky in a couple of subjects. Tutoring tends to exacerbate tutors' insecurities about their own academic performances. Many tutors find themselves driving to their tutoring sites trying to figure out how they will tell students that they have never been good in math themselves.

Many factors may contribute to tutors' evaluations of their teaching abilities. Their high expectations of themselves often lead them to self-doubt when they first start tutoring. As one tutor explained, "Inadequacy is a very hard pill to swallow. I felt disappointed in myself, depressed, and defeated. What if they need help with math and I cannot remember? I never did well in math. What if I cannot come up with innovative and fun ways of teaching?"

Will I Succeed?

Most people get into tutoring because they want to "make a difference," but specific motivations for tutoring vary. Perhaps it is required in a class you are taking. Perhaps you were inspired by a newspaper or television show. Maybe you are trying to make a political or social statement. No matter why they decide to tutor, most tutors have some idea of what they want to accomplish—and usually it is the betterment of their students. But what if the students will not listen? What if they still fail all their tests? What if they go out and get arrested the day after you have a heart-to-heart in a tutoring session? The aftermath of many tutoring situations may look like failure, and many tutors fear that they might have influenced the outcome.

One of the amazing things about tutoring is just how overpowering these fears can seem. What is more amazing is how often they are overcome, and how, in the end, it is usually the tutee's calming effect that helps a tutor's fears disappear. As one tutor wrote, "When I saw the fondness in this little girl's eyes, I realized that I have to let go of my insecurities and occupy my time thinking of ways I can provide these kids with techniques for learning."

As this quote suggests, many of the normal worries and anxieties you may feel as you enter your tutoring site will disappear once you meet your tutee. Yet some ways of approaching a tutoring situation can minimize your worries and fears and often help you overcome them altogether.

ACCEPTANCE

Acceptance means taking your students as they are and suspending any hopes or expectations of what you would like them to be. Although it is important to want your students to learn, to do well in school, and to succeed, your work with them and acceptance of them should not be conditional on these accomplishments. Your interest in your students should not be based on what they could become but on who they are. Although this kind of acceptance usually develops over time with family and friends, you do not have the luxury of time in a tutoring situation. That is why it is important to cultivate this accepting attitude before you enter the tutoring relationship.

The ideal of acceptance comprises a set of attitudes and practices that become apparent in the example that follows. For this volunteer tutor who worked with a different child every week at a children's hospital, all days were first days, and first days are often the scariest. Although this tutor met much more challenging conditions than those encountered by most tutors, the issues raised are typical of every tutoring situation. Brandon's case illustrates that, regardless of the challenges awaiting a tutor on the first day, creating a bond is always a possibility:

> I met Brandon, a seven-year-old liver transplant patient. Brandon seemed frail and very indifferent to his surroundings. He refused to communicate with the nurse in words and only pointed to things if he needed anything.
>
> "Hi, Brandon, my name is Tim, and I am here to spend some time with you."
>
> No response, not even a nod or look my way.
>
> The nurse interjected, "Brandon, isn't this great—we have a volunteer to play with you."
>
> He continued watching the TV as if he couldn't care less about anything that was happening.
>
> "Brandon, would you like to go to the playroom?"
>
> He shook his head from side to side without looking at me.
>
> "Would you like me to bring you a game or video?"
>
> Same response.
>
> Frustrated, I looked around, feeling like a fool, while fighting the thoughts in my head: "You may be making him

uncomfortable. He doesn't like you. Maybe he wants to be left alone. Maybe I should explain to him that I am not a physician or a nurse. What is he thinking? I feel useless. He likes animals, especially dinosaurs and reptiles. Look at his shelf, filled with gifts that had one theme in common: dinosaurs, monsters, and jungles."

I left the room without saying a word. On my way to the storage room, I ordered the King Kong Nintendo game for him. From the storage room I fetched a game called Dynamite (a dinosaur game, in which whoever gets to the finish line first, after going through a jungle full of obstacles, wins). Being insecure in my choice of the game, I also grabbed Battleship. I walked quietly to his room, carrying the games in my hand. I did not announce my entrance, much less the games that I fetched him.

I didn't need to, because he snapped out of his bed and snatched Dynamite with an unfriendly gesture.

While he opened the box and seemingly read the instructions, I sat next to him on his bed without asking him. He did not object, but instead set up the game and chose his green dinosaur. I chose the yellow one, while he tossed the dice. While the game was going on, I asked him questions about the moves, but he refused to utter a word or even make the smallest noise and only pointed to things. His refusal to talk continued even when the Nintendo game arrived and I was desperately searching for an electrical outlet. He finally pointed to a corner of the room where I found one after three minutes of searching.

I had to wonder, "Wasn't he excited about the game? Doesn't he want to get started as early as possible, considering the short amount of time we have the game in reserve?"

He hooked up the system. Then, he gave me the other joystick for no apparent reason, since he set the game on the "one player" mode and kept on playing the next ten games, while I watched and commented on what I thought was cool about the game. Then, suddenly, he handed me his joystick.

So I entered one of the houses but soon dropped off of a cliff and died. Apparently the route I took was a difficult one. Brandon knew that but obviously preferred not to tell me in words. After I died, he took the joystick from my hand, entered the same route, and threw himself off the cliff on purpose. Then, he looked at me and handed me the joystick.

So Brandon did tell me about the dangers of the path I took, but he did in his own terms. He was willing to lose two of the monkeys that he had saved over the past ten games rather than tell me in words, "Do not follow that path." He lost two of his lives to guide me—he sacrificed for me!

This tutor's experience demonstrates that even with the most recalcitrant tutee, a persistent tutor can make a connection. Once the tutor accepted the fact that Brandon was not going to talk, he was able to start working with him, and they found their own way to communicate. Although this is the type of situation most tutors would prefer not to encounter on their first day (and frankly, it is pretty rare for a student to refuse to talk at all!), we have identified a number of attitudes and practices that should help ease your way, whatever the circumstances.

Attitudes

Developing an attitude of acceptance involves giving up expectations, showing enthusiasm and interest, and feeling empathy. These are the most general, fundamental elements in initiating a positive tutoring experience; they lay the foundation for successful tutoring practices.

Although it may be hard to imagine developing your attitudes toward tutoring before you even reach the site, it is worth trying to do so. Some tutoring sites give you time to acclimate yourself and to get to know the students and staff, but tutors are often immediately matched up with students—before you even know what is going on, you are tutoring. So it is useful to have already established some sort of mindset.

As you will see, beginning to work out your mindset and attitudes before you begin tutoring does not mean you should try to figure out your teaching techniques and goals for your student in advance. As each tutoring scenario is different and tutees generally will not conform to your expectations, such preparation would be a waste of time, even detrimental. But you can still mentally prepare yourself. Before you reach the site, you can give up any expectations that you may have, and you can work toward orienting yourself to the positive emotions of enthusiasm, interest, and empathy.

Giving Up Expectations

Start out with minimal expectations. This means giving up visions of what you expect to happen and what you think you will know and feel or not know and not feel. Expectations can cause tension in the tutoring session. When such expectations are not met, the tutor can become disillusioned and disheartened, emotions that can harm the relationship.

Our expectations are constructed through our value systems, upbringing, and past experiences and can be very different from those of others. These expectations can become major sources of frustration when not met by others' behavior, such as that of our tutees. The best thing to do is to try to enter tutoring without any expectations at all. This, of course, includes giving up expectations you may have of your future students and their personalities, their academic skills or progress, and their motivation and attitude toward you. All children are different. They have different backgrounds, different strengths, and different weaknesses. Some may be thrilled to be tutored; others may be suspicious. At the first meeting, a tutor's conception of a student should be a blank slate. Tutors must be prepared to accept and to work with any students to whom they are assigned.

Giving up expectations is not always easy, especially when tutors have worked with other tutees in the past and attempt to hold their new students to the same expectations. In the following example, a female tutor got off to a bad start with her new seven-year-old tutee because of her preconceived expectations:

> [The student was struggling with subtraction.] I tried to teach her a shortcut that is always helpful to me—see what gets you to ten, and take it from there. I spent several minutes trying to explain this shortcut to her, but she didn't understand. After correcting her more than a few times in this part of her homework and others, she said to me (still in her small voice), "I don't like it when you talk." Ah! "I'm sorry," I apologized and smiled eagerly. I didn't like it when I talked either! But how was I supposed to teach her? I didn't know what to do. I wasn't expecting nor was I prepared for any of this.
>
> We continued for a few more moments, and I stopped correcting her and let her make mistakes. Thank goodness it was almost time for her to leave, and as she started packing up her stuff, I tried to make more small talk with her. I asked her ques-

tions like who was picking her up, what days she came to the center on, etc. Everyone else was lining up at the door, so I said my good-byes to her, told her I was excited to see her again next week, and saw her leave.

Reflecting back on my first tutoring experience, I certainly was taken off guard and was unprepared to tutor Jocelyn. My most recent experience with children and teens had been my mentee, who was fifteen years old. My mentee, Vicky, has a very different personality than Jocelyn. Vicky is not very talkative, and she really enjoys hearing my stories and what I have to say. She also especially likes it when I get really into my stories what with voice variation, hand gestures, etc. Coming into the family center, I expected my tutee to react in the same way. I expected Jocelyn to be like Vicky and for her to welcome my lively explanations and meanings.

After the first tutoring session ended, the tutor knew she had come unprepared—not unprepared as far as the material she worked on with her tutee, but unprepared in that she expected working with Jocelyn would be the same as her relationship with Vicky.

Giving up expectations of how a tutee is supposed to act or be does not, however, preclude you from holding high expectations for your tutees' educational potential. It does not mean that you should not challenge your tutees to work as hard as they can and to excel. Tutors need to form, through tutoring, a picture of where they would like their tutees to move educationally. (These informed or educated expectations can really help you be an asset to your students.)

But giving up expectations applies to far more than just your tutee. It means giving up expectations of yourself. It means giving up expectations of the school system, the teachers, and tutoring in general. It means giving up expectations of success. Although every tutor can help a student, no tutor is superhuman. You cannot expect to know everything or to know how to teach everything. And every tutoring partnership can be a success, but not all tutees will land a scholarship to Harvard. Big successes are wonderful, but so are little successes. In fact, little successes make up the bulk of a successful tutoring relationship. Every tutor can make an impact on a child, and any positive impact you make is a success. It is up to the individuals involved in the relationship to determine just what the successes will be.

Giving up expectations is hard. When you make a commitment to tutor, it is difficult not to start thinking about what you will be dealing with and trying to prepare yourself mentally and emotionally. But as you can see, shedding your expectations will also help you shed many of your fears. Will you be able to teach? Of course. You may not know everything, but you are not expected to. Being rusty in trigonometry does not make you a bad tutor. Not knowing Spanish does not make it impossible to relate to a Spanish-speaking child. You will be perfectly capable of teaching many subjects, and beyond helping with school-work, every tutor can teach students about motivation and hard work, about enjoying learning, and about the existence of teachers who care. It is comforting to remember that just being there, reading with students, and talking about what you have read together can help improve their comprehension and vocabulary.

Forgive yourself if you do not live up to how you want to teach. The tutor in the example that follows, a Persian female who seemed to be a perfect match for her Farsi-speaking third-grade student, found it hard to forgive herself and ended a session extremely frustrated:

> I asked Ahmed what he wanted to do, and he said, "Let's study English." I was surprised, considering he had not done such a good job last time around. However, this time around, instead of asking him for the other letters in the alphabet, I went straight after the letter "M" [which had been troublesome for him in previous sessions]. I could not believe my own two eyes when I saw that blank look on his face. I thought to myself, "How stupid can someone be? I don't understand. What am I doing wrong?"
>
> I hesitated to help him. Instead of helping him, I decided that we would sit there for as long as it takes, until he remembered the letter "M." Little did I know that we were going to sit there for a long time. I started to give him hints, pronouncing words that start with the letter "M." However, he still did not know what I was talking about. I told him to write down whatever he thinks looks like "M." He wrote the letter "N" instead.
>
> When I looked at him, he was playing with his fingers. I could not believe it. I was furious. In an angry yet strong tone of voice, I snapped at him. He jumped out of his chair. Tears were circling his eyes. He looked at me as though I had just hit him

or something. I felt really bad. I kept on apologizing, but it was not good enough. From that moment on, he would just look at me. Not that he talked much before, but now he did not even say a single word.

I tried to make it up to him, but I guess it was useless. I calmed myself down and wrote the letter "M" on the piece of paper in front of him. He stared at it for a bit and then started to write the letter "M" until the last line of the paper. I focused his attention on other letters, and when I got back to the letter "M," surprisingly enough, he remembered. He had a smile on his face.

I cannot make any excuses for my behavior. All I can say is that I was very frustrated by the fact that we had spent the entire past two weeks studying the letter "M." I also know that this is no excuse to snap at a child. I wish he knew how sorry I am.

This incident, although not ideal as far as tutoring methods go, is an excellent instance of a tutor getting upset with herself and her teaching skills. It shows how tutor expectations of how quickly a tutee can learn and how well tutors should teach can fill a situation with tension. The important thing to remember is that even though Ahmed's tutor was not at her best in this situation, he forgave her, and he was still able to learn. You must try to be as forgiving with yourself.

Like Ahmed and his tutor, allow your tutees to help teach you how to teach. Teaching someone an idea, concept, or skill can be extremely challenging, especially when you "just know" how to do it. You will find that many skills you have to teach are ones that you learned through rote memorization. Finding more constructive and creative ways to teach these same skills can be difficult, but here you and your tutee have the most to learn from one another.

Will you be able to succeed? Again, forget your notions of what constitutes success. Success is different for everyone. Every tutoring scenario, regardless of the caliber of the student or the tutor, can be a success.

More than allowing you to calm some of your fears, approaching tutoring situations with no expectations lets you view the scene more clearly. Your lenses—that is, your expectations—will not cloud or color what is going on. Looking back at the hospital incident, one can see that what the medical volunteer expected from his interaction with Brandon was bound to defeat him had he not relaxed and dismissed it.

Accepting your tutee means dismissing your preconceived notions about how your tutee should react toward you and learn. In the following example, a heterosexual female tutor working at a gay and lesbian center was terrified by her own expectations:

> At first I was worried that my intentions for tutoring at a gay and lesbian after-school program would be misunderstood and questioned by the students. I am heterosexual and was afraid that they may think I am tutoring at the center because I was homosexual myself. I was also afraid that once they found out [that I was heterosexual], they might not let me into their lives and accept me. I guess I was projecting. My preconceived notions of how it would be were momentarily confirmed by a question that my female tutee [seventeen-year-old Latina] asked me on the first day, "Do you have a boyfriend?"
>
> This question threw me off balance. I was shocked that she asked me such a question right away; I knew that she was trying to find out about whether I belonged to her world.
>
> Hesitantly, expecting a cold reaction, I said, "Yes." To my surprise, the answer didn't seem to change her behavior. Instead she went on telling me about how every time she gets into a fight with her girlfriend, her parents use it against her homosexual relationship. Then relating to me, she asked, "Don't you and your boyfriend have major disagreements?" Embarrassed about my shaky and obviously nervous reactions toward her, I said, "Yes" and explained to her an incident I had with my boyfriend.

This tutor's preoccupation and anxiety sprang from her own fears and misconceptions about homosexuals. Her expectations not only made her nervous; they could have damaged her relationship with the tutee from the very beginning. Can you get along with a tutee who is different from you? Can you make a connection? Yes, you can, but you must be willing to give up your preconceived notions and accept your tutees as they are (and accept yourself as you are).

In the following example, a white male tutor reflected upon a tutoring partnership in which he and the tutee came from dramatically different ethnic, religious, and class backgrounds. The tutor was raised in an upper-middle-class, strict Jewish household; the tutee, a seven-year-old Latina, came from a working-class background. This tutor eventually came to realize that his preconceived notions kept the two of them from forming a relationship for several weeks:

> I was assigned to tutor Marta, a second-grade Latina, who came from a family with low socioeconomic status. As a university tutor, I was confident about being able to help my tutee with any problems she might have. But ironically, the problem was my inability to immerse myself in her life, see her problems, and perceive her actions in the context of her surroundings. I was so preoccupied with how I would affect her life the way I had learned how to, and teaching her from my experiences, that I ignored the greater problems in Marta's life. She seemed "impossible" to teach and focus. . . . I could see that she did not identify with me and really ignored my concerns. It took me a while to realize that I could not expect her to understand my concerns, because they were so foreign and irrelevant to her life.
>
> I didn't find out about her mother physically beating her, her teacher yelling at her in class, and the students in the bus calling her "stupid" until the sixth week of tutoring, once I finally learned how to listen. Once I was deemed deserving of a pass into her world, we learned to grow together and learn from one another by putting things in the context of our lives.

As we see later, once the lens of expectations is removed, you will be able to make important observations about your tutees that will allow you to better understand their world. Your careful observations should enable you to connect with your tutees and the world that impacts their lives, to approach and interact with them on their own terms. If you make no or few judgments beforehand, it is easier to learn what it means to live in their world, even if it is completely foreign to you.

Going back to the hospital example, we can see that once the volunteer gave up his expectations regarding Brandon's nonverbal responses and his lack of enthusiasm toward the volunteer's presence, the volunteer could focus on Brandon's surroundings and seek some way to approach him. The environmental cues, such as toys and books surrounding Brandon's bed, enabled the volunteer to fetch a dinosaur game that Brandon liked. The volunteer was also able express his interest and enthusiasm for interacting with Brandon by paying attention to what Brandon enjoyed doing.

Displaying Enthusiasm and Interest

It is crucial that you show interest in your students' work and in their lives. Your students can see through you, and the care you show for your work—your tutoring—will translate into sincere relationships with them. Tutees know that you cannot start caring for them deeply right away (human relationships do not operate that way), but your obvious love for your work and interest in them will illustrate your potential for bonding with them.

Do not worry about whether a student will like you. Students will be able to tell if you are genuinely interested in them, and their impressions of you will flow from that perception. It does not matter whether they immediately like your personality or the way you tutor. What matters is that they understand that someone cares about them and that they can feel safe responding and building a relationship with you.

Furthermore, by showing your enthusiasm and interest, you demonstrate your flexibility and ability to meet students on their terms. Many adults fail to do this when they interact with children or other people whom they are helping. Because your tutees may have been denied passion and enthusiasm from other adults, they may at first see you as just another authority figure. You may also struggle with tutees dealing with the legacy that other tutors have left behind, meaning they have already experienced tutors showing up late or not showing up at all. As a result, they may test you. They will check your sincerity. The only way to prove that you are trustworthy is to show sincere and open interest in them and their progress.

In the following example, the tutee did not show any enthusiasm toward his assigned tutor. Nonetheless, the tutor sat down and got involved right away, parrying with his own interest the second grader's attempts to push him away:

> I asked him if he had any homework and what he wanted to work on. He said he had math, but it was easy and he could do it by himself in five minutes. I told him, "Show me, it's no rush, I know you could probably do it in five minutes, but I want to do it along with you."
>
> He acted as if he did not need me for the first thirty minutes. He was trying to prove how smart he was. When he got stuck on a problem, instead of asking me for help, he would tell

Practical Matters: How Do You Display Excitement and Enthusiasm?

It's hard to imagine getting excited when the major emotion that you feel is nervousness. But, remember, your enthusiasm will be contagious, so try the following tips:

+ Get excited before you go. Listen to your favorite song on the way to tutoring, have a great exercise session beforehand, or get psyched with your best friend—do whatever it takes to get excited about tutoring.
+ Don't be afraid to "get into" the material you're teaching. Students are often "too cool" to be interested in school work, but if you get into the subject, they often will as well. Be excited about what you read—connect it with your life or something else you know. Show the students that what they are learning is interesting and fun. Sometimes they'll "pretend" to be interested just so you won't be embarrassed about being a nerd and liking it, but even that's a start.
+ Find out what gets your students excited about school work. Do they like certain subjects? Do they really want to get good grades? Are they trying to move to higher reading groups? Will their parents give them treats for improving? Encourage them to love learning, but make sure you also get excited about what excites them.

me how good he was in math and how he could do it so fast, trying to get off the subject. When I was showing him how to do it, he would snap and say, "I was getting to that." I told him that I was just trying to remember and was just discussing the problem to myself.

Although this was no idyllic start for a tutoring session, the tutor stayed involved. After thirty minutes, the tutee started to sprinkle the session with personal comments, letting the tutor into his life. The tutor could then demonstrate his desire for a sincere tutor-tutee relationship. By the end of the session, the math homework had become a game designed to prevent the child from making small talk.

Although I encouraged our getting-acquainted conversations, I needed to have him complete the assignment also. I knew he could do it, but up to this point it was taking him five minutes to complete one problem.

He said, "Wait until the next line." I was fooled. He picked the line with two-digit problems as opposed to three-digit ones on the previous lines. I told him he was so smart, how he fooled me, now he could show me how well he knew his math. He was excited when I discovered he fooled me; he started cheering and almost ran out of time. . . . We were really comfortable with each other at this point, joking and teasing. I knew I had succeeded in gaining Javier's trust.

This tutor's enthusiasm for his work and interest in the child allowed a connection to be made. Javier's ability to fool the tutor and to show what he knows and can do, and the tutor's acceptance of his way of expressing himself, allowed the boy to feel more trusting. It also indicates the success you as a tutor can achieve through passion for your work and interest in your tutee.

Feeling Empathy

One of the biggest fears that tutors face, and one that can be the most crippling, is expressed in the question, "Will I like my tutee?" It is hard to imagine working closely with a person you do not like or do not approve of. But it is important to remember that tutors do not have to like their students to be effective. Your student may not be the person you would choose as your best friend or a child you would want to adopt. Your tutee may be involved in activities or do things that you consider wrong. None of this matters. Liking your tutee is not essential. Feeling empathy for your tutee is.

Empathy differs significantly from sympathy. We can empathize with people regardless of whether we like their actions, because we can understand why they do what they do. For instance, when a student cheats on an exam, we may empathize but not necessarily sympathize. We do not have to approve of cheating. We do have to try to understand why the student cheated. Was it too frightening to take the exam? Was the student unable to study because of a lack of help or because a factor in the home environment was too distracting the night before? Was the student simply afraid to fail? If you can understand why the student cheated, you can work with the student and talk about the situation and still maintain the relationship.

In this example, a Latino tutor caught his ten-year-old tutee, Geraldo, cheating and tried to understand the situation from the child's point of view:

> I saw Geraldo as he was copying the answers from his neighbor, looking through the corner of his eye. I didn't want to make it obvious to the teacher, but I also wanted him to stop cheating. So I stared at him every chance I got. When our eyes met, almost at the end of the period, I could see the embarrassment on his face.
>
> When the bell rang, he collected his stuff very quickly, to avoid talking to me, but I managed to catch him before he left. I did not need to say that I was disappointed in him, because his behavior indicated the acknowledgment of my disapproval and disappointment. But I told him that I understood why he was cheating and told him about an incident I had in my elementary years. Together we explored some other ways around the exam-induced anxiety he was facing as well as his lack of preparation.

This tutor's empathy allowed him to explore and to understand his tutee's situation without excusing the wrongful act. The result: new and effective lines of communication between the tutee and the tutor, through which they can arrive at a deeper understanding.

Once students discern that their tutors understand them and their situations from their perspectives, they will be more eager to work with the tutors and more open to advice and suggestions. Being a good listener signals to tutees that you understand them. Empathy—understanding the tutee's position—is therefore fundamental to the development of a strong tutoring relationship.

One way to develop empathy is to believe that your tutees are doing what they can to succeed. With this mindset, you will be less critical.

It is hard to criticize or to condemn someone who cheats because he or she is afraid of failing and being beaten, ridiculed, or left behind a grade.

Even in situations where you disapprove of students' values or actions, you can empathize and try to see where they are coming from. Then you can respond to them in a way that makes sense to them. In the following example, the tutor was working with the probation department, tutoring male juveniles who had just gotten out of lockup.

Although, as a middle-class white female graduate student, she was continually surprised to learn of her students' crimes—which ranged from robbery to murder—this interaction really dumbfounded her:

> We were reading an article on police brutality, and I asked the guys if they had been abused when they were arrested or while they were in lockup. They said that of course they had, but that it hadn't been as severe as what we were reading about. We went on to have a really stimulating conversation about when brutality might be justified and when it wasn't. Byron and Trang were arguing over whether murderers have rights. Trang says that they don't, that they forfeit them when they kill someone. Byron wasn't so sure.
>
> Later I asked Byron if he thought that all cops were bad. He said yes. Then he changed his mind. He said that not all of them were, but that he thought that the longer they had been on the street, the worse they got. I asked why he thought that was. He said, "Well, they scared. They see so much. They tired of seeing it all." We talked about peer pressure from other police and if he thought that he could be a street cop. He struck me as so intelligent. He read really well and was really interested in talking.
>
> I asked him what he had been in for. He seemed so friendly and actually kind of sweet, and I figured it would be minor.
>
> "Burglarizing a house," he told me.
>
> "Did you do it?"
>
> "Yeah, I did it. But I would've gotten away with it if someone hadn't snitched on me. I'd have gotten away with it." I was kind of shocked. No remorse. Then he added, "But that just gonna slow me down."
>
> I was really shocked: "What?"
>
> "It just gonna slow me down." I could tell by his voice that he planned to keep right on at it when he was done with his house arrest.
>
> I kept flashing back to my friends who had just had their house robbed twice in one week and who had lost a lot of valuables that they couldn't afford to replace. What could I say to this kid? Somehow I knew he wouldn't care about that. He wouldn't sympathize with my friend whose laptop computer had gotten ripped off. He'd never owned anything that valuable

in his life. But I had to say something: "There are more honest ways to make money Byron. And the scariest thing about robbing houses isn't getting caught—it's the fact that the owner might have a gun, and he'll blow you away. No problem."

"Yeah, I guess you're right," he conceded.

It is hard to know whether this tutor's reaction was the best one or if what she said would dissuade the student from committing his crime again. Perhaps she should have been stronger or more insistent. The point is that she did not walk away, indignant. She did not lecture or moralize. She tried to think about the crime from his point of view and to suggest reasons why he might choose to avoid the activity (an outcome that would affect him). We do not know whether the tutee understood, but his tutor expressed her concern for the consequences of his actions in a way that showed her concern for him, not for her values and beliefs, which left room for further discussion—on this or other subjects the tutee might have hesitated to bring up.

This tutor continued to teach Byron, even though she disapproved of his behavior. Rather than preaching to him, she wanted to try to be a role model and to show him, rather than tell him, that he could choose a better way to live. This tutor did not need to like her student, but she needed to see where he was coming from and to try to understand him. Then she could continue to interact with him and to leave open the possibility of influencing him positively in the future.

Practices

These attitudes—giving up expectations, displaying enthusiasm and interest, and feeling empathy—form the foundation for several successful general practices. These practices are being patient, being observant and asking questions, and interacting with your student on as equal a level as possible. For instance, being patient becomes a necessity once you give up your expectations. Because each tutoring partnership is unique, you must wait to learn about your student and yourself. What sometimes seems to require an infinite amount of patience is worth it in the end. Being observant and asking questions are inherent in displaying interest and enthusiasm, the basic tools that show children that you are interested in and excited about working with them. Finally, you need to have empathy to understand students and to work with them on an

⯖ Introductions

Take a minute to get to know your student. Don't start on schoolwork immediately. Instead, start off with a few personal questions and an ice-breaker or two to set an enthusiastic tone for the day.

- Ask your students about their days, about what they like to do, what subjects they enjoy, whether they have been to tutoring before, or what they think of the environment in which you're tutoring.
- Tell your tutees some things about yourself. Don't dwell on yourself too much, but try to find a way to establish some things you may have in common.
- Comment on the students. You can remark on the books that the students are carrying, their shoes or hairstyles, or even the games you saw them playing before you began tutoring. Compliments go a long way. And sometimes simple comments get the conversation going. Pay attention to clothes, doodles on notebooks, conversations you overhear them having with other kids, and other clues. Try to figure out what they like. And pay attention when they drop little clues, such as wanting to tell you what happened on their favorite cartoons or about the baseball game they saw over the weekend: These details could be your entrée into relationships with these students.

equal level. Each of these practices builds upon the other: Being patient gives you the time to observe and to ask relevant questions that bring you into the tutee's world.

Practicing Patience

Patience can mean being willing to wait, being understanding or tolerant or enduring problems without complaint, or persevering in the face of adversity. In tutoring, patience means all these things. It is the ability (or the state of mind) to cope with discouraging situations and distracting environmental factors while focusing all of your efforts on your tutee. It means being willing to let the student set the pace for the growth of the relationship and not being too pushy. It requires being steadfast and trying one method after another until something clicks.

In the hospital case, the tutor showed patience by not allowing Brandon's refusal to talk to discourage him. The tutor took his time and eventually came up with an effective way of interacting with Brandon, through his observation of environmental cues. Furthermore, he did not take the situation personally, realizing that Brandon's behavior had many possible causes.

In the same way, you do not know what is going on in your tutees' lives, and you should not assume anything. Children are often more sincere and expressive than adults. They lack the adult ability to mask their problems and to pretend that nothing is wrong. Remember, as discouraging as the situation may seem, your patience will allow your tutees to enjoy your company and to see your sincere interest in them.

As the hospital volunteer reflected, "Although Brandon seemed not to care much about my presence, his actions talked a different language as he sacrificed two of his monkeys to guide me in the game. He also played Dynamite with me, which was indicative of a connection or a bond." The volunteer was patient, not presumptuous, and let Brandon lead him.

Sometimes getting to know a student requires gentle probing, especially if you are thrown into a situation in which you know nothing about the tutee. Gentle probing is not always as easy as it sounds, so patience is necessary. A student who is unhappy about being tutored or apathetic about schoolwork can shut down a shy tutor easily. You will not always get, nor should you expect, immediate results. Sometimes an entire session or two may feel awkward, but every bit of information that you gather is a potential window into the student's life; store it all away, for it will eventually prove useful.

In the following case, a female tutor felt somewhat lost when her tutee arrived with no homework to work on and gave only terse answers to her questions. But in persevering, the tutor made some small connections, learned a little about her tutee, and was more prepared to get through to this student the next week:

> My next student was nine-year-old Kim. There was no formal introduction except for names, so I fished for information. I asked, "Do you like school?"
>
> Kim replied, "Some parts."
>
> I went on, "What is your favorite subject?"
>
> She replied, "Math."
>
> Kim's answers made it really difficult to continue a conversation, but I forged on. "Do you like art?"
>
> "No."

"Do you play sports?"

"No."

"Do you like music?"

"Oh yeah, I like music."

Finally something I could talk about. I mentioned to her that music and math are more alike than she probably thinks. For a moment she looked amused but then took on the boredom face again. I asked her, "Do you like any particular instrument?"

"No."

I thought, somewhere, she's got to give. "Okay, so who do you listen to?"

"I like Mariah Carey."

This tutor was not very familiar with Mariah Carey, so the student's comment did not lead to a serious connection. But the two kept talking, and the tutor finally found out that Kim had a boyfriend that she liked to talk about and that she liked to go to the mall and would talk a little about those trips. Through a lot of effort on the tutor's part, the sessions eventually became more comfortable. The tutor only needed to gather up enough parts of her student's life to try to understand her and to make her feel comfortable. Exercising patience and observing details about your tutees may likewise help you forge connections.

Being Observant and Asking Questions

Once you have given up expectations and developed the practice of patience, you are in the best possible mindset for making observations. You can learn a lot about your tutees by noticing their body language, clothing, stickers on their binders, or the songs in their iPods. By being observant, you can pick up details about tutees that can help you connect with them. In the hospital case, for example, the tutor's observation of the dinosaurs on Brandon's shelf helped him choose an effective activity. Being observant is not limited to what you can see, however; it includes what you can learn through interaction. For instance, in Kim's case, the tutor learned of Kim's interest in music through their conversation.

In the following example, careful observations, questioning, and building on the tutee's expressed interests allowed the tutor to turn fatigue and fidgetiness into interest and excitement:

A Worksheet for Introducing Yourselves

If you feel uncomfortable having a conversation upon first meeting, try a worksheet like the one below (adjust it for the age of your tutee). It can be hard for a shy student to talk openly with a new person, but writing things down can help break the ice. Be as corny or as serious as you like—just make sure that your worksheet fits your personality. Notice that this worksheet is designed for you *both* to fill out. Each of you gets to fill out a form for the other. Do not worry if the worksheet is silly; it is precisely the silliness that can get your conversation started (and let the student see that you are not too cool, too old, or too boring to be silly).

Draw yourself!	Name:
	My tutor/My tutee:
	Age:
	Grade:
	Hometown:

If you were any animal, what would you be and why?

Favorite subject in school:

Favorite sport:

Hobbies:

Brothers and sisters:

What do you want to be when you grow up?

What do you want to work on most with your tutor/tutee?

Near the beginning of our tutoring session, Rizzo told me he likes rocks. He likes that there are so many different shapes, colors, and sizes. Although it was just a brief comment in our introduction, I took this to note, among other things he revealed to me, and continued on with his English homework. A while later, I noticed he was getting a bit antsy around me and looked a bit uncomfortable. First thing I thought to ask was whether he needed to go to the bathroom, and oh yes, he did. Anyway, we got to the bathroom I think is closest, one which Rizzo had never visited, and it happened to be in the Geology building next door. . . . The walls contain a gallery of rock sam-

❖ Pay Attention, Ask, and Observe

After you get to know your tutees a little, it's a good idea to jump into work. It's actually helpful to have something to focus on. As you look at students' work, get a sense of what they like and don't like, what they want help on and what they don't need help on, what their academic goals are, and what they want to learn from you.

- Figure out what you want to get done during that tutoring session (find the work that the students need help with, not just the work that they want to get done—there's no point to your sitting there watching students do work that is easy for them).
- Ask about everything that is due tomorrow. Students notoriously like to do easy work first, and by the time you realize that they need help with something, your time could be up. Get a sense of the entire day's work before you begin. A great way to start is to have a look at the students' agendas (many schools provide agendas, calendars, or homework books for students). If the students do not have agendas (or did not write the assignments in it), write down the day's assignments together. Talk with the students, subject by subject, and try to write down each task and assignment the students are supposed to complete.
- Ask about everything that students are supposed to do, not just "homework." Students often disregard assignments that do not include tangible products to be turned in. But when students are supposed to read (either a novel or a textbook) for homework, it often presents a great opportunity for a tutor to help them read and understand the content while they read. Reading together

ples ranging from pyrite, fossils, obsidian, and so on. Rizzo got very excited about this, and something clicked. The next week, I came back with a PowerPoint slideshow on how the three types of rocks are formed (sedimentary, igneous, and metamorphic), which he greatly enjoyed. He memorized the three processes, and I took him to the [Geology] hallway again, where I quizzed him on which of the three types each rock belonged to. We did this until all the rocks in the hall had been covered. He said this was the most fun thing he had done the entire day, which made me very happy. Just a little bit of effort on my end and a little bit of listening went a long way. Toward the end of the tutoring

---

(out loud, no matter how old the students are) is often an extremely effective tutoring technique. And the reading assignments that students skip can be the most consequential assignments of the evening.

◆ Talk about long-term projects or work that you should be thinking about a little each session. These could include book reports, research reports, science projects, or any long-term projects. When you talk about these projects, be specific and ask a lot of questions. Students often don't think about assignments until the day before they're due—even when they require a lot of work. For instance, if the students have book reports due at *any* time in the future, start choosing books and reading.

◆ Ask whether any subjects require review (even if no homework is assigned at that moment). If you know what skills the children should be able to execute (from a teacher, a textbook, or even from a list of state standards), you can compile a short pretest.

◆ Ask whether any tests are coming up that you can help the students start to study for.

◆ Decide whether you would like the students to bring certain materials to the next session (old tests, textbooks, homework, notes, and so forth).

◆ Find out whether you should bring specific materials to the next tutoring session (for example, some schools don't use textbooks, but you might have a reference book or old textbook that you want to bring so you can look things up).

◆ Ask whether the students want to focus on particular subjects or types of learning with you.

session, I asked him what else I could teach him about, any
other sciences he was interested in, and so on. He responded
that he'd just like to go back to the hallway and get quizzed
more. I guess he's found a niche.

Being observant takes effort, practice, and concentration. Yet it pays
off, for every cue serves as a brick that builds a successful tutoring
experience. Observation helps in first-day situations especially, when it
can alleviate much of the tension and awkwardness associated with
stilted interaction. These crucial initial stages lead to a more effective
learning environment, especially when tutees feel that you are involved
in their lives. The cues you gather will enhance your understanding of
your students so you can fine-tune an individual, appropriate approach
for each tutee.

Interacting as Equals

Interacting with your tutees as equals requires pulling all the attitudes and practices we have talked about together. It means patiently
observing your tutees and trying to understand what motivates and
excites them. It means accepting them and giving up your expectations
of how they should be or how your interaction should proceed. Although
this equal interaction is not easy to achieve, it marks the beginning of the
success of your tutoring relationship. It proves to your students that you
are really interested in them, not in disciplining, harassing, or changing
them.

Tutoring is not an easy experience; as a tutoring relationship pro-
gresses, tutors are forced to face their own shortcomings and insecurities. But they also learn to work through them. In other words, tutor and
tutee learn and grow together. As one tutor reflected, "It is the best feeling in the world. I am a part of him, and he is a part of me."

Setting Boundaries and Goals

Every tutoring relationship is different, but by giving up expectations
and accepting your students as they are, you set the stage for a relationship that is optimal for your students' learning. However, as the adult,
you are responsible for making sure that tutoring is positive and productive. Many students, especially those facing work that they do not
want to do, would rather hang out. And, many students (and tutors!)

Get Started Tutoring

Remember the reason you're there: to be a catalyst for your students' academic success. Get some work done (ten minutes per hour is probably plenty of time for chatting).

◆ Feel free to help, but don't do the students' homework for them. You're there to help, but the homework is still the responsibility of the students.

◆ Watch to see whether the students might have academic gaps or be working below grade level. If it looks as though the students might need some remedial help, ask a supervisor or teacher for materials to help fill those gaps and get the students up to speed. Most teachers don't have time for one-on-one intervention, so you have a unique opportunity.

◆ No homework? Look for an interesting book or newspaper that you can read. Most students can use help with reading. Have the students read to you (or take turns), and talk about what you're reading. You can also give the students a writing prompt or look for an academically focused computer program to engage them (although, be careful—often the fastest way to lose students' attention is to put them in front of the computer).

◆ Too much homework? If your students have a lot of work to get done, focus on the most essential problems. Try to teach the students how to do a problem or two of each type, and work carefully so they can use their work as examples for future work. Also, work on teaching not just the material but the ways to study so the students can continue to work without you. Even if you run out of time during the session, encourage students to bring calendars or planners the next time you meet so you can plan for important assignments in the future.

have trouble tuning out distractions. So, when you first start tutoring, take responsibility for one of the most difficult parts of the tutoring relationship: keeping the tutoring relationship focused.

Setting Boundaries

Setting up the notion that your sessions will be more than hanging out and that you plan to get schoolwork done is just as important as making a connection with a student. You do not want to make a false connection, leading the student to believe that tutoring will be all fun and games. Your goal is to help the student academically, so it is honest to build your relationship within that context.

In the following example, a tutor felt conflicted over how much time she should spend getting to know her tutee and how much time she needed to dedicate to doing the work:

> When we finally finished her homework, I really tried to get her to open up and talk, and I wanted her to like me. Of course, at first she was a little shy, but when I was asking her questions about herself, you could tell that she wanted to talk. I only had a chance to ask her a few questions, but she told me how she loves to hang out with her friends and how she wants to be a veterinarian when she grows up. I'm hoping that as the weeks pass, she will start opening up more. But at the same time, I feel like do I/we even have time to just sit and talk, or am I just supposed to help her with her homework? I mean, isn't that the tutor's job? I'm pretty sure she doesn't come to the community center to become friends with her tutor; she probably just comes to get help with homework. But then, is that the problem? Is it my job as the tutor to not only be someone who helps with homework but to also be a mentor and somebody that the tutee can go to to talk? I feel like I really need to sit down and figure out how I can connect with Edith or make learning more fun.

Setting Goals

Giving up expectations of how your tutees will behave, what their achievement levels may be, and whether they will like you is the best way to begin a tutoring relationship. However, tutors should set some realistic goals and boundaries with the students early in the relationship. Sometimes you and your tutee will set these goals informally in the course of getting to know each other and working through your tutoring sessions. Other times, you will set these goals more formally. In the following example, a tutor set up contracts and communicated her realistic expectations on first meeting her tutees. Most tutors do not begin with a contract, but it worked well for this tutor:

> I spent all night wondering how I was going to establish relationships and trust with my students. So on the first day with

Looking Ahead

Ideally, you and the student will get to work together for a while. Leave your students with the following:

- Clear instructions about what tasks they need to complete after you part (finishing up an assignment, reading another chapter, studying the words that they struggled with in spelling practice).
- Clear instructions about what materials they should bring next time (especially if they forgot to bring something important, such as a textbook or worksheets from school).
- A confirmation about when and where you will see them next.
- A smile—and confidence that you enjoyed working with them today.

my tutees, I brought a letter, a contract, and a fact sheet for the kids to fill out. The letter that I gave them was for their parents, and I introduced myself and explained that I was excited to begin working with their children. The next thing I did was the contract. It basically gave the children the opportunity to tell me what they needed help on and how together we were going to try our best. The tutees were taken back and amazed at the fact that they didn't need their parents to sign it. I told them that together we are responsible for what we want to accomplish. After this was completed, we did a sheet that asked the kids for their "4-1-1" (information). This was a fun activity, because it allowed the children to get to know me and the other children in the tutoring group. They got really into the assignment, and they opened up to me and shared some personal information about their lives.

The tutor set up parameters of mutual responsibility and made it clear to the tutees just how important they would be in making the tutoring relationship work. With the separate contracts and letters, the tutor made clear that although the students' parents were important parts of the students' academic lives, they were not the ones signing their contracts. Not every tutee will agree to sign a contract, and you may not feel comfortable starting your first day with this technique; nonetheless, it is helpful to communicate realistic expectations early in the tutoring relationship to indicate the purpose of your meetings and the goals of your relationship.

The possibilities for realistic goals to set on the first day are numerous. Introducing a good system for you and the tutee to inform each other in case of an absence or tardiness can help in establishing a sense of trust and reliability. Asking what your tutee expects from you is also a good way to set up realistic expectations. Nevertheless, remember that keeping an open mind and a clean slate for tutees and their personalities, learning abilities, and commitment levels is essential for building an effective relationship with your tutees.

RECOMMENDED READING

A number of excellent books describe teachers' efforts to work one-on-one or with small groups of students, and many tutors will find the experiences of these gifted tutors and teachers rewarding and inspiring. In *36 Children* (1967), Herbert Kohl, a white male teacher, succeeds in an all-black classroom in Harlem. In *Teacher* (1963), Sylvia Ashton-Warner, a white British teacher, finds effective ways to teach Maori children in New Zealand. A Brazilian educator, Paulo Freire, develops an active model for teaching adults in *Pedagogy of the Oppressed* (1989). For a model of how Japanese teachers approach and impact children, read *Educating Hearts and Minds* (1995), by Catherine Lewis.

Torey Hayden, a white female teacher, has written extensively on her experience teaching special-education students (see, e.g., *One Child* [1980], *Somebody Else's Kids* [1981], *Just Another Kid* [1988], and *Beautiful Child* [2002]). Each book reads like a novel but chronicles Hayden's experience with a classroom of special-needs students. Even when tutors do not work specifically with special-education students (or elective mutes, Hayden's specialty), they can benefit from hearing about her experiences, her patience, her teaching techniques, and the spirit with which she fails and tries again.

Educating Esmé: Diary of a Teacher's First Year (2001), by Esmé Raji Codell, is a fun read by a twenty-four-year-old new teacher. The book is funny (from the teacher's standpoint and due to quotes from the kids) and realistic at the same time. It is a great read for anyone who thinks that he or she is going to change the world and wants to be prepared for the life of a teacher as it really is. *The Essential 55: An Award-Winning*

Educator's Rules for Discovering the Successful Student in Every Child (2004), by Ron Clark, delivers fifty-five quick tips for teachers (and anyone who works with students). Not every tip will be useful for everyone (and some seem a little silly), but it is a quick read, and the stories about his teaching experience make it an educational book for anyone who wants to work with kids.

In *Teach Like Your Hair's on Fire: The Methods and Madness inside Room 56*, by Rafe Esquith (2007), the author seems to teach his Los Angeles fifth graders as if his hair were on fire. He provides specific tips, examples, and lessons that he teaches, and, although no teacher or tutor will find all the tips or strategies useful, his enthusiasm and inclusive approach to teaching should be inspiring to anyone who works with children and hopes to make them love to learn.

Vivian Paley's book *You Can't Say You Can't Play* (1993) describes a creative way of teaching children through storytelling. In recognizing that children in kindergarten are already prepared to exclude other children on the basis of race, gender, class, and weight, Paley develops a storyline to use as a proxy for her students to discuss their own feelings of inclusion, exclusion, rejection, and dominance. After six months of deliberation and discussion with her students, Paley and the children implement the rule "You can't say, 'You can't play.'" The book describes how the children struggle to practice and to internalize this rule. Tutors can learn from Paley's emphasis on inclusion and the evidence that exclusion can inhibit learning.

RESOURCES

We recommend three videos that may be difficult to obtain but would be well worth the effort. They inspire tutors and teachers, who are amazed at what can be accomplished with students who had been failing.

A *60 Minutes* description of Marva Collins's work in an inner-city school in Chicago shows that having high expectations for children—even those considered to be hopeless or discipline problems—can lead to student success. Collins's eight- and ten-year-old students read classics in Western literature, including Dante, Shakespeare, and Charlotte Brontë. A follow-up video, *Too Good to Be True* (1996), shows that many of Marva Collins's students have gone on to college and graduate school, and all are employed: www.youtube.com/watch?v=H7LPpsp_Qh0.

In another video produced at PBS, teachers, students, and parents all become involved in ensuring that their children learn and work extremely hard. KIPP teachers, parents, and students all strive to create a learning environment that demands high commitment to reading, studying, doing homework, and testing. See *KIPP on Making Schools Work*: www.youtube.com/watch?v=VAKBnR-QSls.

2 Building Relationships

ONE OF THE MOST VITAL STEPS in the development of the tutor-tutee relationship concerns exactly that—creating a relationship. Tutoring looks easy, particularly if the students are young and the material is simple. But answering tutees' academic questions may be the easiest aspect of tutoring; the more difficult part is providing moral and emotional support and discovering exactly what areas the student needs help in. What would be an extremely difficult process between strangers occurs more easily between two people who have come to know and to care about each other.

Creating a strong personal relationship with your tutee is vital. Without it, a tutor can, at best, scratch the surface of a student's needs. Helping tutees with assignments may improve homework grades or even raise test scores, but filling in long-standing gaps in knowledge or helping students grasp more complex concepts requires the tutor to understand what the students do not know so they can devise teaching methods that are appropriate for those particular students. The best tutor will find ways to use students' natural curiosity and interest to motivate them to want to master challenges and to learn.

Although some tutoring relationships are long and enduring, many are relatively brief encounters: a semester, a few weeks, or a few months. Often, the biggest impact that tutors can make reveals itself not in higher test scores or better spelling papers but in the learning techniques and confidence that one-on-one work can instill in a tutee. Built on a personal connection, the tutoring experience can leave a lifelong impression on tutor and student, but making this connection and achieving this level of intimacy requires forging a strong relationship with the student.

Not all tutor-tutee relationships are easy to build. Myriad potential barriers stand between any particular tutoring pair and a strong tutoring relationship. Many tutors work with students of different genders, races, ages, or socioeconomic backgrounds than their own. Tutors often find themselves working with tutees with emotional and family problems that the tutors do not feel fully equipped to handle. Other tutors find that they struggle with the educational system, either in conflicts with teachers or in dealing with tutees whose confidence suffers or who have been incorrectly placed in an academic program that is either too advanced or too easy. (We explore these potential problems, and the ways many tutors have chosen to handle them, in later chapters.) Our experiences show that most of these barriers can be overcome; to create a successful tutoring situation, they *must* be overcome.

In the following example, a tutor was confronted with a seemingly insurmountable situation. She was frightened about her tutee's illness and whether she would be able to teach and to connect with her tutee:

> I worked with Jonnie, a ten-year-old leukemia patient. During our time together, we learned that his condition was terminal. At first, I wasn't sure whether or not I could continue to work with him, as I didn't feel qualified to deal his illness. However, I realized that I had established a relationship with Jonnie and to walk away was not an option. Jonnie had the right to have as normal a life as possible, despite his disease, and learning was an integral part of his life. I had to honor my relationship with Jonnie and to walk through my personal fears and inadequacies in order to be there for him.
>
> My tutoring with Jonnie revealed his interest and fascination with life during the colonial period. Whenever we had free time, Jonnie wanted to research and read about this historical period. He was particularly interested in their brick-making process. On my next visit, Jonnie was excited to see me. He and his uncle had done more research about making bricks, and they had dug a pit in the backyard. They had made molds for the bricks out of wood, involving measuring and mathematical calculations. Jonnie was set to go, but I suggested that we go back onto the Colonial Williamsburg Web page to review all

about brick making so that we would be prepared. I asked him to read the information to me, and he did! We then set out for the backyard and made a *huge* mess in the pit. We dumped the dirt mixture and water into the pit. We rolled up our pants, took off our shoes and socks, and took turns mixing the dirt and water with our feet. We then took the mixture out of the pit and packed it into the twenty-four molds. They had to dry for days, so we cleaned up and went back into the house for a snack. Although there wasn't much reading that was done this day, the "experiment" that we did was sparked by Jonnie's interest in the colonial period. He read, researched, and used his math skills in order to get to this point. I had a wonderful time with Jonnie, gratified by his enthusiasm. My fears about how I would deal with Jonnie were unrealized. I learned that I need to trust my instincts and to have faith in myself and in my ability to give what is needed to Jonnie, when he needs it.

Despite the limited time she had with Jonnie and her fears that she could not help him through his illness, this tutor built a strong tutoring relationship. Her example raises the issues addressed in this chapter regarding making connections, building trust, motivating students to work, and going beyond the academic work.

Like other relationships, each tutoring combination offers a unique experience, but having followed the experiences of hundreds of tutors, we have a great deal of confidence in tutors' abilities to bond with their students and not only to help them improve their schoolwork but to shape and to inform their lives.

MAKING CONNECTIONS

The first thing that a tutor must do with a new tutee is make some kind of connection. How tutors make connections differs according to the personal interaction styles of student and tutor. But, as with any relationship, some common ground must be established to create the space for the tutoring relationship to grow. Sometimes these connections are purely academic: A student needs help with math or some kind of homework assignment, and the tutor provides it. Other times connections are more personal—a favorite food, sports team, music group, or an ethnic background that the tutor and tutee share. To establish a connection, a tutor must be a careful observer, particularly at the outset of tutoring. An astute tutor can usually find some way to achieve that magical moment in an early session when things seem to click with a student. However, some tutor-tutee relationships require a great deal of effort.

Responding to a Request for Help

A tutee's request for help is often the first step in building a relationship with a tutee, especially with an older or adult student. But neither the relationship nor the academic help stops once the question has been answered. Talk to your students; if they do not understand a concept, move back a step—they likely do not understand the preceding concepts either. Students, especially when they first meet tutors, are reluctant to ask for clarification. They may tell you that they understand even when they are still confused. Encourage them to keep talking and to explain processes back to you. Ask them to talk through their work or to show you the steps that they take in solving problems. Make it clear that you will explain as many times and in as many different ways as it takes to help them understand.

Many tutors find that this process of simply providing help, and being willing to provide more help if necessary, serves as an icebreaker. Even if the student does not open up immediately, your kindness and questions open the door for future contact, making it easier for the student to interact more in later sessions. Sometimes a student who leaves the first tutoring session still shy and reserved will ask for help right away the next week. Tutees may wait to see if you appear again before they begin to trust you. Just showing up again can prove that you are there for them.

Picking Up on an Interest

Picking up on a tutee's interests is not always easy but is a very useful practice in making a connection. Many tutors try to make an immediate connection to get tutees smiling and ready to let down their walls a little. Comment on a baseball cap with a team name on it or a T-shirt with a Disney character. Show the tutees that you are interested in who they are and what they like. In the process, you demonstrate a great deal: that the tutoring session does not follow the same rigid structure as school, that

Where to Find Hints about Your Student

Building relationships is all about making connections, but where do you start? Hints are everywhere!

- Clothing. Characters, sports figures, brand names, styles, even colors give you starting points in conversation. Sometimes just saying something like, "I love your hairbands," can jumpstart a relationship.
- Notebooks and backpacks. Students often write and draw on their notebooks and backpacks. See-through notebooks that can hold pin-ups and pictures are even better. Take a look at your students' notes and doodles, and you'll probably learn a lot.
- Books, magazines, iPods. Your students' free reading materials and musical choices may give you a launching point.
- Friends. Pay attention to the other students with whom your student talks. You can ask questions about them that will help you learn about your student.
- Ask about the most recent weekend or vacation. Asking, "What did you do this weekend?" gives you lots of openings, and it's an easy conversational question.
- Tell a story. Kids love to tell stories. If you tell one of your own, you'll probably elicits lots of interesting stories (it may be hard to get the student to be quiet!).

you are interested in more than just the tutees' academic progress, and that they can relax and be themselves around you.

The next tutor found that, although commonalties established a thin connection, she needed to work harder to build a strong bond with her tutee, a fourteen-year-old ninth-grade Latino student:

Among Marco's books, I noticed he had a sketchpad containing some amazing works of art. One in particular, an intricate drawing of a joker, contained the words, "Breathe in, breathe out." It comes from a song by the band Bush, so I immediately asked Marco if he listened to that type of music (alternative), and he said yes. We smiled at each other approvingly, making our first connection. At first, he did not look me in the eyes either, but as soon as I asked him about his work, everything changed.

"What is that?" I asked, referring to a leather-bound black notebook.

"Oh, I draw sometimes, you know."

"Can I see one?" I dared, hoping I wouldn't be rejected.

"If you want." I breathed a sigh of relief as he handed the book over.

"It's a joker," he said pointing to it.

"That's really good, Marco!" I said with sincerity.

His eyes met mine for the first time. He even smiled, "Thanks."

One tutor who was having a particularly hard time getting through to a shy ten-year-old girl in the fifth- and sixth-grade class she was working with had a breakthrough when she complimented the child:

I complimented Brianne on the white shoes she was wearing and told her I liked how her name was painted in different colors on the outside. I asked her who made those for her, and she replied her aunt. She then began to say how her aunt does her hair and braids it for her. I told her that her hair was so beautiful and long. She told me she would braid mine like hers if I wanted her to. I said, "okay," not thinking she wanted to braid right there and then.

Brianne was very talented, and she braided my hair in two minutes. I praised her over and over again on how good my braid looked. She then said, smiling, "We look like sisters and twins, too."

Brianne's statement, "We look like sisters and twins, too," demonstrates the strong sense of identification that a child can have, often over commonalities that adults might dismiss as silly or simple. Remember that making a connection can be much easier than it looks at a first glance.

If nothing triggers a connection immediately, talk to your students. See what they like and dislike. Ask them what they do for fun, who their friends are, and what they like to do outside school. Take mental notes (and jot down the notes after the session ends, if that will help you remember details). Remembering a topic from one session to the next can serve as proof that you care and are truly interested. Even if your tutee is not willing to discuss something immediately, you may be able to bring it up or to work it into an activity later and make a connection.

Other times, as you work toward making a connection, something will fall into place. Because these two female tutors not only persisted but remained relaxed with their first-grade African American student, they found a commonality with her that they never could have imagined:

After school, I tutored a first-grade African American girl named Tumaini. She was very quiet at first. She sat down and kept her head down even when she talked. When I began talking to her, she answered almost in a whisper, with her face down and her hands in her face.

She was the only tutee to come after school, so Sara and I decided to tutor her together. We introduced ourselves and then asked her questions, such as, what was her favorite color and how many siblings did she have. She answered, "Pink, and my sister who goes to another school and takes the bus will pick me up at 3:30 P.M."

When we asked her, "Do you have homework?" she brought out two handouts. One was a picture of a flower with four blank squares at the bottom. The assignment was to draw the steps showing how the flower grew. We began by asking her what was needed first to make a flower, and she responded, "Seeds." She then drew them and continued by drawing a person planting them and watering them. During this assignment she was still very quiet. She did answer our questions, but only in a whisper with her head down and her hands in her face.

Her second assignment was to write the months on a long gray paper with wide lines. As soon as we saw the paper, Sara and I began reminiscing about our school days when we used that paper. We told Tumaini that the paper always tore when you erased. She laughed and said that that happened to her, too. It was this discussion that helped her feel comfortable with us, because she began to speak louder. She removed her hands from her face when she spoke to us and even made eye contact.

As in this example, patience usually leads to a breakthrough or a connection. Sometimes this "getting-to-know-you" period can also act as a gateway to a more enjoyable school activity that the student would be reluctant to do otherwise. In the next exchange, a male Filipino tutor remembered an interest of his nine-year-old Latino student and used it to get him interested in reading in the extra time that they had together:

> I thought maybe we could read a book like *Goosebumps* or something like that. He had mentioned reading one of R. L. Stine's *Goosebumps* books in a previous session. I recalled the story he was explaining to me called "Be Careful What You Wish For" and got him talking about it again. Like many of the other stories he had told me up to that point, he was really excited and tended to stutter over words.

Later, drawing on his student's interest in myths and science fiction, the same tutor brought in Filipino fables and myths, because he found them to be interesting reading material and because he wanted to share some of his culture with his tutee.

In some situations, creating a connection proves difficult, and the tutors have to exert greater effort, sometimes for fewer rewards. But even without speaking, it is possible to create a link between yourself and a tutee. For instance, in the case of the hospitalized child discussed in Chapter 1, the tutor tried everything he could think of to get the boy to open up—to no avail. He finally took some visual cues from the child's personal effects and went to work trying to find some game or activity to break the child out of his shell. Although the experience ended without any words exchanged, the tutor left with some feeling of accomplishment. He had managed to show the child that he understood where his interests lay and that he respected the child's decision not to talk at that moment. Without words, he had made a connection.

Avoiding Gifts and Bribes

Many tutors try to establish tutoring relationships by giving their students gifts or incentives. Although most children respond well to gifts, gifts can be counterproductive in establishing an effective, long-term tutoring relationship. Using little gifts and treats to gain the friendship of your student is an easy trap to fall into: Tutors find that even the most stubborn child will crack when presented with a candy bar or stickers. Many tutors consider a little sack of candies or pretty pencils part of their standard "tutoring kit."

But gifts create a superficial bond between tutor and tutee, and returning the following week without candy or gifts will endanger the relationship. Gifts or rewards presented regularly can undermine the tutoring, because the tutee begins to focus on the goodies rather than learning. Constant gifts can also hurt the relationship; they tend to preclude a deeper partnership built on trust and common interests. At its core, tutoring works because tutors teach children academic material that they want to learn (even if they are not always excited to learn it!). But most tutors also find that, because their tutees like them and value their relationship, they can set high expectations for students and encourage them, even cajole them, to work hard. Many tutors use the trust that they build to push their students to challenge themselves and to excel. You hurt that trust when you build a relationship on bribes.

The following example shows how fragile a relationship built on bribes can be. This tutor found that she had no emotional or personal leverage with the ten-year-old African American girl she had been working with. Her requests meant nothing. Summer only wanted the candy that she had come to expect:

> I said, "Summer, come here and sit down. The teacher wants you to read this short story and answer the questions on the back. We only have twenty minutes left, so you better start reading it."
>
> Summer placed her hands on her hips and stated, "I don't want to read that stupid story."
>
> While she walked away, I replied, "Fine, then, I won't give you the candy I brought you."
>
> "You better give it to me!"
>
> "Nope, not until you read."
>
> With an angry look, Summer left and went to sit at her desk.

Although students usually respond to bribes, the loyalty that results is often short-lived and not based on the tutee's involvement with the tutor or learning.

BUILDING TRUST

Making a connection is key to establishing a good tutoring relationship, but it is only one small step. The process of creating a relationship builds from that connection. One of the main foundations of this relationship must be trust, which a tutor can build in many ways. Sometimes it is just

How to Be a Trusted Adult

It's not easy to build trust with a student, but some simple dos and don'ts exist.

Do:

- Be consistent. Show up and show up on time. If you say that you'll bring something (or do something), do it.
- Remember details. Everyone appreciates it when people listen to them and remember what they say. Remember who your students' friends are, what they like to do, and how they like to learn. Keep a folder or notebook and take notes if you need to, but prove to your students that you care by remembering important details about them.
- Prove that you think about them when you aren't together. Little things like bringing in magazine articles that you thought that they would like or looking up something on the Internet that they were wondering about prove that you think about students even after you go home. Those little gestures go a long way in building a relationship.
- Be honest. You don't have to keep all your students' secrets. Sometimes you have to tell. Sometimes you have to "rat" on your students and tell parents or teachers that the students misbehaved or struggled. But when you have to tell a secret or "tell on" students, give them warning. Let them know that you're going to tell and, ideally, "tell" in front of them so they know you aren't going behind their backs.
- Admit when you make mistakes. No one is perfect. When you make errors, admit them to your students. They'll respect you for it.
- Apologize. If you do something wrong, say you're sorry. You will have moments when you'll get frustrated. You may snap or raise your voice. It's okay to be human, but don't forget to apologize when you do something wrong.
- Be the grown-up. Don't get into battles, especially attitude battles, with your students. You are the grown-up (or at least the authority figure), so act like it. Take the high ground. If a student gets insulting, remain calm. If a student puts you down, accept the opinion and respond calmly. Try to keep your voice even and calm. Be the adult.
- Use a clean slate. If students misbehave or let you down, don't hold it against them. Start tutoring sessions with a clean slate. Give students a new chance each time you see them. Most students are embarrassed when they do something wrong but can get defensive if you keep bringing it up. So be the adult and let it go.

Don't:

- Make false promises. Some students will come right out and ask if you'll take them on field trips or come to their house to play. Explain that you can't by explaining your role. Don't promise things you can't deliver.
- Give false assurances. If your students study hard for a test, tell them that you are proud of how hard they worked. But don't promise them an A grade. You can't control the grades. If test grades aren't what you hoped, promise to help the students study harder, but don't promise an A on the next test either.
- Put down your students' choices. "In my opinion" is an important preface. If your student chooses not to do a homework assignment, you can say, "In my opinion, that's a bad choice—why not just do the work, get it over with, and not ruin your grade?" But show that you understand that your student will not always make the same choices you do. You can disagree and disapprove, but you still have to respect that the student ultimately gets to make choices about his or her life.
- Sulk. When a student lets you down, act like the grown-up. Don't be passive aggressive and punish a student for letting you down. The student probably feels bad as it is. Acknowledge the issue and then move on.
- Pretend you understand something that you don't understand. Ask questions if you have to. Be sympathetic if you can. But don't pretend to understand a life that you can't understand. Your student can accept the fact that you don't fully get it (but want to). However, the student will distrust you if you pretend to be someone you are not.

a matter of proving that you, as the tutor, want to help and that you care. Other times, tutees demand some kind of reciprocity before they will open up. In still other cases, the tutor must "prove," by remembering facts about a tutee's life and showing genuine interest, that the tutee is an important part of the tutor's life.

In the next example, a tutor realized what her absence might mean to her tutee. She was able to change her plans to prevent undermining the trust that she had already established. She was rewarded by her tutee's response to her arrival:

A few hours before my tutoring session, I found out I had to attend a meeting and miss my session with my tutee. It was about 5:15 P.M., and a fellow tutor text messaged me to make sure that I wasn't going to tutoring, and she asked me whether or not she should tell my tutee, Kalifa, to find another tutor. I became overwhelmed with disappointment with myself; I could not believe that I had even considered leaving Kalifa on her own or with another tutor who did not know a thing about what she needed help with or how to help her. I immediately got up and began walking toward the tutoring site. What was even more surprising to me was that after I left my meeting and was walking toward Kalifa, I was so happy! I knew that at that point Kalifa needed me much more than any meeting did, and I was not going to be the one to disappoint her. As I was walking to the building, Kalifa saw me and ran up to me, almost knocking me over.

As you go about the process of building trust, you are trying not only to get your tutee to depend on you but to be worthy of the dependence. Of course, you will make a conscientious effort not to disappoint your student (as in arriving late or not at all), but you also have the obligation to make sure that the new ideas you pass on contribute to the ultimate goal of tutoring: a student with an increased sense of strength, independence, and love for learning.

Overcoming Past Experiences

Trust is the most precarious aspect of a tutoring relationship. Although some students give it easily, many are suspicious. Establishing trust can be especially hard when students in tutoring programs have seen several tutors come and go, some without saying good-bye. Other students have experienced apathetic tutors and do not know how to even go about establishing a real relationship with a tutor. The following is a conversation that one tutor had with a staff member as she was introduced to her site, a private school for emotionally disturbed adolescents:

As Torey continued to tell me about the school, there must have been some sort of excitement in my eyes, because he asked if I was nervous. I said no, but that I was excited to begin working with the school. I asked why he thought I was nervous. He indicated that previous tutors were never this excited to work with the students. I said, "What do you mean?" He said that a lot of tutors signed in and went to their corners to read their books or magazines.

The same tutor experienced a rude awakening on her first day of tutoring at this school:

Ms. Smith's [the teacher] students seemed well behaved: They quietly attended to their work. When I mentioned this to Ms. Smith, she laughed and said, "You haven't seen nothing yet." I continued monitoring the surroundings. A young lady raised her hand, her eyes directed toward me. Ms. Smith asked her what she needed. The young lady asked Ms. Smith who I was. Ms. Smith told her that I was from UCLA and that I would be helping her out in the classroom. I said hello. She said hi and asked me what my major was. I responded, "Sociology and psychology." She responded with, "Oh, I get it, another lab experiment."

Young people often express their opinions directly and without embarrassment. And this student's reaction to her new tutor demonstrates that every tutor who works with a student leaves a legacy. When students have bad experiences with a tutor, they remember. This memory can affect their progress not only with that tutor but with every tutor they come in contact with. That is why, as you move through your tutoring experience, it is important to bear in mind that you are creating a long-lasting impact on your tutee.

Tutors can leave a good or bad tutoring legacy. Many students remember good experiences with tutors, and their memories show that these relationships are often important to them. A Latino sixth grader who opened up fairly easily to his new tutor. The tutor reported that, as they discussed the student's former tutor, "[My student] shared with me that his old tutor had gone to Switzerland and that he had sent him a postcard. He seemed really touched by that."

Some of the best ways to gain the respect and trust of your tutees (even leery ones) are to be straightforward and honest with them, to respect their individuality, and to lay out the parameters of the relationship from the start.

Showing Respect

Demonstrating respect for the tutee starts off with interest, curiosity, and attention as well as communicating the importance of doing the work. In doing these things, you are saying two things: "You are important to me" and "I expect you to do your work." Tutors need to generate an atmosphere of mutual respect. They serve as role models for tutees, so it is important for the tutor to be someone whom the tutee can look up to and admire. The tutees' respect for their tutors also plays an important role in how well they listen to and follow their suggestions regarding academic work.

It is just as vital for tutors to respect their tutees. Student capabilities vary widely, but it is not for the tutor to judge whether students are up to par. The tutor is there to help and to encourage the students while still giving them the respect and autonomy that all people, including children, deserve.

One of the hardest things for tutors to understand is how difficult it is for many students to ask for help or to receive criticism. Often their reluctance stems from pride, and the same inhibition that prevents students from raising their hands in class to ask questions can cause them to be shy with a tutor. Why should students make themselves vulnerable to a stranger? Tutors must be patient and not push too hard but make sure that students know that they are open to and available for questions. Tutors should explicitly tell tutees that they will not think any less of them for asking for help—that, in fact, they welcome questions from their tutees.

One tutor working at a community center geared toward teaching leadership to mostly minority high school students found that she had to be very tactful about offering her help so she did not offend the students she was working with:

> The black male, whose name is Jesse, said that he was doing fine and that he did not need a tutor. "Tutors make you feel stupid," said Jesse. I looked quickly at him and asked him what he meant by that. He just said that some tutors can make you feel stupid by the way they talk to you. I asked him if I had made him feel stupid by asking him if he needed help. "Nah," he said.
>
> "Okay, well, if you need help, then I'll help you; if not, that's okay too," I told him. He smiled and then went about his work. I just sat there and laughed—hoping to ease the tension.

It was a rocky start, but because this tutor backed off and respected the pride involved in this young man's asking for help, he did ask her a question a few minutes later. The following week, Jesse asked for help again as soon as his tutor walked in. Showing mutual respect allowed this tutor to form a respectful relationship with a student who was not sure he wanted help.

This tutor's willingness to allow a student to determine his own needs created the basis of their relationship. Respect is a major part of the tutoring relationship. Unlike teachers who have to manage a classroom full of students, tutors get to individualize their attention. This means that they can negotiate teaching styles and subjects with their students, giving the students a sense of autonomy and making the academic help much more valuable.

In the following example, a tutor went too far in determining her tutee's needs by automatically correcting her mistakes. Even though the tutor thought she was helping her tutee, she did not realize how a six-year-old child would interpret her constant interruptions and corrections:

> My tutee began reading in a soft voice. She was able to pronounce the majority of the words; however, there were also a good number of words she did not know how to say. I found myself being didactic and trying to explain the meaning of every word she didn't know how to pronounce. I would spend a good thirty to forty-five seconds on each of these words. For example, she didn't know how to pronounce the word "hissing." So first, I sounded the word out for her. Then I asked her if she knew what that word meant. She shook her head. I explained, "'Hissing' is a word to describe this sort of sound: 'Sssssss.' For example, snakes sometimes hiss. (I clasped my two hands together and waved them in the air.) 'Sssssss.'"
>
> I did this for many other words. I always tried to stay animated and used my hands as much as I could to keep her attention. Initially, she loved it when I explained the meaning of the words to her, as she would giggle and smile at me. Towards the end of the story, though, after I had been explaining many words, she started to just give me blank stares. I interpreted her new lack of interest in my definitions as typical of children, as they often get bored easily. Plus, we were almost done with the story, so I continued to explain the meaning of words for the remainder of our reading.

When we were done, she got up and went over to get a sheet of paper. I didn't know what she was doing at first, but once she returned, I realized she had gone to get a "Summary" sheet to fill out. The first question asked what the title of the book was. The book that we were reading was a compilation of stories, and we had only read one story. She wrote down the title of the book. I commended her on that but was eager to teach her the difference between a story and a book. I had wanted her to write down the name of the story, too. So I proceeded to try to explain that we were reading a story, and there were many stories in the book. I told her that she could underline the title of the book and put the title of the story in quotation marks. At first, she thought I was trying to tell her that she got the title wrong. So she crossed out the title she had written, put a huge "X" over it, and drew a girl stick figure saying "No!" next to it. I tried to explain that she was right; I was just trying to say that she could also add something to her answer. I must have spent about five minutes trying to explain this to her, but she didn't understand. Both of us ended up frustrated, and finally, I gave up and let it be.

When she crossed out the title, drew that figure, and wrote those words next to her "incorrect" answer, I was really shocked. I couldn't believe that she had reacted so rashly.

This tutor was faced with a difficult situation: She had a student who needed a lot of help, and she desperately wanted to be a good tutor. She did everything she thought she should: explaining, correcting, helping, and staying upbeat. But how do you provide all that help without completely undermining the child's sense of competence? Tutoring is all about balance. Obviously, you need to correct a student who is struggling with academic material: That is why you are there. And, if a student does not know what words mean, he or she is going to struggle to understand a story. But tutors must juggle the necessity of providing academic instruction, the child's (often fragile) ego, and the need to complete an assignment (as completing an assignment well is often what makes a tutee come back for more help!). In this case, the tutor was right to make vocabulary work fun. But she also needed to listen to the student's cues and to pick up the pace (either let a few words go, or quickly give an easy definition) when she realized that the student was getting bored. Children, especially young children, are apt to give up on a task if they feel like it is impossible. So, it is important for tutors to "pick their battles." In this case, an experienced tutor, already sensing the student's frustration, would have let her write the book title rather than the story title, perhaps just mentioning that next time, they might write both. If the tutor had planned ahead and asked the student what she needed to accomplish in the course of the tutoring session, she would have also been better prepared to budget her time and energy across the reading and the summary. In the end, the tutoring session was a good learning experience for the tutor. She did everything right as a tutor, but she needed more balance to make the tutoring work for this particular student.

Another problematic area that tutors may run into is a tendency, perhaps because of their own discomfort, to treat their students as "less." Sometimes tutors forget that students are capable in their own rights, and they treat them like babies or like students who are less intelligent or less motivated than they actually are. When we provide assistance, we often start to talk down to people, which is the opposite of giving students respect and autonomy and allowing them to determine their own needs. Sometimes tutors resort to using baby talk with their students, or they hover over them, giving the impression that they consider them incapable of working on their own. Such behavior not only strips students of their independence but demeans them and deprives them of the notion that they even deserve respect.

Although tutors often enter the tutoring site expecting to sit right down to work with students, it may take students a while to get used to the presence of other "teachers." Tutors should not appear standoffish, but by giving students the space they need, tutors can help establish themselves as people with whom the students will want to form relationships.

Tutors can also actively foster mutual respect in their relationships with their tutees by showing that they value them—their feelings, their progress, and their friendship. In the following example, a white female tutor was able to show respect for Estella, her seven-year-old Latina tutee, in two ways: by respecting the possibility that Estella might be jealous of her tutor's other tutee and by asking for a piece of her artwork:

> The time went by very quickly, and before I knew it, it was 5:00 and almost time for Jake to arrive. I politely told Estella that we had to finish up, because it was almost time for her to go home

and my next kid to come. She did not know that I tutored someone else. The last thing I wanted was for her to think that I was
trying to get rid of her.

"You tutor someone else?" she asked.

"Yeah, after you go home, a boy named Jake comes and I help
him out with his homework and talk like we do. But you know
what? He doesn't like to draw beautiful rainbows like you do."

She smiled and then asked, "Can I take that picture [that
her tutor had drawn] home?"

"If you get to take one of mine, then I get to take one of
yours." I asked her what pictures I could keep, and we
exchanged pictures and she went inside to pack up.

In allowing her tutee to keep her drawing, the tutor gave Estella something of herself to hold onto until the next week. By the same token, by
asking for Estella's drawing, the tutor demonstrated that she valued her
time with Estella and wanted to keep part of that interaction with her.

Establishing Reciprocity

Another way a tutor can create trust in the tutoring relationship is by
sharing personal stories and experiences with students. As a tutor, you
are in a position of authority. But as the personal helper of a student, you
stand to be much more than just a smaller-scale teacher. Good tutors
can hope to have students open up to them and expose their passions
and interests. These insights form the basis for a relationship, and they
are also what makes individual tutoring so rewarding. But before students open up, they often need to see that sharing is a two-way street
and that the tutor is not just another authority figure there to exploit
them or to make them vulnerable.

Many tutors find that students respond well to shared personal
information or anecdotes if they are relevant and if the tutee is interested. Sharing personal information can be a delicate part of the tutoring relationship; students like to get personal. And when you have a
successful tutoring relationship, in which you are a mentor as well as a
role model and friend, this is natural. Some students are just curious.
Others may be testing you to see whether you are who you say you are
and you are willing to play an equal role in the relationship. It is a fine
line for a tutor to walk. How much do you want to tell your students?

You do not want to bore your students by talking about yourself too much. And, even if they are interested, you have to be careful how much you can share without undermining the tutoring relationship or the tutoring process by wasting too much time or by making yourself look too silly. Nonetheless, sharing can create a more personal connection with the students, particularly if you find that you have something important in common or if you have some expertise in an area they are interested in.

This tutor, for example, drew on resources from her personal experience to advise her tutee, a student at an alternative high school:

> We talked about where he wanted to go, and he said he is first going to a local community college and then wants to transfer to UCLA. I told him that's the best way to save money and get all your G.E.s [general education requirements] done before transferring, but I told him not to be one that gets caught in the community college forever. I continued to say that it is easy to slack off, because no one is there to motivate you but you. I shared that I went to community college and then transferred to UCLA as a junior. I told him that he should follow the IGETC [a form that tells junior college students what classes are transferable and count toward a major at a four-year university].
>
> We figured out that he will be able to transfer after a year and a half if he continues to take the right amount of units. He got excited, and I recommended that he can even take summer school to lessen his load during the year. He started laughing because I was so into it. I think that Bob was willing to hear my advice, because I think he realized that I went through the system and was able to transfer.

Other times a tutor can offer personal information as a reward or a validation that the friendship is in fact a two-way street. Little intimacies that prove a true relationship exists can be the most rewarding parts of tutoring. In the following episode, Juliette, the tutor whose tutee, Jesse, told her that some tutors can make you feel stupid, established a bond through the validation of their friendship:

> When I approached his table, he [Jesse] moved over so I could sit next to him. He continued to work on his algebra problem

but stopped halfway when he realized he didn't know what to do. "Hey, Jul, can you help me here?"

"Sure, what's the problem, Jes?" I responded with a laugh.

He looked at me strangely and said, "Huh?"

"Well, you did call me 'Jul,' so I figured I could call you 'Jes,'" I said to him. He responded with a smile.

Even though Jesse was a little taken aback when Juliette called him by a nickname, she remained calm, explained herself, and took one more step in proving that she was trustworthy.

As you work to build relationships with your students, remember that they do not always show their trust in the same ways. Sometimes a student who is shy in tutoring will reveal that he likes you in an unexpected way, as did a six-year-old tutee who acted like a gentleman and a

---

❖ What's Okay to Share?

How do you decide what information to give your students and what to keep to yourself? Every tutoring relationship is different but here are some guidelines:

- Share preferences. Talking about music, movies, and television stars is a great way to open up conversation.
- Share stories about friends and family. Everyone has stories of friends and family. They are universal and good ways to start conversations.
- Share stories about when you were a kid. Stories about what you liked, problems you had, and struggles you had can help you explain to students why you understand what they are going through. These stories can be priceless in building relationships.
- Be careful with politics. You never know the political persuasions of a student's family. Even simple comments can be offensive. Avoid these conversations. Or, give nondetailed answers and move on.
- Be careful with religion. Even such simple questions as, "Do you go to church?" can be difficult. If you don't attend, it can seem very strange to a student who goes to church every week. Sometimes the best way to handle these questions is quickly and nonchalantly: "I don't go to church much. So, what do you have for math today?"
- Be careful talking about relationships. It's fine to mention a boyfriend or girlfriend, but know that students often find these relationships

friend: "Soon we went back inside the center, because it was getting dark and cold. Jose had taken off his large sweatshirt earlier and offered to let me wear it, because I was cold. It covered my arms, and for that I was grateful." Jose's offering of the sweatshirt and his tutor's gracious acceptance, although not a practice customary in a teaching relationship, reflect the types of mutual respect and personal regard that tutors and tutees can create.

Sometimes students' questions cross a line, and tutors feel uncomfortable. It is up to tutors to draw the line wherever they feel it is appropriate. Some students will push their tutors as far as they can, as did this eleven-year-old male student:

> Juan asked me a lot of personal questions, although not all at once or right off the bat. One of the first questions he asked was

---

very interesting. And they may have lots of questions. It can be awkward to explain to a third grader that you live with a partner to whom you're not married. Sometimes, if you want to talk about a partner, it's easier to talk about that person as a friend.

- Try to deflect comments about drugs, alcohol, parties and other things that parents might disapprove of. Sometimes you'll talk frankly about these topics with older students, especially when you feel like they need some guidance. Sometimes, if you know a student is drinking, you have to share your own experiences to have credibility. But most students who ask these questions are just asking out of curiosity. And your answers will probably bring up more questions. The answers also run the risk of being repeated to parents. When possible, a general answer works best: "Most people drink at least some in college." Smile and change the subject.
- Be careful with any subject you're sharing just because you want to show how cool you are. If you're trying to impress your student, think again. That story could very well be inappropriate.
- Clean up your stories when appropriate. Sometimes you'll want to tell a story or example that is not entirely appropriate to the student's age. It's okay to sanitize a story to prove a point (yet keep things G-rated). Just don't go overboard. The student might remember the story and ask you questions later. Stick as close to the truth as possible so your story is consistent.

if I lived with a roommate. I answered that I lived with my boy-friend and found myself feeling a little embarrassed. He didn't ask anything further about that; he went back to his work. He asked if I was "a volunteer or doing tutoring through school." I told him through school, and he asked, "How old are you?" And when I told him thirty, he said, "Shouldn't you be done with school?" I explained that I decided to go back to college because I hadn't finished my degree.

Putting the tutee at ease by sharing personal information does little good if you feel uncomfortable. In the case of Juan and his tutor, even though the tutor did not feel completely comfortable sharing all this information, the exchange formed the basis of what became a close tutoring relationship.

Deciding what is comfortable or appropriate for tutors to share is not always easy. A Persian male tutor was enjoying his interaction with his eight-year-old Persian tutee because of their similar ethnic back-grounds and her natural curiosity about college life. In the course of the conversation, Mary said that her mother would punish her if she men-tioned even the mildest bad word. The tutor, feeling confident about being able to further their camaraderie, offered the following story:

"My father never physically beat me except once in my entire life."

"What did you do?" Mary asked.

"I called him a very bad name."

"What did you call him?"

Soon I realized the hole I had dug for myself. Had I not told her, she would be disappointed in me and not share anything with me. Had I told her, I would run the risk of teaching her a bad word. This created a serious dilemma, so I explained to her why I couldn't tell her the word, but she insisted and threatened to not tell me anything. So my only way out was to choose one of the words that she was throwing out there (which she obvi-ously already knew) in guessing what I called my father.

In this case, the release of too much information created an awkward situation for the tutor that only a white lie could alleviate. In sharing personal information, you must use discretion and, sometimes, careful maneuvering. In the end, tutors have to make their own choices about how much to share—but tutors who expect children to open up to them will probably have to trust them with some of their own personal experiences. At the same time, tutees—like friends and other acquaintances—are not entitled to know everything about you. So do not be afraid to say that a question is too personal. Most students, even children, will respect boundaries if you set them (in fact, they may be more shocked if you tell them everything!). So be straightforward and maintain the lines that you feel are appropriate and necessary.

How quickly students open up to their tutors varies considerably, sometimes along age and gender lines, and sometimes according to students' personalities. These fifth-grade girls were eager to let their new female tutor into their circle: "When I was leaving, the four girls from my group ran up to me and gave me a hug and asked if I will be here tomorrow. I told them not 'til next week, and they said they can't wait. I was really excited when I was leaving, because I felt like the children really enjoyed me being there, and I felt a close friendship forming with them."

A Few Practical Concerns

With the myriad complex and personal issues that affect building and sustaining trust in a tutoring relationship, a few practical concerns must be kept in mind. The building of trust is a long and careful process that can be destroyed easily. When you create a relationship, you ask your student to trust you, which carries some obligations on your part, including (1) showing up for tutoring sessions, and showing up on time; (2) calling ahead and rescheduling if for some reason you must miss a session; and (3) keeping your promises—if you promise to bring something to a session, such as a book or some information, do it.

The following tutor found that her failure to follow up compromised some of the progress she had made in their previous session with her tutee, a fourteen-year-old Latina:

> Laura was more pleasant with me this second time around, touching me on the arm when she arrived. As I was already on the computer, she went ahead and sat down with me. She said she wanted to compose something again. I was a flake. I had promised Laura that I would type up the letter about her late

friend Joaquin but had not delivered on that promise. I told her that I would get it to her definitely by next week. She just kind of smiled and nodded, not upset and not necessarily disbelieving. I don't know, I couldn't read her reaction. I was so upset with myself though, that I had already broken that promise.

As intuitive and personal as tutoring relationships are, sometimes it is the concrete stuff that proves their solidity. Keeping promises can mean a lot to your students. It proves that they can count on you.

MOTIVATING STUDENTS TO WORK

For a tutor, forming a relationship can sometimes feel like a waste of time. Shouldn't a tutor use every second to help with the child's schoolwork? Not necessarily. Often, time invested in getting to know a tutee can make the time spent learning even more valuable. Once relationships are formed, tutors can work within them to help their tutees overcome their academic problems.

Most students want to learn, and they like doing well in school. However, many students dislike school work. They hate to fail, and they resist doing work with which they struggle. As a tutor, your job is often to help students with work that is hard for them or work that they find difficult or tedious. No matter how much children want to learn and to be smart, they may fight you when confronted with work that they do not like or know that they are "bad at." And, to be honest, when students come to tutoring, they often come to specifically work on skills and subjects that they have been "bad at."

Having a strong relationship with your tutees helps mitigate those problems. You can use your personal knowledge of them to gear schoolwork toward particular interests and learning patterns. You can provide moral support just by being there as they work. You can bargain with students and use the relationship as leverage. And you can use your educated expectations of your tutee to set goals for learning. All these techniques contribute to the tutoring experience, because tutoring is much more than sharing academic knowledge. Tutoring includes motivating students to enjoy learning and to feel good about themselves while they do it. One woman who has been a tutor for almost ten years stated it this way: "The most important aspect of my job is to be a good cheerleader."

Applying Tutee Interests

Drawing your tutees out and getting them interested in learning can prove to be one of the most difficult parts of tutoring. It is very difficult to orient people to tasks that they fear or are not interested in. And yet most people do not receive tutoring in things that they are good at. They get tutoring in subjects that they struggle with—and often dislike. You, as the tutor, have to help them get over their discomfort, fear, and, sometimes, hatred, of a subject, just to begin to approach the academic material. One of the best ways to overcome students' negative feelings toward a subject is to apply the task to something that they are interested in or that they feel confident about. This tutor, a white female who aspired to be a special-education teacher, finally got her fourth-grade African American student, Brad, to open up to her by indulging him and letting him tell stories. Terrified at the thought of reading or writing, Brad was an eager and competent storyteller and quickly lost his inhibitions when he got into a narrative mode:

> Brad started to turn away from the table, but I wanted to get the tutoring session under control, so I immediately asked him if he would like to read one of the books on outer space. Brad, however, had something else in mind: "I would like to tell some stories."
>
> The teacher suggested that he wanted the students to direct their own sessions whenever possible. So, since today was our session, I thought it would be good to let Brad lead. I also was curious about this virus he had mentioned, and so I thought that if I were to listen to his stories, I might have a better idea of where Brad is coming from and where his interests lie. So I said, "Brad, why don't you tell me a story?" Brad responded by saying he had a really good story to tell me.
>
> He walked away from the desk, stood about ten feet away from me, and then started to tell a story about UFOs that were coming down to Earth to fight the bad people. I faced my chair toward him and leaned forward so that he knew I was taking interest in what he was telling me. Brad began to pace back and forth on the carpet and showed no signs of nervousness as he told his UFO story. Sometimes Brad would look down at the floor and other times he would look up at the wall, and he would

always look over at me to make sure I was listening. I couldn't even pick up on everything he was saying since he was talking so fast.

Brad would tell his story in third person, and then he would have his characters talk in dialogue form. When Brad liked a certain part of the story he was talking about, his eyes would get big, and his voice would change to higher tones; even spit would start coming out of his mouth. Brad stopped pacing on the carpet and began walking around the room as he continued to tell his story. I got the impression that he was gathering ideas from the props, books, posters in the room to help him add to his story. I kept saying to myself, "Is this the quiet, underconfident boy that I was helping last week in math?" I couldn't get over Brad's imagination, which brought him to life and gave him confidence and an automatic smile across his face.

After about twenty minutes of storytelling, the tutor began to feel guilty, because she had been working with Brad all morning without getting him to do any reading or writing; she had been letting him tell her monster stories. She came up with the idea of having Brad tell his story into a tape recorder and then write and illustrate his own book. Brad, who had said only a few words to his tutor before he got into storytelling mode, was thrilled the next week when she arrived with a tape recorder and book-making materials:

I told him that not only was he going to tell another story but that I would record him telling his story. At this point, he was sitting down at the desk, and a wide smile came across his face and his eyes got really big. Brad seemed very excited about the idea, and I asked him if he had ever heard his voice recorded. He said that he hadn't and gave a chuckle as he put his hands on top of his head.

Brad asked me why we had these school supplies with us. Now I could explain to him that not only were we going to record his story but that we were also going to make a book about his story. Once I told him the plan, he couldn't stop talking about what we could do with the book after it was complete. He made some suggestions like, "Yeah, let's make it really good so I can sell it to people."

This project turned into one in which Brad drew his own illustrations, put together the book, and sounded out the words of his story to write it down. Brad was reading, writing, and drawing, and he was excited about it, something that never would have happened if Brad's tutor had not listened to his stories and found out what got him excited—what would make him eager to learn. Taking the time to form a relationship allowed this tutor to peer into the mind of her tutee and to focus on the best ways to motivate him into doing activities that intimidated him. This is another example of how respecting the wishes of tutees and giving them some autonomy in their learning processes can open doors to fruitful relationships.

Paying attention to what your tutees enjoy can also lead you to how they like to learn and what methods will be the most effective. The following tutor was frustrated at the lack of motivation his seventh-grade African American student displayed. They struggled so much to do weekly fractions assignments that the tutor feared that the student just did not care about learning at all—and that perhaps the tedious work of fractions was something that the student would never consent to learn (he could do it—he just did not seem to want to!). In some of their free time, as he watched his student draw and teach some other students to draw, he gained insight into his tutee:

> He reached once again down into his oversized pockets and pulled out a folded-up piece of paper. He opened it and showed me a drawing that he made with a friend's instruction that morning in school. This was a really good drawing. I don't mean good as in "a nice attempt"—I mean good as in it had objective quality. So we talked about this art friend of his and how he was teaching Jonathon to draw all sorts of cool monsters, three-dimensional shapes, and fancy lettering of all kinds. It was something he talked fondly of and looked forward to every day in school—the fifteen minutes in homeroom when he was learning to draw. I asked him to draw me other things, and without much hesitation he proceeded to draw his name in creative bubble lettering. Then he drew a dog and some other animals.
>
> It was clear that each figure he drew was not just a natural inclination he had to draw but a deliberate form taken on through learning. Let me explain: The puppy dog that he drew started with two round circles, and I was stumped as to which

part of the dog they would end up being. Then with a few more strokes of his favorite three-dollar mechanical pencil, the animal started taking on recognizable shape. He had learned patterns and could incorporate them into different figures and characters. While at first I thought this was a diversion, it later appeared to me to be the very thing that weekly fractions were not, an activity by which Jonathon could be motivated to learn.

By watching how meticulously Jonathon drew and by realizing that Jonathon was following careful, learned steps, the tutor knew that his tutee was not opposed to learning. He realized that Jonathon could learn, master, and implement a complex set of steps (similar to the ones he needed to compute with fractions). He found out that Jonathon could be eager to learn, as long as he was interested in what was being taught. Armed with this information, the tutor was ready to move to the next, even more difficult step: turning fractions into something that Jonathon would be willing to learn.

Tutors who can personalize material have a great advantage over teachers, who must teach to a classroom full of students. Tutors can tweak work in a million different ways to try to engage students who "don't care" about their work. The following problems were written for Amber, a ninth grader who, having already failed Algebra I once, resolutely refused to turn word problems into equations. Nearly in tears, the student argued that she absolutely could not do the work and that she would not graduate from high school because of it. Her tutor resorted to *American Idol,* the student's obsession, to try to draw her into the work. Some problems from her new, tutor-created worksheet read:

> Turn the following word problems into variable equations. Then solve.
> 1. This season Paula rejected 7 more people than Randy. Simon rejected 80 people this year. They rejected 120 people all together. How many people did Paula and Randy reject?
> 2. Simon got mad at Paula for wearing too much hairspray. Paula used 3 times as much hairspray this season as last season. This season she used 46 bottles of hairspray. How much hairspray did she use last season?

3. Simon got Paula 1 puppy for each person she rejected
and 2 puppies for each time she made someone cry on
TV. At the end of the season, she had 42 puppies. She
rejected 14 people. How many people did she make cry?

To even the tutor's surprise, Amber was able to write and to solve equations for her *American Idol* word problems. The transition to regular word problems was still not easy for her, but at least after completing a page of *American Idol* problems, she could no longer claim that the work was impossible for her.

Providing Companionship

Doing schoolwork with a "friend" sometimes makes the work more fun—even if it is just a math worksheet or something that would otherwise be boring and rote. As the tutor quoted earlier suggested, the most important part of her job as a tutor is being a cheerleader. She said that she knew that she could not make much of an academic difference with children in just a few weeks or months but that improving their confidence and pumping up their self-image mattered a lot. Simply getting students excited about learning has proved useful for many tutors:

> Julia was not very fond of math, especially for a lesson that
> asked you to subtract using the concept of borrowing.
> "You and I, my friend, are going to work on subtraction!
> Just you and I, okay? Are you ready?" I asked.
> "Yeah," she responded.
> "Okay then, let's have a high five to get started." At which
> point she gave me a high five and smiled.

Tutors can also provide important support and encouragement as they help their students learn concepts they struggle with. Sometimes a little advice and some positive feedback is enough. The following white female tutor found that her fourth-grade Mexican American student tended to give up, because she was afraid of what she did not know. The tutor gave her not only a tip on how to get around those kinds of problems but some confidence along with it:

Inside the gym, I sit in between two girls and have them work on independent problems. They both get to the same question about ears of corn that I have to admit is a little tricky. I have to read the question several times over to understand what it is asking. (I wonder if the girls notice I'm struggling and tell them I think the problem is tough also.) I go through the problem step-by-step, learning as I go along. We get to a part that requires them to multiply twelve times eight. Jennifer turns to her own booklet and works away at the problem. I'm watching her carry the one, when I notice that Gina is not looking at her book.

"Do you need some help?"

Silence.

"Do you know how to multiply twelve times eight?"

Small tears roll down her cheeks as she looks at her lap and puts her hand to her face. I am totally confused. Did I do something? Did I not do something? What do I do? Jennifer is still working when I have Gina take a walk with me to the gym's stairs. I didn't want to ask her why she is upset in front of Jennifer. I don't think she will tell me the truth.

"I don't know my twelve times tables," she ekes out with a silent sob.

"Do you know how to multiply eight times two?"

"Yeah, sixteen."

"What is eight times one, plus one?" There is a long pause. "Nine."

"Well, you've done most of the work. You can multiply twelve times eight."

By this time, Jennifer is around us showing me her completed problem, and Gina has stopped crying. I remind her that she can do anything and then remind both of the girls that they are smart.

In this case, the tutor simply broke down the multiplication problem for her tutee. But this act of understanding and the fact that she was there to help made all the difference to Gina. Rather than simply reassuring her and responding to the tears, the tutor helped Gina tackle the problem.

Bargaining on the Relationship

Forming a friendship with your tutees allows you some influence over them. For instance, many tutors report how eager their tutees are to share good grades with them. Students want to impress their tutors and to show that they are working hard in school. Once you have formed a relationship with tutees, you can take advantage of these desires and make some demands upon them. Tutors are often surprised at how well this can work.

After three sessions in which this female Vietnamese tutor's Latino student forgot to bring his homework, she tried implementing a technique she had learned in an education class:

> I turned to Gilbert and said, "You know, it's been three weeks, and I have not been able to help you with your homework. Will you promise me that you'll bring your homework next week?" He quickly responded with "Yes."
>
> Somehow I was unconvinced. I continued, "And what if you forget to bring your homework? Do you know what's going to happen?" He was curious. I said, "I'm going to be really disappointed that you didn't keep your promise to me." He didn't say anything and returned to gluing tissue paper on his piñata.
>
> After several minutes, Gilbert asked, "What if I forget next week?"
>
> I answered, "Then I'm going to be very disappointed."

This tutor did not scold Gilbert. She did not reprimand him or punish him. She used the trust that they had developed in their relationship; this technique would not work between two strangers. But the tutor was pleasantly surprised when, one week later, Gilbert proudly pulled his homework from his backpack. Obviously, Gilbert cared enough not to let her down.

Educated Expectations

We have stressed that tutors should avoid entering tutoring situations with preexisting and unfounded expectations that can cause disappointment and erect a barrier between tutor and tutee. Once tutors have formed relationships with their students and have some insight into their capabilities and how they are best motivated, they can begin to form educated expectations. Educated expectations are goals that tutors can set with their students. They are expectations that are ambitious yet realistic for the students, in the judgment of informed mentors.

When tutees learn to trust their tutor, they can also learn to value their tutor's opinion. As that tutor, your opinions can have an important effect on a student's ambitions and motivations. The following example is from a tutor's experience with Ben, a sixteen-year-old high school student, who was passing but not excelling in any of his classes. When his tutor asked Ben about his grades, he replied that they were "good, I'm passing." The tutor encouraged him to work harder, citing his strength in math and suggesting he could probably get really good grades if he tried. Ben replied that his teacher had told him that if he did his homework, he could probably get an A in the class, but he still resisted doing more work than was necessary:

> It was obvious that he did not understand the benefit of getting good grades, because he commented, "I don't see why I should do the homework if I know how to do the problems, and I am passing."
>
> I found myself in unfamiliar territory. When I was younger, I did not understand the importance of homework either. I was the one who was always asking why I had to do my work, not the one explaining the importance of it. Luckily my parents were there to insist that I did it and to explain why.
>
> They told me, as I in turn told Ben, "Homework is not the hardest thing to do in the world. But to master something, you need practice. Homework is like a way of practicing in order to master a subject. While the subject may have no real bearing on your life, an A in a class shows not only intellect but self-discipline as well. Colleges are inundated with applications every year, and an important way to distinguish people is their grade point average, which is directly affected by doing homework."
>
> Ben thought for a moment and then said, "Yeah, I never thought of it that way. I don't really like to do homework, but I guess I have to in order to be a [UCLA] Bruin."

His tutor's advice made an impact on Ben not only for that day but for the rest of the time the two spent tutoring together. Ben continued to cite becoming a Bruin and going to UCLA as the reason he needed to work hard and to finish his assignments. His tutor had become a guidance figure, someone whom Ben could look up to and respect, and because of that relationship, the tutor was able to place these demands on his tutee.

A tutor can also use educated expectations to push students further than they are at first willing to go. As we mentioned earlier, tutoring is a balancing act. Once tutors know their students, they learn when to push and correct and when to pull back. In the following example, a white female tutor knew that her Latina first grader was capable of sounding out words that she did not know, but she refused to exert the effort. Because they had been working together for several weeks and the tutor knew her capabilities, she made it clear to her tutee that they would learn the trouble words, even if they had to dedicate extra time to it in future sessions. In this way, she was able to motivate her student to try a little harder on the task at hand:

> Estella was reading, pronouncing each word at a time, but whenever she got to the words "things," "was," "where," "were," "there," and "saw," she had problems. "Sound the letters out," I told her. But rather than even trying, she would look up at me and wait for me to start. I tried to explain about "th" and "wh" words, saying the sounds that they make, but it wasn't helping. Every time she got to one of those words, she would immediately look at me, as if to tell her what it was. "Remember, sound it out, that's the best way," I said.
>
> "Sssss . . . aaaa . . . wwww," I tried to get her to sound it out with me, but either she was tired or she just didn't know, and I knew she knew.
>
> She grabbed a piece of paper and wrote out each letter of the word so she would be able to sound it out. "W+h+a+t = what; w+i+t+h = with. . . ." She did this with all of the words she was stuck on. But rather than having it help her, she began to get very distracted and anxious and was writing them very big on the paper and still asking me how to say it.
>
> Then I noticed that some of the times she was looking at the picture to see if that helped her figure out what the word was. For instance, things became all the objects she could find in the picture on the same page, words that had none of the same letters.

"Where is the 'd' in this word? Where is the 'p'?" I felt bad, but I knew that she knew how to figure out what the words were. I told her to stop and take a break, because it was getting too difficult, and maybe she needed to rest her eyes.

I began to write down words she did not understand, and she became very interested in them: "What are you writing?"

"I am writing down the words that you are having trouble with so next week I can bring them back and we can study them again; maybe you can make some flash cards." I could tell by the unhappy look on her face that this did not sound very appealing. And it was just then when she opened up her book and began reading again. This time, she sounded out the words she did not recognize and got them, her speed and confidence level increased, and she raced through the sections. I had to stop her to tell her that she was reading the part she was supposed to read with her parents.

This tutor called her tutee's bluff. She knew Estella was not trying, so she explained to her that if she was having so much trouble reading, she would have to do some extra studying and maybe make flash cards for the words she did not know. Faced with extra work, Estella was motivated to work harder at sounding out words. By learning what her student was capable of, this tutor was able to push Estella to work up to the educated expectations she had formed throughout their time together.

GOING BEYOND ACADEMICS

Not only are tutors more effective academic helpers if they form relationships with their tutees; the relationships may also give them a chance to help students with other problems. Teachers in a classroom of thirty rarely have time to deal with a student who appears troubled on any particular day. As a tutor with only a few students, you have the opportunity to lend some valuable support:

Ms. Lerder stood in front of the class and told them they only had a few more minutes to get their ideas together and finish everything up, so we began to focus back on the subject. It was good, because Christine did not get a chance to speak yet. She was very quiet the whole time, and I asked her if anything was wrong. She said she was just having a bad day. Joanne responded by saying she always had a bad day. I quickly replied, "Maybe there is something really bothering her, Joanne."

I told Christine if she wanted to talk to me after class, I would stick around. She said she didn't feel like talking about her legend and that she would do it on her own for homework. I asked if she had any ideas for homework, and she said she just wanted to explain why it thunders. She did not sound happy. When we were walking out to lunch, I talked to Christine and asked if there was anything I could do to help and just let her know someone cared.

Here, the tutor was able to venture outside her regular duties to provide some moral support for a problem that the teacher hadn't noticed and that Christine's peers dismissed.

For many students, tutors are mentors and role models. For others, they may be the only grown-ups whom the students can rely on or trust. Sometimes students merely need to know that someone is genuinely interested in being involved in the activities of their lives. For this fifth-grade Latino student, having his tutor participate in his soccer game was important to him:

Desiring to have a good time and win the respect of Jason's peers on the field, I played hard while simultaneously trying to keep an eye on Jason. He was one of the least aggressive players on the team and rarely kicked the ball. He seemed almost to disappear out there among close to fifteen others his age. He never made a sound and didn't seem to be one of the more outgoing and well-known kids on his team. In fact, a couple of times when I passed by his area closely, he looked at me with delight that I was noticing him and tapping him. It seemed as though he felt special to have me out there with him even though I was playing against his team.

Tutors can also use their unique positions in their tutees' lives to help fill them with confidence and new experiences. The following female Persian tutor was able to teach her male tutee, a new Persian immigrant, not only how to play basketball but how to interact with his peers and to believe in himself:

Ahmed was standing in a corner of the playground all by himself. I called him over and asked him if he would like to play basketball with me. For a moment, he was hesitant. Then he ran back to the classroom, grabbed a ball, and was ready to play. He dribbled down the court, went up and down the basketball court until he got tired, and stood next to the basket and said that he does not know how. I asked him if he knew how to play; in response, he shook his head.

I explained the game to him. Then, we decided to play again. This time around, he actually knew what to do, but the game was a little boring with just the two of us. I could not help but notice Dylan and Joshua walking toward us. They approached us and asked if they could play. I said, "I don't know, Ahmed is in charge." They went up to him and asked him if they could play, and since Ahmed did not understand them, I translated for him. He smiled at them and said yes.

Once again, Dylan teamed up with Joshua and Ahmed with me. Dylan named their team the Chicago Bulls and our team the Los Angeles Lakers. We began the game. Joshua passed the ball to Dylan, and Dylan made a basket. Ahmed grabbed the ball, threw it at me, and asked me to make a basket. Obviously, since I was taller than them, I was able to make a basket. Ahmed was filled with joy; he had a huge smile on his face.

Ahmed grabbed the ball again, threw it at me, and asked me to make a basket. However, this time I passed the ball back to him and asked him to make a basket. He stood there motionless for a while. He dribbled down the court and just stood right there. I was jumping up and down and telling him to shoot, but he would not. He yelled back at me, "I cannot do this! I don't know how."

From the look on his face, he was obviously frustrated. I really wanted him to make a basket. The only thing that seemed appropriate was to give him some words of encouragement. I yelled out, "You can do this. Just remember what I taught you!" Ahmed looked at the basket and then he looked at me. Dylan yelled out, "Shoot already!" Well, what do you know, he made the basket.

Beyond this kind of moral support, a tutor can serve as a grown-up who cares, sometimes in stark contrast to the other adults whom the student may meet in an overworked school system. One tutor was shocked when her tutee said that her teacher had told her she was not good enough to apply to the University of California (UC) system:

"So, did you get your UC application finished?"

Jessica said hesitantly, "Uh, no. I decided just to apply to private schools and Cal States. I just got lazy."

All at once I was upset, shocked, and saddened. She had worked hard on her essay, and I had invested time in helping her improve it. "What do you mean, 'you got lazy'? You had an essay all ready to go."

"Yeah, but I talked to a teacher who told me that my SAT scores aren't good enough to go to a UC, and she said that maybe I should go to Cal State L.A."

"No, Veronica. You can go to a UC. You have to at least apply. You know you can do this. Do you have the application? We can fill it out right now."

"No, I got mad and tore it up."

"Okay, when is it due, Friday?"

"No, Thursday."

"Well, can you get an application by tomorrow?"

"Yeah, I think so."

"I'm going to come back tomorrow at four o'clock, and we will fill out a new application and send it off, okay?"

"Okay, Rebecca, I will do that."

In this case, Jessica's tutor knew that Jessica had a chance at the UC system because of some of the intense one-on-one work they had done together. She was able to apply this unique knowledge and encourage Jessica in directions she would otherwise have been forced to abandon. The votes of confidence and subtle pushes tutors can provide often make the biggest difference to the students.

ESTABLISHING BOUNDARIES

With strong tutor-tutee relationships, as with any relationships, come some problems. Tutors have to find their places on the relationship spectrum—somewhere short of an authority figure on one end and short of total and equal friendship on the other. It is a delicate balance that each student and tutor must negotiate. Personal issues sometimes threaten that balance, such as a student's jealousy of other students, tutees' overdependence on their tutor, and the ever-present possibility of separation.

Dealing with Jealousy

Once they have formed particularly strong bonds with their students, many tutors find that they have to deal with students' jealousy. Such jealousy might focus on other students that the tutor works with, other aspects of the tutor's life, or other people or distractions at the tutoring site. As a tutor, you need to be aware and honest with yourself about insecurity issues and how your behavior affects your students.

If you are working with several children in one classroom or station, it is your responsibility to make sure that all the children know you are there for all of them, but they have to respect each other's time. Carefully but firmly, you can let them know that your working with other students in no way diminishes your friendship with each of them, but they will have to wait their turns. Here is how one female tutor handled the jealous attachment of a nine-year-old Mexican American student:

> The other kids had already begun working on the second page of the worksheet [on why immigrants come into the United States], but Jade was stuck and asked me a question. "Why are new jobs a pull?" As I began explaining the reason, Kathy kept yelling, "Help! I need help! Help me." She was being really demanding and was just trying to be the center of the table's attention. "Why are you helping Jade? I want you to help me."
>
> I was sort of ignoring her, because I thought that Jade needed my help. Kathy didn't like this at all and began to pout with her chin on the table between her clenched fists. She wouldn't answer any of my questions. I asked her, "Kathy, what's the matter? Is everything okay?" She wouldn't even look at me. I tried to explain to her that when we work in groups, I need to be able to help everyone equally; I can't just concentrate on her. The period was over, and it was time for me to leave. I said good-bye to the students, and as I was leaving, I looked at Kathy's desk; she didn't even turn around to wave a good-bye like she usually does.

Even though Kathy did not seem to accept having to share her tutor, by the next week she was eager and excited to see her. She was also much more gracious when her tutor explained that she would be spending some time with some other students.

Preventing Overdependence

Overdependence is another challenge that many tutors struggle with, especially tutors who get heavily involved in the lives of their students. There is a big difference between a healthy, temporary dependence and overdependence. Tutees need to depend on their tutor to gain the skills to make their own transition to independence. However, tutors often find it easy to fall into the "Super Tutor" trap, in which they feel they can help students in every aspect of their lives and believe it is their duty to do so. And, because tutors often act as role models for their students, students sometimes idolize them and expect them to be perfect. This position creates a double bind for you as a tutor: A tutee may ask for help with a family or school problem, and it will be hard to deny this student whom you feel has no other recourse. Remind yourself that no better way exists for a tutor to create an overdependent tutee than by stepping in and taking care of problems.

Solving students' problems for them can raise false expectations. This practice also increases their disappointment when they realize that their tutor is not infallible or that they are not the main focus of the tutor's life. The following tutee, Justin, was a first grader who needed special help because he was being treated for cancer. Because he had been in and out of the hospital a lot, he was behind academically and in learning to socialize with other children. Justin invited his tutor to his home many times, and she did visit once, even though the psychologist at Justin's elementary school had recommended against it. The tutor could tell that Justin came from a troubled family and that he felt neglected. Wanting only to make a positive impact on him in as many ways as possible, she may have created an unhealthy relationship:

> At 4:25 P.M., Justin called and asked if I could come over and play. I was flattered but a bit uneasy, since the psychologist had asked me not to. I asked if his mom was there, and I told her I am a tutor in Justin's class and that I live four doors down from them. I also informed her that Justin had asked me to come

over several times, but when speaking to the school psychologist, we agreed that I talk with his parents first. She seemed delighted and told me that I was welcome to come over anytime this weekend. I told her I would come over tomorrow, because I was on my way to work.

[*The next day*] I came home, and there was a message from Justin reminding me not to forget to come over. [I went over, met Justin's parents and played tetherball with Justin and his sister.] I hope Justin will not call too much and that he does not expect me to go over to his house too often. He is a nice kid and I want to help him, but I have many obligations, and it will benefit both Justin and me when he makes more friends his own age.

 How to Handle Extracurricular Invitations/Requests

When you work with children, they will often invite you to be part of the rest of their lives. For kids, a "friendship" means certain things, including birthday parties, recitals, soccer games, and other events. What do you do if you receive an invitation to an extracurricular activity? Or what if you're asked to buy fundraiser items or to donate to a team or school project?

- Don't say you'll go unless you will. If you can't attend or don't want to attend, say so. Don't get students' hopes up and then disappoint them.
- Don't allow yourself to be guilted into going or giving. Going to a baseball game or a recital is above and beyond tutoring responsibilities. So is buying the overpriced gift wrap that every school tries to sell. Don't commit if you feel that you don't have the time or money or if you'll feel uncomfortable. And do not give in just to make the situation go away. A tutor who buys one order of overpriced gift wrap will soon be approached with a plethora of other fund-raising items.
- Give a reason. True reasons are best, if you have one. Feel free to say that you're busy or that you don't have any extra money to donate. Also feel free to say that you have a lot of students, so it just wouldn't be fair for you to go to some students' games and not others. Or, if you can say it with a smile, say that you think your student would have a lot more fun in the bounce house without you (you might

[*A week later*] Let's see, Justin has called twice today asking me to help with his homework or to play.

[*The next day*] Justin called and asked me to come over to help him with his homework: "My mom and dad are not here, only the babysitter is here, and she only does the dishes and cleans." I got the babysitter on the phone to ask her to help Justin. She handed the telephone back to him. "Oh, I forgot to tell you," he said. "The babysitter only speaks Spanish."

[*A few days later, at the tutoring site*] As I was leaving, Justin grabbed my leg so I would not leave—it was like he dove to the floor and pulled it. Luckily I did not fall. I told him to get off, but then Ms. Bowling, his teacher, intervened by raising her

---

bust it!) and then change the subject. A white lie (for example, that you have another event) isn't awful, but you really don't want to encourage them to keep inviting you. Don't give the impression that you would definitely go "except I have to go to my brother's game." Be as absolutely honest as you can without being cruel.

- If you do want to attend, make sure that you're allowed to. Some tutoring centers and schools don't allow teachers and tutors to participate in students' extracurricular activities. Check with your supervisor before you commit.

- If you want to go, give a very honest assessment of how much you'll participate. If you plan on just "stopping by" a party or recital, make that clear. You don't want to ruin a child's party by leaving early after he or she told everyone that you were going to stay, do magic for them, play football with them, or whatever.

- If you go, say hello to the parents if you can. Many parents are very grateful when a tutor takes extra time for their child. But some can be suspicious. They might wonder who you are and why you are spending time with their child. So, introduce yourself, explain why you are there, and you should not have any problems.

- Remember that invitations are ways that children show that they like you and think that you are part of their lives. They invite you to show you that they care. Be respectful of that. But don't think that it will be the end of the world if you can't accept. Be thankful and respectful, and remember to ask about the event afterward. You probably will not harm your relationship by refusing.

voice. He listened to her. I felt strange trying to discipline him, so I let her do it.

This tutor had only Justin's best interests at heart, but in thinking that she could make up for the attention Justin craved at home and at school, she created not only an inconvenient situation for herself but a relationship in which a line had been crossed, and the process of defining boundaries with a demanding first grader became ambiguous. The tutor's other obligations made it impossible for Justin to be her first priority, but how was she to explain that to a child with whom she had worked so hard to build a strong, trusting relationship?

Justin also referred to his tutor as his "best friend" and preferred to play with her rather than with the other children at school. By allowing this, Justin's tutor reinforced his reluctance to form peer friendships. Rather than helping him, she inhibited the socialization process that he needed to learn, and his overdependence on her caused his further alienation on the playground.

Students in need, particularly children, will often want more from their tutors than just tutoring. Tutors need to be clear about what they are able and willing to give and to do and what they cannot. Even though it is tempting to play hero to people you are helping, especially younger, troubled, or disadvantaged students, the greater gift is to allow them or to help them learn to work out their problems on their own. We cannot repeat this too often; tutoring is for your tutees, not for you. The greatest gift you can give them is to provide them with a relationship they can learn from. Teach them that they can do more than they imagined possible. Show them that, with the skills and confidence they built with you, they can accomplish more than they could just a few months ago. Most importantly, help them develop the strength that they have within themselves. For a temporary tutor to step in and to solve things for them not only raises unrealistic expectations but robs them of learning this life skill. An overly dependent relationship also sets students up for severe disappointment when the tutor must bow out.

The relationship you form with your student will be the basis of your tutoring, and the trust you build is exactly what makes the process more than just a passing on of knowledge or of techniques for passing tests. A tutoring experience can impact two or more lives for a lifetime—and that impact starts right there, in the relationship.

RECOMMENDED READING

Tutors usually have a difficult time understanding that rewards and gifts, no matter how small, can undermine the tutoring relationship. This struggle probably results from that fact that the tutors grew up in classrooms where rewards (stickers, stars, candy, treats) were used constantly. When people have spent their lives striving to get on the honor roll or to receive "incentives" from their parents for good grades, it is often hard for them to realize that rewards can be destructive. But often, these same people can reflect upon the fact that they do not often read books that are not "required" or pursue learning without someone else (a teacher, a parent) pushing them. Could those incentives have undermined their intrinsic motivation to learn? In the article "Stars and Bribes Forever" (1992), Joan Roemer argues that all rewards have the same effect: They dilute the pure joy that comes from success itself.

No one, including children, needs a reward for learning, because the desire to learn is natural. Just as adults who love their work invariably do a better job than adults who work for rewards, children are more likely to be optimal learners when they are interested in and fascinated by what they are learning than when they are merely striving for gold stars. Alfie Kohn, in *Punished by Rewards* (1993), explores why behaviorism based on rewards is ineffective in the workplace and at school.

Alice Miller describes the most destructive consequence of child rearing that links a child's performance to parental affection and love (rewards) in *The Drama of the Gifted Child* (1997). Miller calls "gifted" those children who are totally oriented toward figuring out what their parents, and later on their bosses and their friends, want. Once they have figured this out (because of their special ability to do this—their gift), they proceed to give the others what they want. This skill and ability is achieved at the expense of their developing genuine selves that can determine and respond to their own wishes, desires, values, and goals.

In *The Power of Mindful Learning* (1998), Ellen Langer argues that all-nighters and rote memorization are not enduring ways to learn and that what is central to deeper and enduring learning occurs when the learner is allowed or encouraged to bring something of him- or herself into the process. Allowing the tutees to bring themselves into the process of tutoring should be balanced by an awareness of what the tutor brings. Of special concern is the possible sense of privilege that a tutor brings, whether it is class, race, gender, sexual orientation, or education. In "But You Aren't White: Racial Perceptions and Service-Learning" (2001), Ann E. Green argues that preparing tutors to understand their race and class privilege—prior to their encounter with students who may be of different races or classes—is critical for their success.

3 Teaching Techniques

ONE OF THE MOST remarkable things about tutoring is that in working with students one-on-one or even in small groups, tutors get to experiment in ways that few teachers have the time to. As a tutor, you have the opportunity to see how your students learn best and to adapt your teaching to their individual learning styles. You have the chance to tailor your sessions to the exact needs of your students.

Although many tutors enter their tutoring situations somewhat bewildered and insecure about their teaching abilities, after only a few sessions, many tutors come up with creative ways to teach and to motivate their students. Methods vary from using puzzles and games to slowing down and reteaching concepts. No matter how or why teaching techniques are developed, their uniqueness is one of the best arguments for forming a strong relationship with your tutee. Teaching strategies developed specifically for particular children demonstrate how important personal attention and understanding can be to the learning process. Tutors sometimes find that, with a little ingenuity, they can accomplish a great deal in only a one-hour session.

Most tutors discover particular teaching techniques that work with their specific tutees as they work together. Just as every student and tutor is different, so are solutions—no problem has one, sure-fire solution. A suggestion from a friend or fellow tutor may work perfectly for you and your tutee, or it may fall flat. Something that you read in this book may seem like pure genius the night before a tutoring session but provoke no reaction from your student.

The examples we present are not intended to be templates for your tutoring sessions. There are no guarantees. But we have found a few guiding concepts that underlie most successful teaching techniques. The most effective tutoring techniques: Get students involved and interested, ease students' fears, let students lead, challenge students, and recognize students' ploys to get tutors to help "too much." We present each of these guidelines with a variety of examples that demonstrate another important aspect of tutoring: the creative process of basing your teaching methods on your unique insights into your tutees' personalities, motivations, and interests. In a strong tutoring relationship, recognizing effective teaching techniques is often easy, because you have become familiar with your tutee's personality and learning style. It may take a great deal of creativity to develop effective techniques, but you can almost always find activities that will motivate your students and challenge them to work as hard as they can.

GETTING STUDENTS INTERESTED AND INVOLVED

The best way to get students to work is to get them involved and interested in the assignment—a simple goal that is not always easily accomplished. If the subject is a play, a novel, or a history project on a subject the student is already moderately interested in, the tutor's excitement and enthusiasm can motivate the student to get more involved. When tutors have to help with subjects or assignments that are difficult for children, however, it is often hard to get kids to pay attention and really want to understand concepts that are giving them trouble. In these situations, students will often push for the tutors to just give them the answers (or show them shortcuts). It is the tutors' job to make anything and everything as interesting as possible and to do everything they can to make students want to master and to fully understand the material at hand.

A multitude of possibilities for making schoolwork more interesting and exciting exists. Sometimes it is merely a matter of incorporating something that the student enjoys or is interested in into the lesson, such as art, animals, or sports. Other times, making the lesson a more hands-on or visual experience can grab a student's attention. Tutors have found that many students respond well to friendly competition, either with the tutor or with other students in the classroom or tutoring

The Fun/Work Balance

Although many of the examples in this chapter show ways to make homework more fun, you've probably noticed that they also make homework slower and take away from learning time. Not every student needs to draw during homework or take a lot of breaks. Techniques that dramatically cut down on your work time should only be used in extreme situations. To make sure that fun time doesn't take over work time:

- Introduce fun activities slowly and only when needed. If students are working on assignments without complaint (or without too much complaint), let them work.
- Set limits on fun activities when you introduce them (such as, "We'll draw the outlines for the comic that will go with your story, but you'll have to do the details and coloring at home").
- Try to make fun activities a reward for completing work rather than breaks in the middle of work.
- Keep breaks short.
- Pay attention to when your student may be manipulating you (for example, pretending to be really interested in something to distract you from homework).
- Remember, you're the adult. You have to set the limits and to make sure that your time together is productive.

site. Such possibilities are endless, but they all mean getting the student (and yourself) involved in learning in ways that go beyond looking at a page in a book. Students respond best to dynamic learning, where they get to think and be creative.

Drawing on Student Interests

One of the best ways to motivate students is to incorporate their interests into the learning experience. (We have said this before, and we will probably say it again.) A tutor needs to demonstrate how learning can help students do the things that they want to do and how using their special talents and interests can help them learn. Many tutors have successfully used sports statistics and counting money to teach math or an interest in clothes shopping and sales to get students interested in percentages. Tapping into a tutee's interest in art or music is another popular way to make learning more fun.

The tutor below found that his student, Peter, an African American seventh grader, was often drawing when he was supposed to be doing his work. The tutor decided that Peter's interest in drawing might be the key to pulling him into other school activities and getting him personally involved in his math lessons:

> I brought in an assignment to help Peter learn about fractions that incorporated his desire to practice drawing. I presented him with a list of objects found in a large broom closet (represented by a blank piece of paper). I told him that there were twenty-four items in all and that he had to figure out how many of the

---

❖ Tutoring Materials

One of the hardest aspects of tutoring is finding materials to use when a student does not have homework, needs extra practice, or just needs to be able to continue practicing a skill in between your tutoring sessions. What do you do when you feel like a student is "just about" to master a skill and then you reach the end of the assignment (and the student hasn't really had a chance to do any problems completely independently)? Ideally, you would work on a few more problems. But where do those problems (or writing prompts, or reading comprehension questions, or whatever you need) come from? You can call on a variety of sources:

- Use the students' textbooks. Often, teachers only assign odd problems, but you can assign evens. Or, if you're doing review work, assign from problems from prior chapters. Math textbooks often have extra practice problems at the end of each chapter and at the end of the book, in cumulative reviews, or in tests. If you're tutoring at a tutoring or community center, look around to see if other students have textbooks that you can borrow to provide new practice work to your students.
- Talk to the teacher. Most teachers have old textbooks stashed away in cabinets somewhere. They might lend you the materials that you need.
- Visit libraries. Tap your public library, the school library, the teachers' libraries, and even your own personal library to find interesting reading

appropriate items to draw according to the clues. For example, one of the [problems said], "One-twelfth of the items are mini-monster guys." He figured out how much one-twelfth of twenty-four was and then proceeded to draw two of them on the sheet of paper. Even though he gave me a funny look when I was explaining the assignment to him, I could see that he enjoyed it and that it tested his knowledge of math while giving him the pleasure of showing off his drawing skills.

In the next example, the male Filipino tutor had a rough time interesting his student, a nine-year-old Latino, in reading. He found a solution by using his own and his tutee's interests. During a session, the tutor happened to pick up on his student's love of monsters and fantasies,

---

material for children. Sometimes children don't like to read because they rarely find anything to read that they enjoy. Get creative and look for good books (or magazines, or graphic novels—whatever you think might encourage the student to read).

+ Buy workbooks. Even regular bookstores contain practice workbooks. If you always work with the same students (and often struggle for material), it might be worth investing in a workbook to use during tutoring.

+ Research options online. Many teacher resources are available online. Use a search engine (just type in what you need, such as "times tables practice printable") to find practice materials.

+ Make up your own problems. Often, tutors will just take a few minutes to write out some more problems or questions of the sort that the student is working on. You know precisely what kind of practice the student needs (e.g., subtraction with borrowing, with lots of zeros in the top row), so you can make the perfect problems. A great technique is to write students a mini "test" to see whether they've really mastered the skills that you've worked on together (if they don't ace the test, keep practicing).

+ Check out www.edboost.org/worksheets. EdBoost has compiled standards-based, skill-specific practice packets (such as math packets, grammar packets, reading-comprehension packets for novels, writing prompts, and more) specifically for tutors who need focused practice work for a wide range of students.

which reminded him of the Filipino myths and folklore he had loved as a child. At the next session, he brought some related books for them to practice reading. This led to more reading and even enough interest to venture into the dictionary:

> Cristobal was fascinated at this world of giants and dwarves. He wanted to learn more, and I felt successful in tapping some of the creative potential that I had seen earlier. He pointed to various legendary creatures, such as mermaids, the aswang or flying vampire, the witches, and each time I would explain it to him in the most provocative way I could. He liked the werewolf stories, so he asked me to find something about it. I looked it up in a book, and I helped him read about it. The reading was a little complex for his level, but I helped him along. Any words he did not know the meaning of, I asked him to look up in the dictionary.

Here, the tutor got Cristobal interested enough to do a little extra research, reading, and work. By sharing an important part of his culture, the tutor also made the tutoring session more fun, which is one of the main aims in tutoring.

Besides tapping into your students' interests, you can also get them involved in their assignments by drawing on their life experiences. As the next example demonstrates, teaching immigration terms to a fourth grader can be difficult, but they make a lot more sense when the student can apply the labels to his own family. This tutor made baffling sociological terms familiar to her fourth-grade Japanese American tutee when she demonstrated how they related to him and his parents:

> I went outside with Hiseo to work on the worksheet. I asked, "Are you an immigrant to the United States?"
>
> He answered, "Yes. I mean, I think so. My parents came here from Japan."
>
> I corrected, "Well, actually, your parents are immigrants, but you are not a first-generation immigrant like what we have been talking about. You were born in the United States, right?" He nodded in agreement. "Then you personally did not move here from another country, which constitutes the definition of an immigrant, but you can be called a second-generation immigrant. Have you ever heard that before?"

Hiseo responded, "Yeah, I've heard the word, but I didn't understand exactly what it meant 'til now. So I'm a second-generation immigrant. Cool."

Hiseo not only learned what the immigration terms that he was supposed to know meant; he understood them in the context of his own life, which means that he will probably remember them.

Relating learning to life experience also works with older students and much more complex topics and issues. In the following example, the tutor, a Filipina, found that her eleventh-grade African American female student worked on an assignment on affirmative action with a great deal of apathy. Although debates over affirmative action were widely disputed and publicized at the time, the tutor found that the student did not really understand the topic and was having a hard time putting the article in context and coming up with an informed response. The tutor framed her explanation in terms that directly related to herself and the student:

> I tried to explain the idea in terms of something she could relate to. I said, "As a woman and a minority, you and I have been historically denied access to certain things." I told her that in jobs and in school, I would have never been given an opportunity to apply for certain positions based on my gender and race, like working at a fire station. I explained that I was not encouraged to apply, because I probably would not get the job. With affirmative action, I was no longer denied but actually given the opportunity to apply for the job. I told her that minority women need to work harder in order to be at the same level playing fields as white males. After we discussed the history of affirmative action, we read over the article again, and she was able to respond to the article more thoroughly. Her response was much more thought out and coherent.

Other tutors have found it useful to incorporate current events or television shows that the students know a lot about. For instance, the O. J. Simpson trial, which was televised and the subject of much conversation at the time, was ideal for many comparisons, from defining vocabulary words, such as perjury, to explaining more detailed concepts, such as the amendments to the U.S. Constitution, as this tutor did with her twelfth-grade student: "After finishing the reading, he told me that he did not understand it. I tried to explain everything by relating it to the O. J. Simpson trial and other things. This seemed to motivate him, and I could tell he was beginning to comprehend the work. He noted, 'Hey, that is why Mark Fuhrman said he wanted to take the Fifth.'" Clearly, the O. J. Simpson trial would no longer be a touchstone for most young people, but any celebrity trial or scandal that your student knows about and that relates to the topic at hand can be used.

Switching roles with students to allow them to explore an unfamiliar job or position of power can also tap into enthusiasm. This female Mexican American tutor hit on a great technique with her sometimes-troublesome African American fourth grader:

> Today we worked on long division. I had tutored before, and the teacher had previously told me that the best way to tutor was to ask the student to explain the material to you. This way, you can find out what they know and what they do not. I did just that. I asked Terrence to explain the steps involved in dividing. I do not think he expected it, but he was excited about it. He looked at me with eyes wide open and asked, "So I'm the teacher?"
>
> I said, "Yes."
>
> He reacted by swinging his arm and yelling out, "Cool!" He seemed to enjoy this method, because he smiled as we worked on the problems. He was very polite and conscientious about others. As he began his explanation, he talked very slowly so I could understand. He also made eye contact, especially after every step.

The possibilities for getting students involved in their work are endless as well as personal for each tutoring pair. The key is listening to students and remembering what they like and want to learn about. A big part of tutoring is making the relationship pay off for the students in greater understanding of their academic work and greater love for learning in general.

Making Work Visual and Hands-On

Drawings, props, and manipulatives can often invigorate boring work or bring highly abstract concepts back down to earth. Children respond to things that they can see and manipulate, so drawing and involving other physical objects in your tutoring sessions often works well. Although props are particularly useful with young children, for whom they also help maintain attention, visuals can also help older students understand complex or hard-to-grasp concepts.

Effective drawings or diagrams range from simple charts or stick drawings to complex illustrations. Sometimes incorporating drawing turns work into play in the student's eyes, as this white female tutor found with her stubborn seven-year-old Latina tutee, Elsa:

> I tried to redirect her back to her schoolwork several times, but her attention span was fleeting, and she continued to color. That was when I figured out how to get her to work without her knowing she was working. I took out a piece of construction paper and a marker, and then wrote the word "perro" at the top of the page and "dog" underneath it. I then drew a picture of a dog beside these two words. "What does this say?" I asked her.
>
> "D . . . aaawwwgg." We painfully sounded out each syllable, but this time she had more fun, because there was an illustration of the work there, too. She giggled and laughed at my awkward stick figures and sketches. For every word or sentence I wrote in Spanish, I translated it in English underneath. This way, she had to practice sounding it out in both languages. I wanted her to see the relation between words and meaning, so I made the sentences fairly self-explanatory—with a rather obvious picture below each one. This made the whole reading process less tedious for her.

In the next example, a Latina tutor found that if she turned the story she and her eleven-year-old Latina student were reading into a more visual experience through drawings, the student became more involved in the work:

> I asked, "Do you want to take turns reading to each other?" She just sat there with a sad, blank face. So I decided to read the first paragraph. Once I realized she was not listening and was not going to read, I began to draw out the paragraph on a white sheet of paper. When the history chapter talked about Magellan sailing on a ship across the Atlantic with all his men working hard to guide the ship through bad weather, I proceeded to

Desperate Times Call for Desperate Measures

There are times when you'll sacrifice work time just to get a student working. When should you forget about trying to maximize work time and do whatever you can to get the student to do any work at all?

- When the student absolutely refuses to do anything (for example, won't even pick up a pencil or look at the papers or textbook).
- After you have already talked with a supervisor and/or the child's parent (or told the child that you will talk with his or her parent).
- When the child is just having a horrible day (and is able to express to you why this day is particularly difficult). If you have some history with the student, you will be able to judge if this is just "one of those days."
- When all the techniques that you have tried have failed to either (a) engage the student or (b) teach the student.

On those days when you feel hopeless and that you need to do more research, talk with more people, and come more prepared next time, just see if you can get the child to do some tiny bit of work. You can also try a fun activity so that you don't lose the child entirely.

draw a large ship, a strong man with a beard (who was Magellan), and all his crewmen on the ship. I made the waves of the Atlantic incredibly huge and drew rain coming down that looked like stormy weather. As I kept reading and drawing more pictures, Carly began to get excited, and she wanted to start reading and draw one of the paragraphs herself.

The tutor in the following example found that giving her non-English-speaking Persian tutee something concrete to base his new knowledge on helped him remember a letter that he was having a lot of trouble with:

Today was a great day, I finally did it. I helped Ahmed to remember the letter "M." A classmate told me that it would be beneficial to relate the curriculum to things that he can relate to. For example, she mentioned that I should sing to Ahmed or bring toys or things I might think he's interested in. With that in mind, before I went to tutoring, I stopped by Pavilions [a supermarket]. I went there to pick up a bag of M&Ms.

When I got to school, I asked Ahmed to write the letter "M." Just as I expected, he had no clue. I reached for my bag, grabbed the box of M&Ms, and laid them on the table. I asked him what he called these colorful circles. He looked at me and thought I was crazy. He said, "M&M." I asked him, what did M&M start with? He opened up his eyes, put a smile on his face, and with a lot of confidence responded, "It starts with 'M.'" He asked me if he could have some, and I told him only if he promised not to ever forget that letter. He looked at me rather uncertainly and said, "Okay."

Another tutor was frustrated even in his attempts to use drawings to explain how the solar system works. He finally got the idea to use three-dimensional objects, which he used to clarify the homework assignment and to motivate his student, a Latino fifth grader, to memorize almost all the material from his work that afternoon:

> He whipped out his ditto on the solar system. The student had to place the solar system in order, from Mercury to Pluto. Surprisingly, Guillermo didn't know anything about planets. We tried to memorize the order of the planets together, but it went slowly, and I felt that he was not getting it. I attempted to draw them, but that, too, was futile. At that point, both of us were hot and tired, and I suggested that we step out for a bit.
>
> With the ditto in his hand, Guillermo and I trudged outside for some fresh air. As we were about to go back in, I spotted a little girl playing with pebbles by the park. I suddenly got an idea to show Guillermo the solar system visually. "Hey, Guillermo, let's try to find stones that look like the planets."
>
> For the next ten minutes we were bent over, searching for rocks. I found a large rock to represent our "sun" and a few stones related to the planets' respective sizes. Guillermo, too, came to me with several stones. I was delighted to see a piece of brick I suspected Guillermo found to represent Mars.
>
> "All right! You knew that Mars was red!" I exclaimed.
>
> He replied, "Well, it says so on the ditto."
>
> I could tell Guillermo was having fun. It was then time for us to arrange the rocks in order. I placed my "sun" stone in the middle, and Guillermo proceeded to place the rocks using the

ditto as our guide. We were missing a replacement for "Jupiter" though. Guillermo had brought a rock that was twice the size of the "sun." I placed a string around the "Saturn" stone, representing the rings.

We took a step back to admire our own solar system and nodded to each other. After our activity, Guillermo still struggled with Neptune and Uranus, but other than that, this little dude definitely learned the solar system and also the relative sizes of the planets.

 Competition for Speed and Accuracy

Sometimes students procrastinate their homework, refuse to keep working, or just work ridiculously slowly. Other times, students do work so sloppily and quickly that many of their answers come out wrong. At still other times, they just won't put any effort into doing the work well. Sometimes a little friendly competition can get them going. Just showing students that you are willing to do the same work that they're doing may also be enough to get them going.

- Tell your students that you will do the same work that they are doing. To give them a head start, tell them that you will copy down all the math problems first and then do them. See who can finish first.
- Compare answers. Don't be afraid to tell your students if they're correct and you're incorrect. For those instances, put a big "X" on your paper and a happy face or something similar on their papers. Adults make mistakes, and it's important to show students that.
- Compete to see who can finish more problems with greater accuracy.
- Compete to see who can write a whole page (or a whole paragraph) first. Afterward, you can read your assignments to each other.
- Compete to see who can look up words in the dictionary faster.
- If the student has to write spelling or vocabulary sentences, compete to see who can write funnier or more interesting sentences.
- Make up games that have students compete against you or against other students (try to make sure games maximize the use and practice of academic material).
    - For instance, if a student needs to learn addition or multiplication facts, you can play a modified version of the card game "War."

Encouraging Friendly Competition

Many tutors have found that a little friendly competition can help get students involved and interested in their homework. Even "boring" tasks, such as memorizing multiplication tables, can become a game your students can enjoy and get excited about, when they involve competition. Tutors might make a *Jeopardy!* game out of math problems or facts from a history chapter. Scrabble and other learning games are also fun and effective for some students.

Tutor and tutee each get half a deck of cards and turn over a card simultaneously. The object is to add (or multiply) the numbers shown on the two cards. The first one to get the answer right wins the cards.

◆ If you are working with several students who are studying for the same test, line the students up. Ask the first student a question (the definition of a word, the symbol for a chemical element, the date of a historical event, and so forth). If the student gets the answer correct, he or she moves to the end of the line (and stays in the game). If the answer is wrong, the student is "out" for that round. When a student gets an answer wrong, explain the correct answer for everyone to hear. This way, students will keep hearing correct answers as they play. Repeat questions to reward students for paying attention. The last student standing wins each round. (For a twist on this game, kids who have been eliminated can get back into the game when they can provide the correct answer after the student at the front of the line gets "out.") Students love this game, because they get to move around and see what other kids know. It's great for teaching, because it provides an incentive to listen and to remember each fact.

When competing against your students, you will often win (that's okay— they expect you to), so you should try to give them some kind of head start so the competition is somewhat fair. But you'll be amazed to see how much the fact that you are working helps keep them moving through their assignments.

The Asian female tutor in the next example found that a game pitting her against her nine-year-old Latino student (putting them on equal ground in the student's perspective) was the best way to help her student get his word search done:

> After a while, I didn't know what to do to help Esteban. So I decided to put a twist into his homework. I suggested that we have a race to see who could find the word first. He agreed and told me that he would find it first. We chose the word "America" and said, "Ready, set, go!" I started from the top of the page, and Esteban started from the bottom. I used my strategy and found it going across diagonally. "I found it," I said, kind of loudly. Esteban asked me where it was, but I told him to look for it and I wasn't going to tell him right away. We kept racing, and he found a lot of them first.

Competing with peers often motivates students as well, and many tutors have a great deal of success using games to quiz kids for tests or on material they are supposed to memorize. This method can be especially useful when a group of tutees are all working on the same material, either in a classroom or at another common site. Again, something as simple as practicing for a spelling or vocabulary test can become fun, exciting, and encouraging. In the following example, the tutor found the method particularly successful in the fifth-grade classroom in which she was working:

> I looked around the room and noticed a sense of curiosity from other children about what I was doing with Kevin and Mark. Soon a few students approached our table to see what we were doing. I explained to them that we were playing a game, a review game for the much-anticipated vocabulary test. The students' eyes lit up immediately when I said the word "game." I incorporated the rest of the children into our intimate study group, and, like the master of ceremonies at an awards banquet, I began the game.
>
> I had Mark start, so he gave the group the first definition: "The bone that connects from the scapula to the ulna and radius." All the children thought about it as quickly as they could, feeling their bones, some at the scapula and some were feeling their ankles. I knew the results would be interesting

when children were guessing bones all over their bodies. But in the end, some students came up with the correct answers.

EASING STUDENT FEARS

Although getting students involved in their studies is a great way to motivate them to work, some need more than motivation. Many students are reluctant to work, because they are afraid of the material or intimidated by difficult concepts they have not encountered before. Even students who are generally motivated to learn can appear lazy or disinterested when, in fact, they are hesitant to try an assignment at which they do not think they can succeed. For these students, a tutor can provide support that will often keep them encouraged enough to work on an assignment that intimidates them. Other times, breaking the assignment down into small steps that they are familiar with can be useful. Tutors also find success in relating lessons to things that are familiar— for example, families or a native language—to make strange concepts more comfortable.

Showing Support

Tutors may only need to offer a little encouragement and personal involvement to keep students going through difficult assignments. Sometimes just having someone to commiserate with and to look to for occasional help makes a hard assignment easier to bear: Tutors are ideal hard-work companions and cheerleaders. As with the following student, an assignment or task that seems difficult becomes possible if students know that someone is there to help if they need it. Not a strong reader, Jonah was hesitant to try to read aloud until the tutor provided moral support and the assurance that if he got stuck on a word, she would help him out:

> I asked Jonah to read. I got out of my chair and knelt down next to him and listened intently when he read. I helped him sound out almost every other word, and little by little he was sounding out the words alone. He was really struggling with pronunciation, and his reading skills were that of a second or third grader. I proceeded to pat him on the back every time he made it through a sentence.

How to Make Reading Faster and More Productive

Although reading seems like one of the easier tasks that we ask children to do, many children struggle with it. When you first work with a student on any assignment that requires reading (even if it's just reading the directions on a worksheet), have the student read aloud to you. Assessing how well the student reads will give you immediate insights into any other academic problems he or she may be having. (And if a child says, "I need help with number 4," the first thing you should have the child do is read the question and any directions out loud to you—often, that reading answers the question before you say a word.)

If a student reads really slowly, helping with homework can be a very frustrating experience, for you and the student. Don't give in and just point out where answers are in the story or passage. However, some techniques do make reading faster:

- Read with the student. Take turns. You read a page or a paragraph, and then the student reads a page or a paragraph. The ratio of what you read to what the student reads should be reasonable given how slowly the student reads and how hard it is for the student to understand when he or she reads. When students need to read for homework, the assignment has two goals: improving reading skills and learning the content of the reading material. By reading together, you can correct the student's reading and model good reading. You also learn the material together. So, even if you do a lot of the reading yourself, you're still accomplishing both goals.
- Tell the student what unfamiliar words mean. Although the dictionary is a great tool, when you want to streamline the reading process, help out with vocabulary as much as you can.
- Choose an easier book. If you have flexibility in terms of what you read, reading is always most productive when students struggle with less than 10 percent of the words (so the student should be able to read and to understand nine out of ten words that he or she reads). If you can choose any book, choose one that is at the right level. Even though reading harder books may be more challenging, they do not provide good, leveled skill practice for struggling readers.

To help children better understand what they read:

- Ask tons of questions. Ask what individual words mean. Ask the student to summarize what he or she just read. Ask the student to predict what will happen next and to guess at why characters act the way that they do. Many students read quickly and without understanding. Any reading that a child does with you should focus on comprehension.

Reading out loud can be an especially difficult task when tutees lack confidence in their abilities to read adequately. Some students refuse to read. Others read only in a whisper; still others guess half the words and pretend that they know what they are doing. Many will tell you that they "read better to themselves" just to avoid having to read to you. In the next example, a student masked his anxiety by reading too quickly. By having the tutee become the tutor, this Latina tutor helped her student face his anxiety and had him focus on his reading rather than showing off how fast he could read:

> Once he finished his math sheet, we moved on to his reading exercise. At first, I could see that he was nervous and reading very fast to impress me, but because of that he was stumbling and not taking the time to actually read the words on the paper. For example, instead of saying "singing," he would say "singer." When I noticed that, I calmly told him that I wanted him to point to the words and read a little bit slower, because he was going so fast that I couldn't keep up with what he was saying. Basically, I made it seem as if it was my inability to keep up with him that brought me to ask him to read a bit slower. Carlos simply smiled and willingly started again. I could see he was so impressed with himself, because he felt like he was reading the story *to* me now rather simply reading the story for me to criticize as a disciplinary figure would. This time, as I expected, Carlos read more easily. He struggled with the pronunciation of words, such as "amiable" and "country," but when he did get stuck, I would help him sound it out.

Breaking Assignments into Manageable Steps

Students often get overwhelmed by large quantities of work. The thought of writing a two-page paper prevents them from even starting the task. The idea of having to read an entire book makes them procrastinate even starting chapter one. Even a relatively simple task, such as writing a sentence in cursive, can seem impossible to a third grader just learning handwriting. In the next scenario, the tutor found that breaking the assignment down into individual letters helped a lot. She then tried to animate the activity for her student to make it seem more interesting. This tutor found that adding a little fantasy to cursive writing made it easier for her student to overcome her fear of it:

Jenna was struggling to write a cursive "D." "I can't do this letter. It's hard for me," she said.

I told her that I knew she could do it and offered to show
her how to do it. I took the pencil from her and said, "Okay, let's
pretend the tip of the pencil is you sitting on a roller coaster.
Okay, the roller coaster is going down the hill. All of a sudden,
we come to a loop. Let's follow the loop all the way up and we
hit another loop. What does that look like?" I asked.

"A 'D,'" Jenna responded. She took her pencil and repeated
the exercise again.

How to Deal with "I Don't Get It"

When working with students, you will probably find that one of the
most common statements they make is, "I don't get it." As adults, we
often take this to mean that students are confused, and we jump in and
start explaining. In fact, when you work with students for a while, you
will realize that "I don't get it" has several meanings:

+ I don't know what to do.
+ I don't know how to start.
+ I'm confused by this task or skill.
+ I don't know where to look in the book for this answer (and I don't
  want to read the whole chapter).
+ This looks like it will take too long.
+ I don't feel like doing this right now.
+ I don't like this kind of work.

Each different "I don't get it" requires a different type of help from
the tutor. When a tutee says, "I don't get it," follow a few key steps to try
to figure out the best way to help:

+ Ask the student to show you exactly what he or she "doesn't get."
+ Ask the student to read that specific question or problem to you. If
  there are directions on the worksheet or page, have the student read
  those as well. Half the time, students "get it" as soon as they actually
  read the problem.
+ Ask, "What don't you get?" If they say "all of it," start breaking it
  down. See what skills the problem involves. Have you worked on
  some of those skills with the student? Have you seen the student

In the following case, the concept of syllables seemed like nuclear physics to the nine-year-old, third-grade Latino tutee. His tutor, an Asian female, found that all she had to do to make the concept manageable was introduce something familiar to the foreign concept. She found that syllables were a difficult concept to grasp for her tutee but that it became easier with names that were close to home:

> After finishing the first worksheet, we moved on to the second worksheet, "Syllables." I asked him if he knew what a syllable was. He told me no. I said his name, Tomas, while clapping, To-mas. "How many different sounds do you hear?"

using some of those concepts (perhaps earlier in the session)? Point out the parts of the problem that the student should get (based on your experience with the student). Try to walk the student through the problem, step by step, pointing out, as you go, how much he or she does "get."

- Ask if the student has read the necessary material to answer the question. If not, offer to do the reading together.
- Ask the student to start trying to answer the question, either by writing down a start to solving the problem (for math) or by telling you everything that he or she does know. Sometimes trying is half the battle.
- Be kind and encouraging but persistent about pushing the student to do whatever part of the problem is possible.

By going through all the steps above, you may figure out that the student is simply not paying attention to the problem or directions, needs to go back and read, or just needs a push to get started. If the student is genuinely confused, the questions above will help you find the source of the confusion and give you a place to begin tutoring. At the end of the steps above, if your student still won't work and you still don't know what is wrong, the student probably just does not want to do the work. Those are the moments when you talk with the student about how it is important to do work, even if the work is boring—and how you are there to help make it more interesting.

Sometimes "I don't get it" is a ploy to get a tutor to do the work: Don't fall for it. But, most of the time, it just indicates that the student needs a little guidance, some support, and a push to do the necessary work.

He said, "Five."

"Five? Why do you hear five?" I asked.

He said, "Because there are five letters."

I told him to try not to think about how many letters were in a word. Then I asked him how many brothers and sisters he has. He told me three, two brothers and one sister. His sister is ten, and his brothers are three and nine months. Then I asked him what their names were. We went through all his siblings' names and talked about how many syllables each one has.

In the following example, an Asian tutor realized that her six-year-old Latina tutee continually made mistakes on her addition problems because she did not have basic counting skills. With a great deal of patience and persistence, the tutor was able to help her tutee slow down and learn what she needed to better complete her assignment and to be prepared for new problems in addition:

The most concrete example of where I used such an approach was mentioned in last week's written assignment. Jocelyn and I were working on a math worksheet that the Mar Vista Center provides for each grade level. As we started to do the problems, she was having difficulty adding single-digit numbers. She kept missing them, so I decided to write out a few problems for her to do on the back of the worksheet. Jocelyn missed the majority of the problems. I knew there must be something she was missing. So I then went even further back to the basics—I had her write out the numbers from one to twenty. I realized that she could not count. By not knowing the sequence of numbers, she didn't know how to approach adding or subtracting those numbers she could not yet get in order. After writing out one to twenty several times, I had her move forward and write out one to thirty. She mixed a couple up again. I had her write them out again until she could do so without making any mistakes. Once we moved back to adding single-digit numbers, it became much easier for her to do the problems, as she had a much stronger grasp of the numbers, or the basics.

Obviously, Jocelyn's skill gaps go back further than just the assignment she brought to tutoring. Once her tutor identified her basic problem

Talking with Parents

Just as students' personalities vary, there are many types of parents. Some don't have the skills to help their children with schoolwork. Some can help but aren't sure how. Others don't have time to help. A few are not inclined to help. However, most parents want their children to do well, and a good tutor will try to get parents on board when trying to work with a student. If you have the opportunity to talk with your students' parents:

- Be honest. If a student did great work, say so. If the child needed to focus more, say that, too. It's important for parents to get honest reactions from you about their children.
- Give updates. Let parents know if the student completed all the homework or if work still needs to get done. Sometimes children will lead parents to believe that the tutor helped them with everything or that their tutor said that the parents should not help. Don't let parents learn about you from the child. Give information to parents yourself.
- Explain to parents how they can help. Even parents who are not very confident in their academic skills can help with many basic tasks. If a child needs help with counting, tell the parents and ask if they can try to practice at home (counting in any language helps build counting skills). If a child needs to read more, tell the parents and, if you can, suggest some books or materials that they might read together.

(a problem that Jocelyn's classroom teacher may not be aware of), she had a unique opportunity and obligation. Each time the tutor met with Jocelyn, they could work on counting and basic math to try to improve Jocelyn's skills and her ability to learn more advanced math. In situations like these, if the tutor sees the student's parents or teacher, she should also mention her discovery to them. Although parents cannot always figure out what is hampering their children's academic skills, they can often help practice skills once the gaps are identified.

Tying in Familiar Concepts

Often just a little simplification or familiarization can help students get over their fear of assignments and get started; then they can see for themselves just how capable they are. This technique can also be useful when dealing with students for whom English is a second language. Tutors who speak their students' native languages, however poorly, often find the ability helpful. Some tutors, like the one in the following example, draw on a relatively limited knowledge of the students' native languages to help make some connections. Here, a Latina tutor was able to help her nine-year-old tutee, who was also Latino:

> Again, he used the glossary in the back of the book, but I could tell that he did not know the difference between a verb and a noun. I defined noun as "a person, place, or thing" and a verb as an "action word." I thought that this definition was inadequate and unclear, so I thought that I would relate it in his first language of Spanish. I told him that a verb "was like 'leer' in Spanish, which means 'to read.'" I asked him if he understood a little bit better and if he could tell me another example. He cited the word "correr," which means "to run" in Spanish.

By using examples of Spanish terms with which the student was readily familiar, this tutor found that explanations about English equivalents became much more solid and understandable. And, although this tutor was a native Spanish speaker, any tutor with a rudimentary knowledge of Spanish could have made a similar connection.

Sometimes students hesitate to get involved in assignments or learning activities, because they get frustrated or are afraid that they will not do well. In the next example, the tutor found that bilingual Scrabble was a good way to get her fifth-grade Latino students involved in vocabulary and spelling, but one of the students, an English Language Learner (ELL) student named Jimmy, got embarrassed while playing. Afraid that Jimmy would not want to continue playing, the tutor instituted a rule that involved something that Jimmy excelled at. She found that this new rule kept Jimmy's morale up and encouraged him to keep trying:

> When Pedro was done, he put the paper away and went to get Scrabble. As we got out the game, Jimmy came in early. I asked him to join us, and he shrugged and sat down. We were all on separate teams.
>
> During the course of the game, Jimmy really struggled with the concept. He would make a word with his letters without

incorporating any of the letters on the board. He made the word "dog" and put it on the board without connecting it with any other letters. I asked him to try and find a spot for the word. He found an "o" on the board and placed it with those letters. I was really happy when he got the concept, but the word "dog" had another word directly underneath it vertically, and the letters going vertically didn't make a word. I didn't know how to break it to Jimmy, because he looked so happy. Pedro told him in Spanish, and Jimmy took his word off the board.

It was clear that Pedro understood the game much more than Jimmy, and I didn't want to offer my help to Jimmy, because he might feel stupid when Pedro didn't need any help. Jimmy is very good in Spanish, so I invented a new rule. I told them that when a word in English was put down on the board, the first one to say what the word was in Spanish would earn an extra point. Jimmy really got into this new rule. Although he was still having a tough time coming up with his own words, every time a word was put down, he would shout out the word in Spanish. He earned a lot of points this way. His interest in the game also increased.

Tutors who are tuned in to their students usually know when the students are scared of the material. Such fear can be crippling for the student and frustrating for the tutor. But sometimes all it takes to allay fears is bringing the activity closer to home or incorporating something that the student already excels at. Students can often break down and understand concepts that at first seem complex and intimidating—with a little help.

LETTING THE STUDENT LEAD

Some tutors go into sessions with lessons in mind and plan far enough ahead to bring along props and materials, but lessons are often ad hoc, and tutors make do with the materials at hand. Often tutors are not even sure what students or subjects they will be working on in a particular day, so they cannot bring materials with them. Although arriving at a session without prepared materials may seem hard, it is not always a handicap. Tutoring sessions often happen in libraries, a rich resource for research on any subject that may interest a student. Classrooms and tutoring centers will often offer up something to use for an activity or interesting reading for a student. One of the greatest advantages of a little ad-libbing in a tutoring session is that it allows the students the chance to tell the tutor where they want the session to go and how they want to work.

When you tutor, both you and the students need to know that you are in charge and that your goal is to get work done. Yet children often work best when they have some autonomy over their tutoring sessions. Students can often give you some idea of how they learn best or at least how they will learn best at any particular moment. A way to let students lead is to give them some choice about how they will learn and how long their learning periods will last. As you listen to your students, you can learn a great deal about their interests and their attention spans. You can also be sensitive to how students are not learning. When techniques that you think ought to work do not, be alert and willing to change tactics.

In the following excerpt, a student organized a tutoring program for immigrant, Spanish-speaking women and made the mistake of not listening to her students or allowing them to guide her in what they needed from the tutoring sessions:

To fulfill a class requirement, several classmates and I volunteered for a tutoring program wherein we tutored adult women in English-language skills. Upon entering the classroom, we were met by a program coordinator, Carmen, who introduced herself and thanked us for coming to class. I looked around the classroom and noticed that there was no instructor—there were only over twenty eager women and Michael, Diana, and myself. At this moment Michael and I looked at one another and said, "What do we do?"

We asked Carmen about the women's prior experience in English classes, and she said that they were all at different levels, from women who could not hold a conversation to women who desired to practice their pronunciation and writing skills. We were stuck.

Immediately we introduced ourselves and asked the women to write down what they wanted to learn in the class in English, if they could, or in Spanish, if they did not yet feel comfortable enough to write in English. Flash cards were passed around, and a light murmur of whispering followed while the women scribbled their thoughts on the cards given to them. The flash cards were collected, put away, and not looked at seriously to determine what we would be learning in the next session. I have never felt more overwhelmed in any other educational or tutoring situation in my life.

We had no idea what do to. Several women could understand English, but as a whole the class needed to be initiated in Spanish. Being the only Spanish speaker in the group, I began to do what I could: Remember my experience in my own language classes and attempt to build from there. From the first day until several weeks ago, we started off with reciting the alphabet, collecting words for each letter and writing out their meaning(s), and discussing how these words were used in sentences. We did not look at the flash cards to guide our sessions; instead [Michael and I] met several days before the tutoring session and decided what we thought would be best for them to learn. The program continued showing very little progress. We worked on verbs, conjugation, making sentences—all topics completely unrelated to their learning everyday communication skills.

Later in the quarter, after many tutors came and went, we finally sat down and had a discussion about our progress in helping the women. Finally, one of the tutors involved noticed we had not really asked them what they wanted to learn and focused on that. For the next session, we were committed to asking and going from there. The first thing that came up (and all of the women agreed with) was writing out numbers correctly so that they could write checks when in stores or at the bank. They wanted to use English for street directions, basic foods, and how to interpret customer orders (for those that worked at fast-food restaurants)—all things I couldn't have known, because I was not one of them.

Although the tutor had the right instinct when she asked the women what they wanted to learn, she did not follow up on that instinct. She focused more on what she thought they should learn than on what they wanted to learn. Until she learned to take their interests seriously, she stalled their progress and her ability to help the women learn what they needed for everyday interactions.

Deciding when to lead students, when to follow them, and when to get out of their way will be an ongoing challenge. But you will find that as time passes, you will understand what makes your tutees work. As you do, your relationship will begin to lead the tutoring sessions naturally. Because you will get to know your students personally and academically, your teaching techniques will develop as you tutor. The more time you spend with students, the better you will be able to adapt your style and add new and personalized teaching techniques.

Listening to Students

Many students, especially those who have worked with tutors before, have some idea of how they like to learn. As great as it is to introduce them to new techniques and to be creative, it is just as important to listen. The tutor in the following case not only used the suggestion of her five-year-old Latina tutee but also creatively incorporated her surroundings to create an active learning experience:

> The director told us we could work on letters and numbers or some coloring, so I led Elsa to the area where the crayons and games were. I searched through the container for some crayons, but I couldn't find any that we could use. But Elsa picked out some flash cards with letters and a picture that began with a specific letter on each card. I then led her off to the side, where there are blocks and other toys. Meanwhile, I was trying to think of how to use the cards she chose. I then noticed that the carpet had the alphabet written around its edges, so I decided that I could have Elsa place each card on top of the correct letter.

An important part of being a successful tutor is taking advantage of the materials and opportunities around you to make learning fun and interesting for you and for the student.

Another tutor who worked with Elsa found that she had to be creative to work around her tutee's relatively short attention span:

> In her backpack, there was a book, *Mi Sonrisa y Yo.* We started going through the easy reader together. Elsa must have read this book several times before, because she clearly knew a couple of the lines by heart. I originally wanted her to attempt every word

before I helped her, but this method was much too frustrating for her. She was up and about, switching chairs and dancing around mine. It was impossible to keep her focused.

When I realized how short her attention span was and how quickly she gave up when frustrated, I began doing more of the initial reading myself and allowing her to repeat after me. Although I think that the learning environment would have been more ideal if she did all of the reading on her own, I do not realistically think we would have been able to make it past the first page that way. When I read the words aloud first, she could still practice reading and seeing how the individual letters made sounds, but she could also grasp the meaning of the story as a whole.

This tutor had to be flexible. Being able to adjust to her student's learning habits made it possible for them to accomplish some reading instead of frustrating each other.

The following tutor also dealt with her tutee's short attention span by introducing a game unrelated to the work. Although she was hesitant to stray away from their task, she learned that allowing her tutee to have small breaks in between the work helped him in the rest of the tutoring session:

Our first couple of sessions together were filled with Dillon's favorite question of, "How many more minutes?" Honestly, it broke my heart to hear him ask me this, but I knew it was up to me to change his view of tutoring. I was determined to make our sessions fun and enjoyable for the both of us. Although I wanted to make sure he was enjoying our sessions, I didn't want to take too much time from actually doing the work. I finally decided to introduce a picture game. After finishing Dillon's homework assignment, I asked Dillon to draw a picture of anything he wanted. I would have to guess what it was, and then we would have to spell out what it was together. He loved the idea at first, but he soon became uninterested in the spelling aspect of the game. He was so adamant in his dislike of spelling that he completely shut down. I knew I had to do something to turn him back on, so I started drawing a picture of Bart Simpson. I knew he liked *The Simpsons,* so I thought I might be able to catch his attention by drawing them. I asked Dillon, "How does Bart's hair look?" He immediately grabbed my pencil and began drawing the whole Simpson family. Dillon and I bonded while drawing together that day. We didn't get back to the spelling aspect of the game, but I realized not all of our sessions had to be about academics. Because Dillon would now enjoy drawing with me, the door was open for new learning possibilities.

Letting your students lead may also mean letting them work on what they want to work on—what interests them. Doing schoolwork with tutees is a big part of tutoring, yet it is also important to encourage students to explore their own ideas. In the next example, the female Asian tutor found that her two fourth-grade students were more interested in Shakespeare than in social studies:

Gillian, Toni, and I went to the auditorium, where there were several tables and chairs set up. After we sat down, Toni said, "Let's read *Romeo and Juliet*! I have the book right here." Toni showed me a small, soft-covered copy of the play.

I asked, "Whose book is this? Is it yours?"

Toni replied, "Oh, I brought it from home." She then pleaded, "Please, please, can we read this book?" I promised her that we would read some after we read some pages in the social studies book that their teacher wanted us to read from. Toni pleasantly agreed to my plan.

Toni and Gillian took turns reading from the book that described the transcontinental railroad. They both read with fluency and ease. They took turns reading a paragraph each, and I was pleased by their enthusiasm to read.

After we finished reading one of the sections in the social studies book, I told the girls that they could read *Romeo and Juliet*. Toni became very enthusiastic then; she gently yelled, "Yay!" then immediately began to flip through her book, looking for the best parts to act out.

Gillian and Toni had fun acting out their parts, especially the sword fighting. Whenever one person was reading her line (there was only one copy of the book), the other person would pretend to jab the reader with a sword. The two girls almost continually giggled and laughed. They had trouble pronouncing many of the words, and they read much slower then when they read the social studies, probably because the sentence structure was unfamiliar. I knew that they were having trouble understanding what they were saying to each other, but they still enjoyed it.

When Toni read a line, "Do you bite your thumb at me?" she literally began biting her thumb in front of Gillian. Gillian followed and bit her thumb as well. They laughed while doing this, and I did too. I explained to Toni that what she read actually meant, "Are you insulting me?" She then understood and both girls stopped biting their thumbs, but they still giggled and laughed as they read their parts.

Even though the Shakespearean play and its concepts were difficult, the girls were involved in their reading and having fun, one of the best aspects of learning that tutoring can introduce students to. The students challenged themselves and became acquainted with one of the great writers of the English language all on their own initiative. All the tutor had to do was let them enjoy reading it—and, of course, help them with interpretation.

Sometimes the best teaching techniques have more to do with organizing and arranging the session and motivating the students than with actually teaching. Most tutoring sessions come after a full day of school for the students, when their motivation may be at its lowest. Many tutors feel guilty if they do not use every moment of tutoring time to be productive, but sometimes a break can do more good than harm.

In the next case, the tutor found that breaking up the session helped his student, a fifth-grade Latino, concentrate longer: "It took no longer than twelve to fifteen minutes before I could tell that I was losing his interest. Therefore I offered him a backyard break when he got to a certain place in the homework. He plugged along as normal until about 5:20, then we headed outside to get a breather before returning to homework."

By paying attention to what a student likes, you may even be able to establish study breaks that are not only fun but constructive: "Gus suggested, 'Let's read another one of those stories like we did last week when we're done.' I agreed. I was thrilled, because I had a great time reading them, too. I said, 'Great idea, that was so much fun, let's hope we have time.'"

Having something fun to do at the end of a session can be a real motivator, helping students concentrate harder and work more efficiently. The anticipation also gives the session a tone of fun rather than of simply work.

Looking at What Is Not Working

Just how far to push a tutoring session is another issue tutors deal with. How much help is too much? How much pushing is too much? At what point does the session go from fun to boring to downright tedious? All tutors and students have to experiment with these boundaries. In the following instance, the tutor found successes and failures in her first session with her student, a Latino fifth grader, but the entire experience helped her establish where to go next:

> As we began to read, I realized the extent of his problem with pronunciation. Rather than decreasing his motivation by continually correcting him, I allowed him to break down each syllable to figure out the pronunciation on his own. Only when he asked, "What's this word?" did I help him. I also told Sam to ask me for explanations if he had trouble understanding the meaning of any word. He quickly nodded.
>
> Whenever he had difficulty reading a certain word, I asked him whether he understood the meaning. He answered, "No." I wondered why he didn't ask me. As we read further, I realized that he did not understand a lot of the words; therefore, I suggested that he write those words down and look them up in the dictionary. He quickly whined, "Naaah, that's so boring! Why do we have to do that? I just want to read." I tried to explain that it's important to learn the meanings of words, and he reluctantly agreed.
>
> Having pondered it, I regret forcing him to use the dictionary. Not only did this process break the flow of the story, but I created a boring environment that was not conducive to learning. Sam was bored and probably didn't care to learn the words at that particular time.

Sam's tutor learned an important lesson: Sometimes the best intentions make tutoring and learning dull. When a child is struggling, sometimes it is best to streamline the learning process as much as possible. Although it is good to be able to learn how to use a dictionary, in this case, tutors should probably just explain what words mean (and look words up together if the tutor does not have a good definition in his or her head). Explaining words is not cheating—it helps students learn new words, makes reading more comprehensible, and gives you a chance to personalize definitions for your students.

Adjusting as You Go

One of the most exciting things about establishing an ongoing relationship with your students is that, as time passes, your techniques usually improve, and you adapt them better to each tutee. In the dictionary case just quoted, the tutor quickly learned that her student had a short attention span and that she needed to put in more effort toward keeping him interested. As this same tutor-student team continued to work together, the tutor found other ways to break up the session to make it more fun and to encourage Sam to work harder:

> Throughout the session, as he got problems right, I would tell him to take a bow as he did. He got a half bow when he completed every question and full bow when he finished every third question. He liked this a lot and enjoyed the physical comedy he could display with such self-approval. I have to admit, it was fun.
>
> When the bowing wore thin, we tried a little missile-launch practice. As we took about a ten-minute diversion from the problems themselves to just focus on the multiplication table, I would make a hit sound (like a siren) when he got problems correct and a miss sound (like the error buzzer on a game show) when he didn't. This simple technique went well, as we enjoyed ourselves and it gave Sam a greater desire to struggle with the material.

As you work with students over a period of time and get to know them better, you can employ a variety of techniques to challenge them in different ways. In the next example, the female tutor found that her third-grade Latina student was willing to work hard but lacked confidence. To address this issue, she changed her techniques even though they had been fairly useful in teaching multiplication in the past.

My fourth week at Mar Vista began with Claudia arriving on time and with one assignment for homework. As usual, the assignment was a multiplication worksheet. A recurring thing I noticed in my time with Claudia in terms of her math work was that she always looked to me for the answers or approval of her results. I am still trying to help her realize that she must learn to trust herself and her abilities. Before today's tutoring session I would watch her do every problem and work with her on each one. If she would answer the problem, she would look to me for approval or correction. . . .

Today I tried to do something a little different. She pulled out the infamous multiplication worksheet, and she started on the first problem. I told her, "Claudia, let's try it this way. Finish

---

❖ Making Math Connections

Many children hate math. But we all use math in our everyday lives. When you can, try to connect math with tasks and activities that children want to do:

- Money. If you need to count, or count by multiples, break out the coins (or fake money, if you have some around). Using nickels is a great way to prove to children that they need to be able to count by fives.
- "Even Steven." Division is probably the hardest math operation to master, so why bother? But children love fairness. Make up scenarios where students have to distribute items, such as cookies, to children evenly, thus requiring that they perform division. Challenge them to make situations fair.
- Songs. Some children just have a very hard time remembering the steps for completing math problems. If you don't mind singing, try making up little songs or rhymes that you can repeat like mantras while the student is doing the problems. The sillier you make the "multiplication song," the better! You will be amazed at how easily students can memorize songs—and how quickly you can get a child to laugh about math when you are willing to put yourself out there.
- Averages (or any kinds of statistics or data work). Think batting averages or other sports statistics. Many kids like sports, so grab a newspaper and some real performance statistics and figure out some averages. You can also make some graphs depicting player performance. Or compare modes, medians, and means of points scored.

the worksheet—don't worry about the problems you don't understand or aren't able to get, because we'll work on them together. But this time, I won't hover over you and I won't help you . . . yet. You know the answers, and I know you can find them." I ended with, "I know you can do it, Claudia."

The sheet was about forty problems, and she finished in about ten minutes. She skipped seven of them, and, when I looked at it, of those done, only about four or five were wrong. I worked on those problems with her, using the "walking" through method. We completed the assignment in about half an hour.

With this new technique, Claudia's tutor not only showed her how to multiply but also proved to her that she was learning to do it on her own.

The sports section of the newspaper (or stats from your smart phone) can provide a huge amount of data that your students might actually find interesting.

- Fractions. Fractions can be depicted in many ways (such as pizzas, cakes, or any size circle), but when do you actually use fractions? Cooking is a great example. What if you need ½ cup of sugar, but you don't have a ½ cup measure? What else can you use?
- Decimals. Again, use money. Children often have trouble understanding decimals and place value lower than one, but most children understand money. Work with whole numbers, tenths (dimes), and pennies (hundredths) for a while until they start to get the concept.
- Percentages. We use percentages all the time: discounts, sales tax, tips in restaurants. Set up some "real-life" scenarios and let your students calculate percentages.
- Integers. Adding and subtracting negative numbers is hard. We spend years telling students that they cannot subtract a larger number from a smaller one, and then, suddenly, we introduce negative numbers and they can: It can be genuinely confusing. Some students need visual representations. Draw a picture of a thermometer or a ladder going into a manhole, and show how the number line moves above and below 0. You can also explain that positive numbers are the amount of money that the student has in his or her pocket, while negative numbers are the amount of money that he or she owes. So, $4 + -7 = 4$ dollars in the pocket, with 7 dollars owed: Where does that leave you? You owe 3, so -3.

CHALLENGING STUDENTS

Challenging students in a way that boosts their confidence and is fun for them is one of the best things a tutor can do. You are there to engage students in learning and to challenge them to learn more. You can challenge them in small, immediate steps, such as daring them to learn a spelling word. Or you can give them longer-range goals, such as improving a grade in a class or getting a good score on a test that is coming up. Other challenges are even more far-reaching, such as being a good, motivated student or sticking to a goal, such as applying to college.

A simple challenge can be effective. In the following case, a second grader had been assigned to use vocabulary words in sentences. This simple activity turned into something more exciting and personal for the child with a few queries from the tutor:

> "How can you use 'grow' in a sentence?"
>
> He thought about it and quickly came up with, "The cow grows."
>
> Although this sentence was grammatically correct, I had seen him come up with better examples. This simple sentence simply reflected William's desire to rush through the homework and did not demonstrate his ability to think creatively. Therefore, I challenged him, "Hmmmm, 'grow' can be used in so many ways! Can't you expand your sentence?"
>
> He looked at me blankly, and I knew I had to urge him further. "Okay, William, think about this. What would you like to be when you 'grow' up? A soccer player, a baseball player, a fireman?" I encouraged him to think more analytically by offering him several options.
>
> He began slowly, "When I grow up I want to be . . . a coach for a baseball team."

You can also challenge students to take pride in their work. Too often they turn in homework without rechecking it for correctness; students are reluctant to put in extra effort to make their work good. But a creative tutor can find ways to make extra effort worthwhile. In the next instance, the tutor found that making accuracy a game compelled his student, a ten-year-old Latino, to take pride in his work and to be willing to check his answers:

I wanted to teach him a skill that he could take with him.
I taught him how to check the answers of his problems to guar-
antee an A+ on all of his math problems. I showed him how to
take the answer and plug it into the problem to see if it works.
I showed him how to do it and then asked him if he would like
to check all the problems. He replied, "No." I then decided to
make a bet with him and try to make math fun. I told him that
if I checked a problem and it was wrong, then we would have to
check all the problems, and if he was right, then we could play
any game he wanted. He won.

Besides challenging their students, tutors have an obligation to allow
the students to challenge themselves. The white female tutor in the next
scenario had been working with her fifth-grade Latino student, Miguel,
for several weeks when she realized that she might not always be pushing him to challenge himself. Miguel was considered a troubled child
and had been called unmotivated and disruptive, labels that the tutor
tried to ignore and even to combat. In this instance, however, she found
that, at times, even she fell into the labeling trap, failing to treat Miguel
as a student who might want to go above and beyond the assignment:

I allowed Miguel to have a few minutes to work on his own,
and then I went over to see how he was doing. I noticed that he
was cutting out portions of articles, and so far only two articles.
I explained to him that he needed to cut out single words from
the newspaper. He seemed to immediately understand. He said,
"Oh!" and threw away what he had already cut out and quickly
began cutting out single words he could use [in the poetry he
was supposed to write with them].

I realized that he had not understood his teacher's directions,
but now that he did, he was right on task. Miguel had received
the "Calendar" section of the *L.A. Times,* so he was finding many
movie titles and entertainment-related words. He began to cut
out the word "neurosis."

I told him, "I think that word is going to be difficult to put
in a poem, maybe you shouldn't cut it out."

"It's okay," he said.

"Do you know what it means?" I asked.

"No," he said.

"Well, your teacher said that you should only cut out words that you know the meaning of, because you're going to have to use them in your poetry," I said.

Miguel looked at me with a "duh" kind of look on his face: "I'll just look it up!"

A little embarrassed that I had not suggested that, I said, "That's a really good idea." And I handed him the dictionary.

RECOGNIZING STUDENT PLOYS

Many students are extremely adept at convincing tutors to do their work for them. The tutor is there to aid the student. Asking questions that will help push a student toward a right answer, for example, falls within that

---

 What to Do When There's Too Much Work to Do

Sometimes children save up all their work for tutoring. Other times, students just have a lot of homework to complete in a day. As a tutor, you'll feel pressured to do as much work as possible. Sometimes, with help, a tutor really can provide the help and motivation to push a child through a lot of homework. Other times, the student works too slowly, won't try hard enough to get the work done, or needs too much help to be able to complete the work well. In those cases, you need to prioritize. And, most importantly, don't start doing the homework for the student or allow the student to take shortcuts just because he or she has a lot of work to do.

- Keep your eye on learning. If you can help in a way that speeds the child along but does not compromise learning, do so. (For example, talking with a child about vocabulary words is much faster than looking words up but still forces the child to think.) Don't help in ways that just get the work done, but do teach the student how to do the work (and if you can teach the student how to do work more efficiently, that's even better!).
- Be practical. Sometimes children with skill gaps need some support as they catch up. You can't teach a child several years worth of work in one tutoring session, so if you can provide support that does not undermine the learning process, go ahead. For instance, when children don't know their multiplication tables, math homework can take forever. You should make it a priority to work with such a student on times tables (and give homework if you can). But if the stu-

definition; filling in answers or writing a paper for the student does not. Tutors sometimes find that their students try to manipulate them. As in the following case involving a male fifth-grade Italian student and a female tutor, this realization did not come until after she had been tutoring the child for a while:

> He was completely aware of how much work we had ahead of us—let me rephrase that, how much work *he* had ahead of *him*. Sometimes I feel like Terry pretends to not understand an assignment when he really is trying to get me to give him the answers. He does it subtly, of course. For example, if Terry doesn't know what a word means or how to spell it, he'll ask me instead of looking it up in the dictionary.

dent is facing forty long-division problems, provide a times-tables chart that the student can use during the homework. Using the chart will help the child get through the division (and learn the division process) and will help reinforce times-tables answers.

- Prioritize. Help with work that the child needs help with. If the student has busywork (such completing a writing standards worksheet or writing spelling words over and over again) or work that does not require your help (such as coloring a picture or doing a simple word search), let the child do that on his or her own, after the session.
- Help the child plan for the future. If a long-term assignment or project is the bulk of the work, talk with the child about planning better in the future. And make sure that the child knows that this project will not be perfect: It needed to be started sooner to be really good. Let the student know that planning ahead is essential and that rushing or cramming will almost always yield an inferior product. If you can, this session or next, help the student plan a schedule to handle upcoming tests and projects.
- Talk with parents and teachers. If you see a pattern in which a student has far too much work to complete, even when working hard and without distraction, talk with the parent. The parent can talk with the child's teacher, and the teacher may be able to cut down on the homework. Cite specific reasons for the workload being too much, if possible, to help the parent make a good argument. Just be careful to avoid making excuses for a student who will not buckle down and work efficiently.

Other students will frankly ask a tutor to do work for them. In these cases, no matter how unsettling the situation may be, it is important to lay down your guidelines right from the start. Set the tone for your tutoring sessions from the first session by being positive yet firm. The tutor in the next example found that, with a little friendly pressure, his tenth-grade student was willing to work:

> Mike pulled out his science book and said, "Will you help me make an outline on photosynthesis?"

≫ How to Help with History and Science

The most common history and science homework assignments involve reading a chapter and answering the questions at the end of the chapter. Students often claim that this work is "too hard," but we find that most of the time, they do not read the chapter. Instead, they go straight to the questions and try to find the answers in the textbook. Often, they simply find a keyword in the text and write the sentence down word for word as their answer. It is no wonder that many children find history and science to be boring and hard. Tutors are ideally situated to help with history and science homework, help students understand history and science, and even help students learn to enjoy history and science. If your student is struggling with science or history homework, try the following strategies:

- Read the chapter. It will be more fun if you read together. Students are often shocked to see how easy it is to answer the questions when they have actually read the chapter. Have the student read out loud or take turns, with each of you reading a paragraph out loud.
- Talk. Sometimes history and science books take for granted that students know the context and background of the chapter. Often, children do not, so, try to fill in the pieces. If you are reading about the Civil War, you might have to provide some background on slavery or Abraham Lincoln. If you are learning about photosynthesis, you might have to take a step back and talk about how people get food versus how plants get food.
- Explain. Textbooks are not always as clear as we want them to be. Children can read an entire chapter about the Constitution and Bill of Rights and not see why they are important, because they take their freedom entirely for granted. Ask questions while you read and

"Sure. Let's start by writing down some facts about photosynthesis. Why don't you tell me what you know about it?"

He began to laugh again and said, "That's the problem that I need help with. I don't know anything about it."

I asked, "Mike, in what chapter in your book is photosynthesis discussed?"

He replied, "Chapter four, I think."

I countered, "Have you read it?"

He said, "No."

make sure that the student follows what is going on. Give examples that pertain to the students' lives whenever possible.

- Help make information visual and tangible. Again, textbooks can be dull. Sometimes they do not take advantage of just how interesting the subject matter is. For instance, a history chapter about the advancements of Constantinople might mention that it was one of the first cities to have a sewer system. For most modern students, this is a no-brainer and not very interesting. But, when a tutor can explain what life is like *without* a sewage system, students can see how big an advance sewers really were.
- Model. Sometimes students just need dense textbook material to be broken down and simplified. Explain. Make connections. When you can, draw pictures and models. Putting things on paper is a great way to help children see how things work.
- Don't give in to the temptation to point. The most common refrain you'll hear from students doing textbook work is, "Just show me what paragraph the answer is in." Don't tell them. Teach them to read the chapter and understand. Then, teach them to use subheadings and keywords to review and to find specific information. But don't give in to the temptation to show students the three sentences they need to read just to answer the three review questions at the end of the book.
- Allow the process to take some time. When you first start reading together, students are going to complain that it's taking too long and that they'll never get their homework done. Explain that if you read and talk and learn as you go, they will not have to study at all for the test, so in the end, they are saving time. And make the work as fun and interesting as possible, which will help them forget that they're still doing homework.

I couldn't believe he was asking me to explain something in order to avoid reading the material himself. I said, "I'll make you a deal. Why don't you read the chapter right now, and afterwards I will answer any questions you have."

"Oh, man, all right."

To give a tutee the answer may be tempting. Tutors get tired and frustrated, too. But to make students do the work is to make them learn. In the next case, the Latina tutor felt frustrated with her nineteen-year-old Latino student but resisted her student's pleas and her own inclination to give up:

Jorge was not familiar with any of these words, so I told him to look them up. He referred to the page that contained the definitions of each of the terms, yet he could not figure out which word belonged in the context. He didn't seem to know the difference between a verb and an adjective. There was a section of the worksheet that required filling in the blank with the right vocabulary word.

I tried to show him a clue that would hint the right answer by figuring out what part of speech was missing. For example, if the sentence read, "The teacher did not want to _____ his students with too much homework," I showed him that the word "to" hinted that the blank must be a verb, so we could narrow down the words on the list to verbs only. When I asked if he knew what I was talking about, he said, "Yes." But when I asked him to do the next problem on his own, he couldn't figure it out.

He kept saying, "C'mon, just help me out. What's the answer?"

"Nah, I can't just tell you the answers. Look it up. I know you can figure it out." Despite my encouragement, he did not do the work without my help. For each of the next eight sentences, I would have to guide him through it, figure out the part of speech of the missing word, and narrow down the choices on the list so he could write the one that fit the context. We finally finished the worksheet but definitely not without my being tempted to just tell him the answer.

By not giving her student the answers and walking him through each step that she used to find the correct word, this tutor may have still been doing some of her student's work. But in the process, the tutor was pass-

What to Do When Work Is Too Difficult

Occasionally, teachers assign work that is simply too difficult for a particular student. The student may not have the English-language skills to read a passage or the underlying math skills to complete an assignment. If students do not understand fractions and are asked to multiply and divide mixed numbers, they cannot complete the assignment. In those cases, parents and tutors often feel that their only choice is to do the assignment themselves or to give the students the answers. Resist this temptation.

- Do the preliminary work needed to learn the material. Learn from the assignment. If the child does not understand fractions, start teaching how fractions work, what they mean, and how to add and subtract them. Work together at a pace at which you can be sure that the student understands some aspect of the lesson (even if he or she only understands the very first step).
- Send work back. Write a note to the teacher. Explain exactly why the student could not do the work. Attach the work that you did instead and include an explanation of what the child understands so far. Make it clear that you are not trying to get out of work and that you do want the child to get to the point where he or she can complete the assigned work, but you aren't there yet. Most teachers will appreciate the effort and will not blame a child for not completing work that is too difficult.

ing on the tools that she herself uses to do her own work to a student who had not learned them. He would have been cheated of that learning process if she had just handed him the answers.

As we have seen, an activity such as looking up words in the dictionary can either encourage or discourage hard work. So no simple rule covers what students should be helped with and what they should be left to do on their own. But, as Mike's tutor did, you will realize that even good kids sometimes try to get away with doing as little work as possible. The key is staying aware and, no matter how anxious you are to help, making sure that your students are doing their own work and learning along the way.

Building on the ideas in this chapter, you will discover many ways to convince your students that they not only can do their work but also enjoy themselves and excel at it. Go into your sessions with an open mind, plan to be creative, and maintain a keen eye for what your student gets excited about. One of the main objectives of tutoring is to encourage your students to continue to learn and to succeed in school after your relationship has ended. To this end, making learning fun becomes one of a tutor's greatest achievements.

M OST OF THE TUTOR BEHAVIORS that we encourage in this chapter are very different from typical classroom teaching techniques. Because most tutors work one-on-one, they have much more freedom than teachers who must teach to entire classes of students (and maintain order among entire classes of students!). Our tutors' successful teaching techniques often involve (1) active learning, with all the noise and movement of students doing, talking, collaborating, experimenting, and experiencing lessons hands-on that go along with it; (2) higher-order thinking beyond just rote memorization; (3) choices for students (in terms of book and activity selection); and (4) more cooperative and collaborative activities for students with their tutor and with their peers. Teaching techniques that incorporate the above strategies often succeed in exciting ways, even for children who have failed to thrive in regular classrooms. In this sense, tutors can help and reach students in ways that classroom teachers cannot. Every new, exciting, and unique technique that you develop enriches the education of your students—and may influence their learning for the rest of their lives.

RECOMMENDED READING

The attention you pay to your tutees, their needs, and the teaching style that works best for them is often an antidote to the contention of many critics of contemporary education that children find school boring and purposeless. In *A Place Called School* (1984), John Goodlad documents the efforts of secondary school teachers to keep students under control and passive. This repression of spirit and curiosity occurs just when adolescents need to be taking control of their educations. Goodlad shows that, by taking them through rote exercises and tedious busywork, our education system often teaches children to give back the "standard" answers rather than to learn and to speak on their own.

Through his work with adult students, Paulo Freire challenges the traditional model of teaching in which the teacher is the source of all knowledge and the student merely a passive recipient of this knowledge.

In *Pedagogy of the Oppressed* (1989), he develops an active learning model in which students learn to take control of their own educations. In contrast to the banking approach to education, a metaphor used by Freire that considers students as empty bank accounts where deposits are made by a teacher, Freire sees his adult students, who can neither read nor write, not as illiterate but as incomplete. As peasants, they understand such concepts as exploitation, unfair wages, and unsafe working conditions. These are words that they use in their everyday lives. By acknowledging that they already use these words, Freire finds that his students can quickly learn how to spell the same words. By building on what students know and value, Freire deconstructs the mystery of writing and empowers students to write what they know.

For a wonderful compilation of active learning practices for teaching a range of school subjects, from reading and writing to math and science, see *Best Practices: New Standards for Teaching and Learning in America's Schools* (1995), by Steven Zemelman, Harvey Daniels, and Arthur Hyde. Not only do the authors put together specific techniques to engagingly teach specific subjects; the book includes a number of general pointers that should prove key to any tutoring partnership, such as less memorization of facts and details; less time devoted to dittos, workbooks, and "seatwork"; more experiential, hands-on learning; and more emphasis on higher-order thinking.

For more specific suggestions about how to excite students about learning, especially reading, check out Esmé Raji Codell's *How to Get Your Child to Love Reading: For Ravenous and Reluctant Readers Alike* (2003). The book offers recommended reading for all ages and a wide range of specific topics (fiction and nonfiction) as well as games, activities, and projects that teachers, tutors, and parents can use to engage students in reading and to build on the material that they learn when they read.

4 Race, Gender, Class, and Background Differences

UTORS MUST FORM close relationships with tutees and become part of their worlds to create successful tutoring partnerships. Not only does a close relationship give you, as a tutor, access to ways to motivate your student; it provides you with opportunities to develop your most successful teaching techniques. However, as discussed in previous chapters, many factors can inhibit a strong tutor-tutee relationship.

Expectations and anxieties that tutors and tutees bring into their partnerships create the most common obstacles to tutoring relationships. Tutoring is easiest and most beneficial for both parties when those expectations and anxieties can be left at the door (see Chapter 1). But many fears stem from a common and real fact of tutoring: Tutors and tutees often come from drastically different backgrounds. Many tutors find themselves working with students of different genders, races, ages, class backgrounds, or sexual orientations. Often the everyday world of the tutee is one the tutor sees only on the evening news.

Ideally, tutors easily overcome these differences. We are all people. Tutors, driven by the desire to help, should not be hampered by simple differences in background, right? But such differences are real and sometimes startling. Tutors who work with children and adults who do not speak English well often feel frustrated and powerless, because they do not understand the students' native languages. Sometimes tutees approach their tutors to ask for help with gang or crime problems, and the tutors have no idea what advice is appropriate. Sometimes the discomfort a thirteen-year-old boy feels about opening up to his female tutor can create a substantial barrier to tutoring. In expressing her relief at her own tutoring situation, the following Latina tutor summed up the fears of many new tutors:

> There were three things about Janie that eased my nervousness about tutoring. First, she welcomed me warmly, with a gentle smile. Her familiarity with the tutoring process made it evident that she must have had a couple of tutors before. Secondly, at the risk of sounding sexist, she was female. The fact that she was a girl instead of a boy made me think that tutoring would not be as stressful, because I was under the assumption that boys were harder to control. Thirdly, Janie was a Spanish speaker. I assumed that because we had language and ethnicity in common, that would facilitate my tutoring.

Just as it seems natural to be relieved that you have a lot in common with your student, it is understandable for differences to make tutors somewhat uncomfortable.

In this chapter, we often refer to students and tutors who are different from one another. We use the term "different" to refer to tutors or students who are of different genders, ages, races, ethnicities, religions, classes, social backgrounds, or sexual orientations from the people with whom they are working in the tutoring situations. Differences can create major barriers to the formation of the relationship before tutoring has even begun, at the beginning of the tutoring relationship, and throughout your time with your tutee. All tutors can work around and overcome these differences to discover common ground between themselves and their students and, as the relationships develop, come to accept and to embrace the differences between them and their students. In the end, differences in background and culture can themselves contribute to making tutoring relationships rewarding learning experiences for tutors and tutees.

ANTICIPATING DIFFERENCES BEFORE
THE RELATIONSHIP BEGINS

Fears about tutoring can be crippling, even before tutors meet their students. Throughout the United States, tutors—often university students or people from the upper middle class—volunteer in inner cities, immigrant enclaves, and poor rural areas. They work with youth who are considered "at risk," prisoners, immigrants, homeless people, and many others with whom they might feel uncomfortable in everyday encounters. Tutoring often brings tutors into neighborhoods and social situations they could not imagine themselves in for any other reason, and tutors sometimes erect mental barriers based on their fears regarding particular tutoring sites before they even meet their students. For many potential tutors, typical "tutoring fears," such as those discussed in Chapter 1, are compounded by fears about safety, discomfort, or the location of the tutoring site. Differences between the tutor's and the tutee's backgrounds may become starkly apparent when the tutor first arrives at the site or meets the tutee. It is hard not to form opinions upon these first impressions. In many cases, a spur-of-the-moment impression will leap to mind, such as, "Oh my gosh, this child is dirty. His family must not take care of him." Tutors have to work hard not to let these first impressions hamper their relationships with their new students.

Organizational factors or pressures at the tutoring sites can sometimes aggravate the differences between tutors and tutees. Some site directors prefer to match tutors and students by gender, ethnicity, or language proficiency. This type of matching can facilitate tutoring, but it can also make tutors who do not "fit" feel terribly out of place. Some sites seem designed to serve only particular ethnic groups, which can make tutors of other races or ethnicities ill at ease. Regardless of a tutor's ethnic or cultural background, walking into a brand-new tutoring site almost always evokes at least a moment of fear and unease.

Quieting Pre-site Fears

When tutors set out on the adventure of tutoring, they usually have very little accurate information about the tutoring site or tutees. If they know anything, the little information they have is often not reassuring. To know that the tutoring population is all minority, non-English-speaking, poor, or in a "ghetto" neighborhood can be disconcerting for a middle-class tutor who does not normally interact with a diverse group of people. As politically correct as our society has become, it is naive to think that stereotypes, prejudices, and fears have disappeared. Many people who volunteer to tutor have had little contact with the communities they want to help. For many volunteers, a desire to see more of the city and to get out of their "bubbles" motivates them to tutor, but even a strong motivation to learn and to help does not always quell their fear of the unknown.

That this ignorance can be unnerving is reflected in the following tutor's candid notes: "I was scared of 'retarded' people. I'm afraid of black people. I do not fear them personally, but I fear my inability to share and relate as fully [to people who are different] as I can to people who have had similar life experiences. In writing this, I feel a great deal of discomfort and guilt. I feel like it sounds prejudiced, or as if I think I am qualitatively better than black people. I do not believe that I feel this way. So here I am."

Feelings like these are hard to express, and many tutors leave them bottled up inside. As much as these emotions are socially unacceptable, they are real. Tutors need to be honest with themselves, to know what their fears are, and to work to overcome them. Students of all ages can sense when a tutor feels uncomfortable (and young students are the most likely to call you out on it). The tutors who are most successful are the ones who can admit that they are not sure how to act. As she began tutoring, one tutor wondered, "Would I be rejected as a white poser trying to invade this community, thinking I was the only way to help the kids here to get the socially defined goal of college? I was suddenly aware of my face, my clothing, my posture. I felt like my smile was fake. It is one of the worst feelings in the world, and people can read it on you—fear and insecurity." Although these fears made this tutor insecure, they also made her honest, and as much as students can sense fear, they also sense and respect honesty.

Many tutors opt for sites at which they feel they can make the biggest impact. Sometimes it is exactly these sites that evoke the most anxiety in the days or hours before the first session. The following comments come from a white female who had signed up to tutor in a program for high school–age students who had qualified for early parole, most of whom were still on house arrest and whose crimes ranged from robbery to assault and battery to murder:

> I met the organizer of the program in their main office in [a middle-class/poor African American neighborhood]. She was really positive and really excited about the program, which made me feel really good. But the tutoring is actually going to take place deep in the heart of south Los Angeles, in an area I've never even driven through before.
>
> Amy [the director] says that they can't move the tutoring to their own facilities, because many of the tutees are gang members

Volunteering Safely

Most of the sites at which you'll tutor will be perfectly safe, but you should remain cautious and avoid taking unnecessary risks. Before you go to a new tutoring site:

- Use your computer to create a map and directions. Make sure that you understand the directions. If you're taking public transportation, be certain about the routes, buses, and schedules before you leave the house.
- Make sure that you have a reliable phone number for the tutoring site, in case you get lost.
- If you are driving, clean any valuables out of your car. Don't leave anything tempting in your car when you may have to park on a street in a strange neighborhood.
- Clear valuables out of your purse or backpack. You might keep your bag with you while you tutor, or you may be asked to stow your bag in a locker or office. You'll be much more relaxed if you are not worried about your stuff while you tutor.
- Think about your clothing and jewelry. You may be parking in or walking through a poor neighborhood. You may be working with students or other tutors from a different socioeconomic class. Make sure that you wear clothing and jewelry in which you'll feel comfortable (and not too flashy or ostentatious), no matter where you are or who you are working with.
- Think about the impression you give with your clothing. Some "funny" T-shirts are context-dependent. Think about any writing on your clothing before you go to tutor. Likewise, clothing that is acceptably revealing on a college campus may be too risqué for a community center. Use your common sense and, for a first visit, err on the conservative (and covered-up) side if necessary.

and are afraid to ride the bus across town through other gangs' turfs. I can't even begin to imagine what these guys are going to be like. I talked to my mom on the phone, and she's convinced I'm going to get caught in a drive-by shooting or something.

Fears like this are real. As a tutor, you may have to drive, to take the bus, or to walk through an area where you feel less than safe. You may even be dealing with students who make you uneasy. Always make sure that you are safe (any time you are in a tutoring situation that does not feel safe, talk to the director) and then try to act as normally as possible. A terrified tutor will not inspire a lot of confidence in a student.

Fear for his or her personal safety is not the only thing about a site that can frighten a tutor. Sometimes social differences are just as scary. Faced with glaring differences between themselves and their tutees, some tutors even question their motives, as did this tutor who had elected to work in a program designed to serve gay and lesbian students. As the time to tutor approached, she became more and more nervous: "At this point, I was slightly overwhelmed. Would I not fit in because I am not gay and am involved in a heterosexual relationship? Would I not be able to relate as well as my classmate, someone who obviously understands and can empathize with the students at this center more than I? Did I choose to tutor here for the wrong reasons?"

Such feelings are not only valid but important to acknowledge. It is hard to enter a situation in which you know that you will be surrounded by people who are different from you, and facing the daunting tasks of forming a relationship and helping someone under such conditions can throw your confidence. But acknowledging your doubts and working to prevent them from interfering with the relationship is one of the major challenges of tutoring.

Even tutors who have ethnicity in common with their future tutees can feel pre-site insecurities, as did this Latina tutor: "I'm scared to death of being rejected by the children. I'm concerned about the cultural barriers; although I am Mexican, I don't look it. I fear I might be considered a 'Pocha,' or a person who denies his or her heritage. I know this to be a very sensitive issue."

Although she understood Spanish and was able to communicate basic ideas, another Latina tutor felt nervous about tutoring Spanish-speaking Latina women:

> Tomorrow will be the first day that I meet the women of the Promotora program. I am nervous, because we are implementing this program to teach these women, who primarily speak Spanish, how to speak English. Having trouble speaking Spanish is one of the things I perceive as a personal weakness when it comes to being Latina. Although I grew up interacting with my Mexican culture on a daily basis, I spoke English with my parents at home. However, as a child, I had been cared for by

Don't Pretend to Be Someone You're Not!

You may be "different" from the people you tutor. If you are, you won't be able to fool anyone. We all accept differences, so don't pretend that they don't exist. If you want to avoid putting your foot in your mouth, try to avoid these common mistakes:

* Don't go out of your way to show students that you "know someone" like them or "are friends with people like them." If you work with a gay student and the first words out of your mouth are about your second cousin Jason's boyfriend, your student will know that you're stretching. Likewise, if you spend five minutes trying to find a Facebook photo of you and an African American friend, an African American student will probably see right through the effort.
* Don't pretend to like movies, music, or stars that you don't really like. And, don't assume that your students will like particular types of entertainment just because of their ethnic backgrounds. So, feel free to engage in conversation about popular culture with your students, but don't jump in just to "prove" your credibility. Think of it this way: If you work with a first grader, you wouldn't pretend to think Bob the Builder is a hunk. The student would think you were silly. A teenager will likewise think you're ridiculous if you gush inauthentically over her heartthrob.
* Try not to pick up accents or speech patterns. Don't start using slang that you don't usually use to try to fit in. Don't start using nonstandard English to sound more like your students. If you do slip up and say something that seems uncharacteristic (such as picking up their slang accidentally) and they look at you strangely, be willing to laugh at yourself.
* Don't lie about your life. Students will like you for who you are and will likely appreciate you for the new information you share with them. Don't dismiss parts of your life because you think they are inappropriate.

Overall, you want your students to be proud of themselves. You should behave in the same way. Have integrity, be honest, and be yourself. In the end, they'll know that you're different, but you'll probably have respect for each other.

a woman who spoke Spanish, and I have grown up with one set of grandparents who only speak Spanish. Thus, although my Spanish is not perfect, I understand it well, and after many classes at UCLA, I know that I can speak Spanish. However, whenever you are interacting with a person who is good at something that you are not good at, you always feel a bit intimidated. I feel as though tomorrow I might be intimidated by the women if I am not able to converse in Spanish properly with them, or they may feel intimidated by me if they do not catch onto the English I am teaching them quickly.

The important thing to remember is that tutoring is a positive thing. No matter why you decide to tutor or to take a class that involves tutoring, you are trying to help someone and to form a fulfilling and positive relationship. If you are sincere in your efforts to relate to people and to help, they should be able to sense it and will probably respond positively. Try not to question yourself too much; instead, remind yourself that tutoring should be an enjoyable experience for everyone involved.

Evaluating First Impressions

We like to think of ourselves as open-minded, yet one of the most common problems tutors face in forming relationships with their tutees is feeling too different from their students to understand and to relate to them. Sometimes the differences are apparent from the first tutoring session, as they were to this white tutor:

> I really wasn't very happy with the school I chose to tutor at, and I was even less happy when I arrived at the school. I thought, "Is this some kind of joke?" I wondered as I stood outside the dilapidated school, "Am I even safe here?" The neighborhood certainly didn't look very rich or even middle class. I noticed the chain-link fences running around the length of the school, and images of drug dealers and kidnappers came to mind. I saw their images talking to kids through the fence trying to entice them off school grounds. . . .
>
> I expected to be teaching highly motivated white students who were not just college bound but Harvard bound. I never even considered teaching students who were minorities who

might not even be interested in learning. . . . I had to ask myself, "What the hell am I doing here?"

Although this tutor's response is extreme and obviously not the most desirable for a tutoring situation, it captures the thoughts that many express (or do not express, but think) when they begin tutoring. Although most tutors have only the best of intentions when they go to their sites, they often develop conflicting feelings, and many doubt that they will be able to help students who are very different from them.

Sometimes, as a tutor, you will be faced with prejudices you did not even realize you had—even ones that you dislike and do not want to have but that taint your impressions and behavior anyway. Upon meeting tutees who are very obviously different from themselves, many tutors feel immediately uncomfortable. A tutee of a different race, gender, or even standard of appearance can exacerbate feelings of insecurity or inadequacy about a tutoring situation. At first glance, the Latina tutee in the next scenario did not look like a child that the Latina tutor would want to befriend, and she found it difficult to want to work with her:

The moment I saw Michelle, I knew that I did not want to tutor her. Prejudging her by her unkempt appearance, I doubted that we would have a cool tutoring session together. Perhaps I placed high expectations on her by hoping she would welcome me with a smile, show me her completed homework, and teach me things she likes [as her first tutee, Adria, had done]. I had expected her to be a "model tutee" like Adria. Nonetheless, I took the challenge and began tutoring her.

My first impressions of Michelle were disastrous, because I could not help but compare her to Adria (they were so similar and yet so different!). She was eight and was in the third grade. She had long black hair that was pulled back but hung out of her ponytail and her bangs were so long that they covered over 50 percent of her dark brown eyes. Her skin was much darker than mine, and though she was Latina, too, she looked almost black. She was short, and her tummy was so chubby that some of it hung out of her pink shirt. What struck me most about Michelle's unkempt appearance were her filthy hands, which, after noticing my staring, she cleaned on the pockets of her sky-blue skirt.

This example underlines the necessity of leaving expectations at the door. Expecting, or even hoping, that a tutee will look or act a certain way makes it hard for your student not to disappoint you. All tutees are different, and tutors must work to accept them. Take your students for who they are, hope that they will accept you, and get to work. You will probably be surprised at how well you can work with someone you might not have chosen to befriend—and at how rewarding that partnership can become.

Adjusting to Organizational Set-Ups

On some occasions, the organizational structure of the tutoring environment can highlight race and gender differences, creating an awkward situation for a tutor, particularly one who is already feeling out of place. In the next case, the man who organized the tutoring programs seemed to favor male tutors for many students, which left this female tutor feeling somewhat discriminated against:

> "Could you tutor Roberto?" the director asked Daniel, not even acknowledging me.
> I felt a little offended that the director asked Daniel instead of me to tutor Roberto. I remembered the progress that Roberto and I had made last week and believed that the director had asked Daniel because he was male. If a male tutor could better help Roberto, then I supported the director's decision completely. Otherwise, I felt truly discriminated against.

In other cases, the tutoring environment is oriented around a particular culture or language, which can be alienating for a tutor who is an outsider. For instance, this Latina tutor found herself surrounded by African American faces at her tutoring site. When she entered her assigned classroom, the emphasis on the race of the children made her feel somewhat alien: "The first floor where the office is located is covered by posters of famous African Americans. . . . The [classroom] library is composed of an array of books dealing with African Americans. The books are mostly biographies, such as Malcolm X, Martin Luther King, Jr., Aretha Franklin, and Jackie Robinson."

This tutor thought it was great that the classroom teacher worked so hard to give his students positive African American role models, but she and her friend could not help commenting, "There don't seem to be any Latinos."

Other tutors find themselves in alien territory when trying to tutor children in bilingual schools that assign homework in languages the tutors cannot read. A number of our tutors were troubled at having to go back and forth between their students and other tutors who could translate the instructions on the tutees' homework before they could get down to work.

In instances like these, it can be hard to feel like you belong in a tutoring situation. As a tutor, it is important not to let your discomfort or frustration get in the way of the relationship that you form with your tutee. Organizational problems do not mean that you should change sites or classrooms. Most of these difficulties fade into the background as you begin to work with your tutee. Sometimes, a different cultural environment, in which both you and the tutee can learn, can even enrich the relationship.

RIDING THE ROLLER-COASTER RELATIONSHIP

Like any relationship, tutoring involves ups and downs, periods of great confusion and of great intimacy. In a tutoring relationship with someone very different from you, you will likely experience a roller-coaster ride with more dips and turns than you experience in your everyday relationships and interactions. When you and your students have different worlds and different perceptions, you may not always see eye to eye or understand everything about one another. If you are prepared for these differences, you are less likely to get discouraged when even an established relationship shows signs of strain. These relationships take a lot of effort to maintain and to coax into growing to their full potential.

In some cases, a student's attitude toward you will make you aware of how different you are. Some tutors are hurt when students are cold with them and exuberant with other tutors, perhaps those of the same gender or race. Other times, students are disdainful of you for having more privileges than they do and will not want your help.

More obvious instances of difference will appear when you put your foot in your mouth with a student. Because many of your assumptions will differ from those of your students, it is very likely that you will say something "wrong" and will feel bad about it. Such faux pas are not only natural but to be expected in pairings such as these.

You may also have students come to you with problems or situations you have no idea how to deal with. Tutors raised in suburban middle-class families can be appalled at the gang activities that some of their inner-city students get involved in. Other tutors find themselves at odds when students approach them with family problems that seem greater than the tutors could have withstood at the tutees' ages.

In spite of the reality of these issues, and the need for taking them into consideration as you interact with your tutees, many tutors overcome them. No matter how badly you stick you foot in your mouth or how naive you seem to tutees, you can still convey that you genuinely care about them and are trying to understand.

Allowing for the Student's Attitude

Not all tutoring pairs are matches made in heaven, and not every tutee will greet you with open arms. Just as the tutees differ from you, you may not be what they expected either, and it may take some time to earn their trust and to establish mutual respect.

Even in minimally awkward situations, something as simple as gender difference can make a tutoring situation uncomfortable. The student's objection may not be overt, but in both of the following examples the tutors felt that gender differences were hampering their abilities to form relationships with their students:

> "Hi Brad," I greeted him cheerfully. He looked up, silent and expressionless. This always bothers me. Although I do try fervently, I don't understand why he consistently acts indifferent towards me. I have been friendly, helpful, and supportive. I always attempt to decipher the reasons behind this indifference, and I conclude that it may be attributed to the fact that I'm a girl. He's at the stage where girls are viewed as "yucky."

The second tutor's student was less subtle:

> He tries to delay doing his homework. He asks whether the playground is open, and when I explain that I don't know, he runs off to go ask the director. I follow him, and he actually asks her if he is going to have another tutor. She says no, and he returns with me to the table. This makes me wonder if he asks this because he had decided that he doesn't like me or whether

he sees that his brother has a male tutor and feels he would be more comfortable if he had a male tutor as well.

It is important to recognize that these types of feelings, by the tutee or the tutor, are not only all right but normal.

Because tutor-tutee pairs are usually assigned, tutors cannot know or choose their students in advance, and some matches are not perfect. But a slight mismatch does not have to be a disaster. Sometimes all that is needed is a deep breath and an attempt to find something in common with the tutee. As a tutor, nothing prevents you from developing a strong relationship with a child who comes from a completely different background than yours. Tutors often find that all they need to do to build friendships is develop some flexibility and understanding.

Putting Your Foot in Your Mouth

Even if your students are not bothered by the differences between you, you may embarrass either yourself or your students, because you are unfamiliar with how their lives differ from yours. As the tutor in the next instance found out, seemingly innocent comments can create a moment of awkwardness with a tutee:

> I unknowingly put a huge foot in my mouth midway through our conversation. Kindra [her adult tutee] works in a restaurant in Westwood. Surprised by the long commute she makes from Hollywood to her job, I exclaimed, "You drive all the way to Westwood every day?"
>
> Her reply shocked me into a reality I had not even considered: "Honey, I don't have a car. I take the bus!" How ridiculous and ashamed I felt to assume she would drive, and how quickly she picked up on my assumption that she had a car.

Although this tutor felt vaguely uncomfortable every time she drove up to the center in her new sports car, it was a moment of discomfort that passed relatively quickly and did no harm to the relationship. Similarly, in the following case, a white female tutor made a slipup in her assumptions about her sixteen-year-old Latina student:

> I was trying to explain the meaning of a "dormant" seed to Jill, when I made a big mistake. I said, "I can figure it out by knowing

Fixing Bad Situations

You will probably have some ups and downs in your relationship with your students. You will probably put your foot in your mouth. What are the simple ways to "fix things"?

- Say, "I'm sorry." We often don't think to apologize to children (or to people we're supposed to be teaching). But if you make an error or cause offense, apologize. People are surprisingly forgiving.
- Admit that you've made an error. Something about saying, "Oh my goodness, I can't believe that I just assumed you liked rap (or spoke Spanish, or liked Hello Kitty)" is very disarming. That admission will be much easier than trying to rationalize your assumption. Admit that you relied on a stupid stereotype and move on. If you keep talking, you'll probably put your foot in your mouth again.
- Ask what's wrong. If your student is acting strangely, don't assume you know what the problem is. Ask. Make sure that your student knows that he or she can be honest, and you won't be mad. The student may or may not tell you about the issue, but at least you will have asked.
- Laugh at yourself. Have a sense of humor and make sure that your student knows that he or she can laugh at you, too! Once that ground rule is laid out, it will ease the entire tutoring relationship.

Spanish from high school. What do you think the root of 'dormant' is?" I waited expectantly for the answer "dormir"—to sleep—but it never came.

"I don't speak Spanish," Jill said with a smile.

"You don't?" I asked. I remembered her telling me that she was celebrating Mother's Day on the tenth instead of the twelfth, because the tenth was Mexican Mother's Day. I remembered seeing her aunt come to pick her up and speaking Spanish with an adult who worked at the center. But, come to think of it, I had never actually heard Jill speak Spanish.

"I'm sorry," I apologized. "I just assumed. . . ." I stopped, feeling bad. If there's one thing I've learned from my class, Sociology of Education, it is that you can't generalize one person's experience to another's. You can't stereotype, because everyone is different, and you shouldn't assume anything about anyone.

"Oh, that's okay," Jill laughed it off. "Everyone does that." She didn't seem to take offense, but I still felt guilty for making an assumption at all. Noting my confused expression, Jill explained, "My dad is Mexican and my mom is white. My parents split up when I was two, and I lived with my mom for most of my life, so I never learned Spanish. I started Spanish 1 before I moved here to my aunt's house, but I felt behind when I got here. I guess I'll take Spanish 1 next year."

I touched her arm. "I feel bad. I hope you weren't offended that I assumed you knew the language."

She brushed it off with a grin: "All my friends are fluent in Spanish, and sometimes they even forget. They'll say something to me in Spanish, and I'll just stand there staring at them. I won't say anything, and then they'll realize and translate for me into English."

As in these examples, most small slips can probably be either ignored or laughed about. But even with the understanding that you and your tutee come from different worlds, it is important to be sensitive to issues and differences.

Coping with Situations You Have No Idea How to Deal With

When university students tutor underprivileged or at-risk students, a telling socioeconomic and education gap often exists between tutor and tutee. Sometimes the differences are apparent the moment tutors enter the neighborhoods in which they will be working, and sometimes fear can get in the way of successful relationships:

What was even more striking was the physical location of the Eagles Center. I admit that the first time I stepped out of my car onto the street and walked to the building, I felt slightly nervous. As I approached the front door, I smelled the stench of urine and garbage. There were homeless men and women, barred-up shops, and dirty street gutters. . . .

As I entered the classroom one day, Billy and Matt were engaged in an intense conversation regarding the outside surroundings. As I listened to the conversation, I realized that they were talking about prostitutes picking up the two boys as they leave school sometimes.

Beyond the obvious surface-level differences, tutors sometimes have to deal with more difficult issues when tutoring students of very different backgrounds. As you establish a friendship with your tutee, you will probably deal with some of your student's personal problems as well. Everyone has bad days, and, as a friend and a tutor, you will find it nearly impossible to sit down next to a sad or sullen student and settle right into math homework. As a friend, you will ask what is wrong, and as a mentor, you will try to help.

Sometimes, when the students talk about their lives, they may reveal situations that seem unfair, painful, or difficult to you. You may not know what to say, and you may not know what your responsibilities are in trying to help them.

For instance, the tutor in the next scenario was extremely troubled by the gang activity at his tutee's school:

> The first day of tutoring, Gabriela and Bonita witnessed a stabbing at their high school, and the police questioned Gabriela, because she dropped her backpack at the scene of the crime. The police would not give Gabriela her belongings until she admitted who committed the stabbing. Gabriela fears for her safety, because everyone saw her talking to the cops, and if she names the guilty people, they will come after her. When Gabriela told me what happened, she looked as though she would break down and cry. I reassured her to let all her feelings out and not to hold them inside.

The tutor comforted Gabriela in the immediate aftermath, but he remained troubled that he could do nothing to protect her in the future.

In the next case, the tutor was shocked and scared about a gang problem that was troubling his student. The tutor and tutee had formed a fairly close relationship. The tutor had been serving as a mentor to the tutee and had been able to help him raise his grades and start thinking about the possibility of one day going to college and becoming a UCLA Bruin—if he continued to work hard in school. They considered themselves friends. One day, the tutee came in upset over a situation that the tutor had no idea how to deal with. As the tutee explained to his tutor:

What to Do When Presented with a Situation that You Do Not Know How to Handle

In any new job, paid or volunteer, you'll encounter situations that are new and different. How do you deal with those problems?

- Ask someone who knows more. Most tutoring centers have directors or coordinators. Those people are supposed to deal with big issues. In fact, those people would rather that you talk with them than handle things badly on your own. If you handle something badly, *they* will be held responsible for *your* errors, so please get them involved. If you're doing private tutoring or tutoring in a classroom, don't hesitate to talk with parents or teachers. Again, they have more experience, and they know the students. Don't take problems on by yourself. Share the weight.
- Talk with your student. Students can often give you guidance on what they want or need you to do. Some will beg you not to tell their parents. Others times, students bring up situations precisely because they want you to bring in an authority figure (for instance, they might want a teacher to know what is going on, but they do not want to be the ones to "tell"). Ask your students whether you can help in some way. Do everything you can to let the students lead. If they want you to talk to another adult, by all means do so. If they beg you not to, try to respect that wish without being irresponsible. (If a student is in danger, is being abused, or threatens someone else, you have a responsibility to tell an adult in authority at your tutoring site—even if the student begs you not to tell.) If you decide you need to talk with another adult, try to give the students prior warning so they don't think that you're going behind their backs. Let the students know that sometimes you *have* to tell someone, even if don't want to or if you know that the students are scared. When you do talk with an adult, try to talk first with someone you trust to guide you in the best direction.
- Talk with other tutors. A tutor with more experience may be able to share stories or examples that help you. Don't be afraid to talk with your co-workers or classmates.
- Use your common sense. Your life may be very different from your students' lives. But if you're scared, they're probably scared, too. Don't let a student's false bravado keep you from doing the right thing. Get good advice, and whenever you feel in over your head, talk with someone who is in charge.

I'm telling you, there's nothing you can do. I was hanging out shooting some hoops with a couple of my friends at lunch, when these gangbangers came up to us and asked us to play three-on-three. Before I could object, my friend Dan agreed to play, and there was no way out of it.

Everything was fine until the game was almost over. We were winning ten to seven, and the game was to eleven. This guy guarding me, I won't tell you his name, said that if he lost, he was going to kick my ass. Even though I did not want to lose and probably wouldn't have listened to him, I had no control over who won. Dan stole the ball from another guy and went in for a layup. Just like that, the game was over. Now this guy wants to kick my ass. Can you believe it?

For a tutor who has no experience with gang-related activities, a situation like this may not only prove overwhelming but leave the tutor feeling helpless. All of the rational solutions a tutor might offer take on a different twist in the world that some of the tutees live in. Sometimes the best thing tutors can do is be good listeners. In situations where you feel that the student really needs advice that you do not have the expertise to provide, speak with the supervisor at your tutoring site. The supervisor may be able to advise you or the student or help you get advice from someone who knows more about those kinds of problems.

When students do reveal surprising problems, tutors should try not to register too much shock. Students often perceive their own situations as normal, and your outrage might be inappropriate and alienate the student. Listen and try to understand the problem from the tutee's perspective. Be sympathetic, but also understand that problems that seem extreme to you may be fairly common for them.

Even when tutors find problems shocking, they may be able to help solve or prevent them. In the following instance, the tutor's young student confided in her that he shoplifted regularly: "In the middle of a spelling lesson, Nathan changes the subject. 'Do you know how easy it is to steal from the 99 Cent store?'

"I ask him, 'How do you know you won't get caught?'

"He responded, 'They don't have cameras or nothing in there. I won't get caught.'"

This tutor was unsure how to handle the situation at the time. But she did a good job in holding her tongue, getting the full story, and not scolding the tutee on the spot. Sometimes it is better not to get involved right away; sometimes a student is testing the waters to see how a tutor will react, and the beginning of a relationship is not always the best time to try to influence a child.

Over time, the tutor realized that Nathan was starved for attention, perhaps even wanting to get caught so his parents would talk to him. He also tended to act out in class to get people to notice him:

> His mother frequently travels to Mexico and leaves Nathan with his stepfather, because his biological father is not part of his life. The catch is that the stepfather works from 3 P.M. to 1 A.M. during the week, so who takes care of Nathan? Who cooks dinner for him, helps him with his schoolwork, or even puts him to bed?
>
> No wonder he's stealing from the 99 Cent store and not completing his homework. He had no direction after school. I wouldn't be surprised if he wanted to get caught shoplifting, so his parents would notice him and pay some sort of attention to him, even if it's negative.

Even if the tutor could do nothing specific to improve Nathan's home life, she had a chance to do three things: She could encourage him not to steal, push him in the direction of some positive ways to get attention, and give him some one-on-one attention that might lessen his need to get into trouble. Nathan's major problem seemed to be a lack of attention from his parents, but, for a few hours a day, he had a tutor all to himself. Do not underestimate the difference that a little personal attention in the form of good tutoring can have on a child.

OVERCOMING DIFFERENCES

Despite all the differences and difficulties in the previous examples, adopting the basic tutoring attitudes outlined earlier in this book can help overcome differences between tutors and tutees. Tutoring often succeeds between two people who seem to have little in common.

As you tutor, solutions will have to come from you, your tutee, and the unique relationship that you have formed. As the following excerpts demonstrate, many tutors find ways to work with their students and to mitigate circumstances that, initially, seem insurmountable. Several strategies will help you move toward a productive relationship with a tutee who is very different from you. First, try to minimize the difference between yourself and your tutee—or at least maximize your "sameness." You are both people. Find out what you have in common and start from there. Even people from vastly different backgrounds can have similar interests or values. By the same token, do not stick out more than you have to, either in dress, speech, or conversation topics. An inner-city sixteen-year-old probably will not have a brand-new car in the driveway on his birthday—so you do not have to mention the one you got. But, as you emphasize similarities, do not create any that are not really there; do not pretend to be someone that you are not. Finding and creating true commonalities is the way to build a solid relationship.

Even differences that will not go away in the time that you tutor your student need not be impenetrable barriers to your relationship. Following the premise of accepting your students for whoever they are, your best solution may be simply to maximize your acceptance of the differences between you. Accepting your differences means working with them and talking about them but still being confident that dissimilar people can create a strong and productive relationship.

The attitude of dealing with your student as an equal also comes into play when tutoring students very different from you. You may not always feel that you can comprehend the lives, problems, and joys of these students, but you can empathize and try to understand. The life situations of your students may seem alien to you, but get your tutees talking and take the opportunity to let them teach you something; with your new information, try to understand them and place yourself in their shoes. You cannot necessarily solve their problems, but an open environment in which to discuss them is a gift that you can give.

Differences can also have a positive impact on your relationship. Most importantly, they open up avenues for conversations. The dialogue that can spring from differences in knowledge, expectations, ambitions, and assumptions can teach both of you something about another world and a person unlike yourselves. Get your students to explain their worlds to you, but do not hesitate to explain yours to them. Show them an alternative to their worlds (while recognizing that no world is ideal for everyone) and a glimpse of what else is out there. And try to see and to understand their lives and environments. One of the best possible consequences of putting your foot in your mouth or encountering a hostile student is the opportunity such situations create for open, honest conversation.

Fitting in and Being as "Same" as Possible

Getting past the differences between tutors and tutees is part of the process of building a relationship. Most tutors are surprised at how much they have in common with their students. One of the first steps in the tutoring experience is finding these commonalities, and many tutors also find it effective to minimize obvious differences right off the bat.

Being "the same" is often impossible, but you can try some tactics to fit in more, or at least to not stick out in your tutoring environment, as this next tutor found:

> I was tutoring at a private school, under contract with the Los Angeles Unified School District, to serve district students who are labeled as "emotionally disturbed." The "emotionally disturbed" label made me very nervous. I did not know what I was getting into. I decided to suit up; perhaps if I looked professional, the kids would take me seriously. . . .
>
> The students standing out front when I approached the school were older than I expected. The students were ethnically integrated, wearing baggy jeans and T-shirts. Nervously, I walked past them en route to the office. In the office, I was greeted by Jim. He was wearing corduroy jeans and a tie-dyed shirt. When I saw him, I wished I had worn my jeans.

When you enter a tutoring situation, it is vital to be yourself, but it may also help to be as neutral as possible. Do not attract attention to yourself, your different culture, or your socioeconomic background. If the students you work with come from cultures in which modesty is valued and you walk in wearing a miniskirt or jeans with holes all over them, effective relationships will be harder to build. Tutors enter their students' environments as guests, and the hosts' values and morals deserve respect.

The following tutor found that the same rule applied when she was working with kids from a poorer background than her own: "I noticed that they immediately spotted my jewelry, and every child I helped kept staring at it. I hadn't thought that maybe I should have taken it off so I would fit in better. The reason I say 'fit in' is because it is obvious that the students at this particular school are from working-class families. At the first chance I got, I took off my rings and necklace."

This tutor felt that the signs of her class status were too blatant and might interfere with her ability to relate to the students. It was easy for her to remove her jewelry and to feel more like she was on their level. Her removal of the jewelry also allowed the tutees to focus on tutoring rather than this sign of difference.

Maximizing Acceptance and Embracing Your Difference

Tutors cannot change their accents, educations, or skin colors. They may simply differ from the students they are tutoring, and that is okay. In fact, it can be very valuable for tutees to develop relationships with people different from them and from the people they ordinarily interact with. Just as you, as a tutor, will learn to relate to students who are different from you, they will learn to relate to you—if you show them that you want them to.

Some tutors fear that it is impossible for them to relate to students who are very different, but that does not seem to be the case. Not only do many successful tutoring relationships grow between educated, upper- or upper-middle-class tutors and inner-city or poor youths; a flourishing private tutoring industry also faces the class-difference problem, in reverse.

Private tutors who tutor in the homes of students much more privileged than themselves often report the same discomfort as tutors who work with students much poorer than themselves, as in this example: "I had to be led out of the house, because it was so big I didn't think that I was going to be able to find my way out on my own. There were three cooks in the kitchen preparing dinner. I asked Aria if her parents were having a party that night, and she said no, that her parents were in London. Three cooks to make dinner for two little girls! There was also a butler and two maids that I saw in the two hours I was there. I felt like the seventh servant in the house."

Private tutors get paid well to form strong and effective tutoring relationships, even though it is obvious that few private tutors live in multi-million-dollar houses staffed with hired help. In the same way, a middle-class or even an upper-class tutor can form a relationship—often a very positive one—with a child from a working- or lower-class background.

Some tutors, such as the one who removed her jewelry, find it helpful to hide the obvious signs of their socioeconomic difference, but this is not the only way—or even the best way—to deal with the differences.

The tutees know you are different. You may come from a university, in which case they probably assume that you come from a different background. In some cases, sharing personal information can break down boundaries rather than create them:

> As I was about to take the children back to the classroom, they noticed my new red Ford Mustang parked outside the school. I try to park it in a spot where no students can see my car, because I feel it's too flashy. I just feel awkward, because I don't want the children to think of me as just some rich college kid. I also didn't want it to be the topic of my conversations with the students. I want to help tutor them, not discuss cars.
>
> Anyway, the lunch table where I gave them their spelling list was in direct view of my Mustang, and Daniel said, "Check out that new Mustang! I think Mr. Mooney drives one of those."
>
> Erin jumped in, "No, Mr. Mooney's is different. Is that yours, Miss Karen?"
>
> I was on the spot, and I had to respond, so I told them, "No, it's not." I feel so guilty about lying to them. Instead I should have trusted the fact that they would have enjoyed knowing what kind of car I drive, as they did about Mr. Mooney's car.

Opening a Conversation

In many cases, being different gives you the opportunity to expose tutees to ideas and ambitions that they may never have come in contact with. Just as working with and forming a relationship with a person quite different from yourself is interesting and eye opening, tutees may have the same experience with you. You are foreign to their world, but that does not mean that they cannot learn something from you.

You have a wealth of information that many students have never been exposed to, especially concerning academic success. You also have resources that they may not have access to. For instance, tutors are often able to give their students valuable information about preparing for college. Sometimes the tutor is the only resource a tutee has for this kind of information. Other times, information about college and higher education is simply more effective coming from someone who is more of a peer and a friend than an authority figure.

When you deal with students from very different backgrounds than yours, you may find yourself cast in the role of "the other." You may be foreign to your students' neighborhoods, even feared there. You may represent employers that they dislike or privileged people who oppress them. Just as you will be forced to confront your stereotypes when you tutor students unlike yourself, they will be forced to confront theirs.

This clash of expectations can cause tension in the relationship, which some tutors like to address head on, often to the benefit of both parties. In the next scenario, the tutor placed himself in a "rich white" category by his familiarity with a posh Beverly Hills restaurant that had donated bread to the tutoring center. When his tutee reacted negatively, the tutor used the opportunity for a candid conversation on race and privilege:

> On the table were several packages of bread from a restaurant called Il Fornaio. I told him, "That restaurant is in Beverly Hills."
>
> He immediately squished his face together, wrinkling his nose, and said, "I hate Beverly Hills." When I asked him why, he made a disturbing comment that "rich people are uptight and rude."
>
> I asked, "Do you think Magic Johnson, who is obviously rich, is rude?"
>
> He responded with an even worse comment, saying, "It is just white people who are rude." I then asked, "Do you think Mike Piazza, the star of the Dodgers who is also rich, is rude?"
>
> He said, "No."
>
> And I explained, "Mike is an example of why you might not want to form opinions about people before you meet them. I understand that historically, white rich men have brought about many inequalities in society, but I want you to know that if you want to be treated equally, you should treat others equally as well. Having a predetermined opinion about an individual based on his or her skin color or income is not right."
>
> He said, "I guess I never thought about it that way. It's just that most of the rich white people I see, like at the television studios [he goes with his youth group], don't even say hi to me. I'm sorry, I know I shouldn't stereotype."

For the most part, tutors find that differences, which at first glance seem impossible to work with, are not that overwhelming. A tutoring relationship does not have to be homogeneous. Furthermore, tutors often find that "very different" students have a lot to teach them, once the lines of communication are open. Like the following white male tutor, many tutors enjoy learning new words in their students' native tongues as they work to increase their tutees' English proficiency:

> The supervisor asks me if I want to teach English. This tutee speaks minimal English. And, even worse, I do not speak Spanish. Of course, though, I am up to the challenge. I go and get flash cards from the rolling bin. I show him the picture, he reads the word. I then correct his pronunciation if it needs correcting. After a few words, I realize it's going well.
>
> I try to explain to him that he can teach me Spanish while I teach him English. He doesn't understand. Another tutor who speaks Spanish relays my message to Julio. He likes that idea. I get out a piece of paper and a pen, and for every word that we do, I say [the English], then he says [the English]. Then he says the Spanish equivalent, and then I say the Spanish equivalent. Then I have him write down the English word next to the Spanish word. He likes this form of learning, and I think it is working well.
>
> After doing about forty words or so, I turn to sentence use. I start with "I am a" and things like that. He catches on fast, and before we know it, we are making sentences about him and me: "I am a man." "You are a man." "I am tall." "You are small."

Many tutors who pick up some Spanish or another language from their students can then to put their new skills to use with other limited-English-speaking tutees.

Beyond languages, tutors also learn a great deal about other religions and cultures by talking to their students about after-school activities and holiday celebrations. Tutors can even learn a lot from students whose differences may seem rather unsavory at first glance. The tutor who worked with paroled gang members found that discussions with her students gave her a broader view of her city and the "other" people who lived there:

I was fascinated as Oscar described to me how the various gangs are broken into subgroups and cliques and what the tags that we see all over the city stand for. That the hierarchy is so intricate and complex was shocking to me. It was not what I had expected from groups of "thugs." . . . In talking to him, I could see just how pervasive this way of life was to him—that he had grown up in a gang and that it was very much of what he knew.

As he explained to me how he could attack someone just for being in another gang, the reasons, completely absurd to me before, became somewhat clearer. Although I can't say that I approve of gang life, I feel like I have a better understanding of what was just a cartoon picture to me before. I also better understand that the boys in them are just that: boys. They aren't monsters. We had the kids fill out a form in which they had to write a bit about themselves. One of the questions was, "Who do you admire most?" From this group of convicted delinquents, one answer was unanimous: their moms. How can we say these kids cannot be saved?

Through tutoring, this tutor gained compassion and understanding for a group of people with whom she might never otherwise have made contact. Her new knowledge will affect the way she sees others, interprets the news, and discusses such topics as crime and poverty. In the end, for all the difficulties that can arise from tutoring those who are different, the benefits are generally greater for all parties involved.

RECOMMENDED READING

This chapter focuses specifically on how tutors can overcome and work around differences that they experience in tutoring situations due to race, ethnicity, gender, social class, religion, sexual orientation, or life experience. A great deal of literature discusses how these differences influence students in their school experiences (accounts range from first-person reports to academic and journalistic investigations of differences between students and teachers; between different groups of students; and between students and parents, politicians, and stakeholders who control school resources).

One poignant work that documents the devastating treatment of poor children and the resistance by middle- and upper-class parents to improving poor schools in their own communities is Jonathan Kozol's *Savage Inequalities* (1991). Kozol began his critique of U.S. public education in 1967 with an indictment of the educational system's response to poor black children in Boston. In *Death at an Early Age* (1968), he describes conditions so horrific that one wonders how Americans, teachers, and administrators can endure their own insensitivity to these children. Kozol has written more than twenty books and has been one of the most consistent and trenchant critics of American public education. He writes with passion, eloquence, and a deep concern about America's children. For a review of eight of these books, see Jerome Rabow and Laura Saunders, "The Legacy of Jonathan Kozol" (1992). And in one of his most recent books, *Shame of a Nation: The Restoration of Apartheid Schooling in America* (2005), Kozol captures how the United States has recreated a segregated public school system.

Many educators throughout the country are also positively addressing the range of students found in the U.S. education system. In *Possible Lives* (1995), Mike Rose travels America and finds teachers in different cities and locales building class curriculums geared to the cultural backgrounds of their students.

In *Affirming Diversity* (1996), Sonia Nieto shows how race, religion, immigrant status, gender, and ethnicity are very significant factors in students' motivation to learn and to become educated.

Similarly, Lisa Delpit's *Other People's Children* (1995) describes the special care that must be taken when teaching children from diverse racial and class backgrounds. For instance, she explicates some of the cultural differences in the ways African American and white parents direct and discipline their children and the repercussions of these differences on classroom management. Likewise, Shirley Heath's *Ways with Words* (1983) and "Questioning at Home and in School: A Comparative Study" (1982) share a number of provocative insights into the cultural-linguistic differences between working-class black children and their often white middle-class teachers. Both Delpit and Heath help teachers and tutors understand how and why students from different backgrounds learn differently—and may react differently to different teaching styles.

For a deep understanding of the differences in social-identity development for black students in contrast to whites, see Beverly Tatum's

"Why Are All the Black Kids Sitting Together in the Cafeteria?": A Psychologist Explains the Development of Racial Identity (2003). This book provides an understanding of why "those students" all sit and hang together. It helps the reader understand that, rather than being cliquish and racist toward others, students of color rely on each other for validation and for a sense of self-worth.

Gary Howard describes in *We Can't Teach What We Don't Know: White Teachers, Multiracial Schools,* second edition (2006), how he, as a white teacher, comes to grips with his stereotypes and his position of "I'm here to help you people" as being negative for teaching students of color. He aims to help prepare a predominantly white teaching force to work effectively with an increasingly diverse student population.

Jerome Rabow has published several articles on how college students can be taught to appreciate the "other":

- When the other is gay or lesbian, see Rabow, Stein, and Conley, "Teaching Social Justice and Encountering Society: The Pink Triangle Experiment" (1999), and Milman and Rabow, "Identifying with the Role of 'Other': 'The Pink Triangle Experiment' Revisited" (2006).
- When helping behavior is involved and judgments about differences are demonstrated, see Wolfinger, Rabow, and Newcomb, "The Different Voices of Helping: Gender Differences in Recounting Dilemmas" (1999).
- For teachers interested in confronting racism, sexism, and homophobia among their students, see Rabow and Yeghnazar, "Transformative Teaching in the University: Uncovering and Confronting Racism, Sexism and Homophobia" (2009).
- For an appreciation of the stereotypes that men of color have about white males, see Conley, Rabinowitz, and Rabow, "Gordon Gekkos, Frat Boys and Nice Guys: The Content, Dimensions, and Structural Determinants of Multiple Ethnic Minority Groups' Stereotypes about White Men" (2010).

5   Other Adults

Parents, Teachers, and Administrators

OGETHER, TUTORS AND STUDENTS create their own learning relationships and environments. However, you almost never tutor in a bubble. Throughout your tutoring experience you will find that the other adults who are integral parts of your tutees' lives will influence your work in many ways. The other adults you will work with most frequently are your tutees' parents and teachers.

The actions and the attitudes of the other adults in your tutees' lives will affect your tutees' academic progress. For instance, when teachers and parents work hard to give students extra help, students tend to learn more. And when teachers and parents believe in students, they can give them support and confidence that enable them to perform up to their potential. On the other hand, when teachers or parents neglect students or label them as "slow," they can harm the students' progress. Although tutors form their own relationships with their students, it is important for them to be aware of the actions and attitudes of the other adults in their students' lives.

When the involvement of other adults serves the best interest of tutees, tutors should welcome it. However, as a tutor, you may also encounter situations involving other adults that seem to jeopardize the mental, emotional, and sometimes physical health of your tutees. You need to be able to recognize and to try to mitigate the effects these influential adults have.

Parents and teachers shape the environments in which your students spend most of their time. Often these influences are positive and flow from supportive attitudes. Parents and teachers can work wonders with students when they act as encouraging and enthusiastic leaders and role models. The students' resulting confidence makes your job as a tutor considerably easier. Even when teachers and parents do not do everything perfectly (they never could), students can tell when their parents and teachers care about them. That support, alone, helps them succeed.

The more parent and teacher involvement you see in the lives of your students, the more positive their learning environments are likely to be. Involved parents go out of their way to know what is going on and to get advantages for their children. Involved and attentive teachers stay on top of what you are working on with your students, monitor their progress, and make sure that the work they give you continues to be challenging.

Another obvious way that the adults in your tutees' lives can help make your job easier is by assigning challenging and interesting tasks. Teachers who assign exciting homework and provide a dynamic curriculum produce kids willing to sit down with their tutors and do their work.

On the flip side, other adults in your students' lives may have negative impacts. A tutor must always be alert to such influences, because they can create obstacles in the tutoring process. Before tutors can hurdle these obstacles, they have to recognize them.

One of the most common negative attitudes that students face, from parents and teachers, shows up in a lack of involvement. Because adults, particularly parents, might seem uninvolved in their kids' education for a variety of reasons, we suggest that tutors spend a significant amount of time observing and trying to understand all the circumstances before deciding that a parent or set of parents is neglectful. Some parents do not get involved, because they are too busy, they lack the education or language skills to help their children, or they have a different orientation to school than you do. For example, although some parents believe that they should challenge teachers if they think that teachers have done something wrong or unfair, others believe that "the teacher is always right" and would feel uncomfortable confronting a teacher (even if, to you, the teacher was quite obviously wrong). To begin with, tutors should work under the assumption that all parents want their children to succeed and want to help them succeed, even if they do not know how to do it. Form judgments about parents carefully and seriously, and be as generous as you can.

Another form of neglect that makes a tutor's job harder occurs when teachers assign students boring, rote exercises and provide students with little motivation to do them. When teachers assign work that does nothing to inspire your students, it is up to you, as a tutor, to inject some creativity and to make their homework fun. It may also fall to you to explain to students why the homework may be useful (and, remember, just because work is boring does not mean that it is useless—think about how handy it is to know your times tables).

As they work with students, most tutors also have to work with (and around) the labels that other adults have assigned to their students. Labels come up a lot, as adults are often looking for simple ways to tell a tutor about a student. When a teacher or parent tells you that a student is an "English-language learner" or "ADD," these labels can be informative (you can know to ask the English-language learner lots of vocabulary questions and not to be too tough on a fidgety ADD student). On the other hand, labels are sometimes sloppily applied, and many labels can give you a bad impression about students before you even meet them. Students who have heard—often—that they are stupid or lazy can be the hardest to motivate. Tutors get especially frustrated at labels when they can see no basis for them in the child. Here again, tutors can try to use their influence as adults in the students' lives to combat the negative stereotypes.

Although tutors can and should be the first to applaud the other adults who fill their students with positive attitudes, they can also be highly disturbed by damaging negative influences that they see. One of the most common questions that tutors ask themselves and each other is "What can I do to help?" The answer is not an easy one. In a classroom, a tutor is a guest in the teacher's domain and does not have the authority to change a teacher's curriculum or attitude toward students. Dealing directly with parents also places a tutor in a position of relative helplessness. Who are tutors to tell parents how to raise their children?

Tutors can nevertheless mediate and find solutions to some of the negative forces in the lives of tutees. Developing a close relationship with the other adults may be the wisest investment a tutor can make, aside from developing a close relationship with the tutee. Building an effective partnership with parents, teachers, and administrators will create understanding and cooperation, which will help tutees. Establishing this effective partnership often requires the tutor's initiative, forbearance, and patience. Although some tutors feel confident in their social skills, others feel uncomfortable developing these relationships. Yet your skills will improve over time. Tutors who keep in mind the best interests of their tutees can always draw strength from there.

ATTITUDES AND INVOLVEMENT OF THE OTHER ADULTS

Involved and supportive parents and teachers can be a tutor's greatest asset. They can give you relevant background information on your students and tell you their areas of strength, weakness, or other qualities that may facilitate your tutoring experience from the start. Beyond that, parents and teachers who are willing to work closely with tutors often form good teams. Tutors are usually the most effective when they have the cooperation of parents, teachers, and other adults whom the child either works with or respects.

Even if the other adults in your students' lives will not or cannot work directly with you, their simple involvement in the lives of your students can create good tutoring environments. When students know that adults care about them, they are more willing to open up with other adults, including you.

Involvement with the Tutors

Many tutors find that their most successful tutoring comes out of strong partnerships with the students' parents, teachers, or both. When the adults in a child's life work together as a team, they can rely on each other to reinforce values and to keep up confidence.

In the following case, the tutor found that interacting with her tutee's mother set a great foundation for their partnership in assisting the tutee. Joe's mom was able to bolster his confidence not only by praising him but by praising him to his tutor, someone else who would be proud of his accomplishment. In this case, the tutor and the parent shared the task of helping Joe with his homework, which made the partnership even more successful:

> Joe wanted to sit at the far round table and said that he had fun homework today. Louise, his mother, excitedly came over and said, "Joe, show Lisa your spelling test."
> I said, "Oh, great, how did it go?"

How to Communicate with Parents

In some tutoring situations, you'll get to talk with parents. Other times, you'll never know anything more about a student's parents than what the student tells you. But you can still communicate with a student's parents:

• Send a note. A quick "Hello" note can be a nice way to introduce yourself to a student's parents. Keep the note short, but explain who you are, tell when and how often you are working with the student, and let the parents know if they should expect homework from you. It's also nice to ask the parents if they would like for you to work on anything special with their child. Don't be disappointed if you don't get a note back, but if you do, it could be helpful.

• Send instructions with homework. If you do assign homework, attach a note to explain what the student should do and when the homework is due. Also, make clear that the homework is from *you* and not the teacher. Instructions will help parents feel involved and informed.

• Send messages through the student. Students are not always totally reliable as messengers, but you can definitely encourage your student to show off to parents. If you're working on times tables, ask your students to "perform" what they know for their parents. If you've just finished a book, ask a student to read the book aloud for his or her mom or dad. When students complete perfect papers, write "100%" and nice comments on top and encourage them to show the papers to their parents.

She said proudly, "Every day last week, I made him sit down and work on those words." It was Joe's first spelling test. He handed it to her and took off to look around the center. She showed me how he got all but two correct, minimizing his errors by showing me how he confused the two words. She seemed very pleased.

Tutors who interact with their tutees' parents also may get a sense of how the parents feel about their children's educations and what teaching methods they would prefer. Although it is not always necessary, it often helps to form a good relationship with students' parents. Knowing and talking with parents can make tutoring sessions, particularly with young students who do not have much official "work," more productive. The following Latina tutor found out a lot about what her six-year-old Latina tutee's family wanted her to focus on by talking with the student's mother:

> Lucia's mother and I had a small conversation on bilingual education that was triggered by my asking how much English Lucia knows. To my questions, Delia responded, "Lucia used to know more English when she was in the Mar Vista preschool than she knows now that she's going to kindergarten." Delia showed some disappointment when she stated this.
>
> Without further questioning, Delia volunteered her opinion on her daughter's education. She explained to me that Lucia is a smart young girl who learns new stuff pretty quickly. She said that she is convinced that if teachers at her kindergarten spoke to her in English, she would learn it rather quickly. Delia told me that the staff at Mar Vista show that they really care about student learning. She said that most of the things that Lucia knows now, such as writing her name, counting to twenty, and the vowels, were taught to her in preschool. Delia feels that Lucia is not being challenged in her new school.
>
> Before Delia left, I asked her what language she prefers that I speak to Lucia in during tutoring. "Speak to her in both," she said.

Similarly, teachers who are receptive to working with tutors can enrich the tutoring experiences of their students. In the following case, the tutor was empowered by the great attitude of most of the teachers with whom she would be working:

> Today I mainly observed, because the teachers wanted me to get a feel of the class to see what I would be comfortable with and to see what it is that they want me to do. I was very welcome in two of the classes, Mrs. Edwards's and Mrs. McCall's. They were both extremely receptive toward me, showed me around, gave me a few things to do and told me what they would be expecting of me in the future. The third teacher, Mrs. Lowry, said nothing to me from the moment I walked in the door.

A close partnership between teachers and tutors can really benefit a student. Teachers and tutors can work together not only to figure out the needs of students and the best way to address them but to monitor their progress and to keep each other abreast of developments that might otherwise be missed, either because the teacher is busy with the other students or because the tutor is only with the student a few hours a week.

The cooperation and help of teachers who have developed relationships with the children whom you are working with can help you develop your own strong tutor relationships. Teachers sometimes use their power to help tutors out, as in this incident in which a tutor was rescued by a teacher she had not even met yet:

> A teacher whose class was outside for recess saw how uncontrollable Gary and Phillip were being and approached the bench we were sitting on. She said to Phillip, with a thick Hispanic accent, "Phillip, what are you doing to this poor young lady? Can't you guys behave for her?" The teacher was very polite and obviously knew them both on a personal level.

Similarly, any other adults who have a relationship with a tutee, from volunteers at the tutoring site or classroom to other parents, can help when a tutor is struggling with a child. As a tutor, do not be afraid to ask for help from an adult who may have more resources or leverage than you have. As the female Jewish tutor in the next example found when working with Elsa, her stubborn seven-year-old Latina student, a little gentle persuasion from someone in power is sometimes all is takes to get a tutor some respect or cooperation:

> Once I had officially said "No" to her, she became more blatant in her defiance. "I not gonna do it," she told me coyly, with a great big smile on her face.
>   I dealt with this by informing her, "You need to do it before we can do anything else." We went back and forth for nearly ten minutes—she insisting that she wasn't going to do it or she couldn't do it, and me replying that she needed to do it and she could do it. I told her that I knew she was smart at math, because we had worked on numbers last week. Finally, I pointed to the line that said "nombre" and prompted her to fill it in. She wrote "Elizabeth" on the line. I reminded her that her name was not

"Elizabeth," it was "Elsa," and that she needed to write her real name down. With a big smile on her face, she declared that Elizabeth was her real name.

There were only so many battles I could fight with her, so I decided to leave the name alone and start working on the math problems. It was agonizingly slow, because she wanted me to just write down the answers for her. She continued to be distracted, to wander off, or to color on her arms. I just kept plodding along, prompting addition by holding up my fingers to help her count.

We mostly worked in Spanish, though I speak very little. The concept of adding seemed to make more sense to her in Spanish. After what seemed to be forever, but was actually only fifteen minutes, we finished the sheet. When Anna [the site director] walked by, I used what is called an "overheard compliment." I spoke loudly enough for Elsa to hear and informed Anna of how well Elsa had done her homework. The only problem, I said, was that she had put the wrong name at the top of the paper.

Anna glanced at the paper and told Elsa to put her name at the top. They spoke in Spanish for a few minutes, and then Anna repeated her instructions. After Elsa erased the name "Elizabeth" and wrote her own, Anna grinned at me: "She likes to play games."

Elsa had been coming to the center since she was a baby. She knew the rules and had a good relationship with Anna. In asking for help, the tutor was not admitting a weakness; she simply used Anna as a resource to prove to Elsa that she had some authority and that her request was reasonable. Some level of cooperation between teacher and tutor is essential, and the more the teachers and other adults involved with your student are willing to work with you, the easier your job will be.

General Interest and Involvement in the Students' Lives

Some parents and teachers do not have the time or the ability to get involved in tutors' relationships with their students. Sometimes tutees' parents are not able to help out in the classroom and be directly involved in their educations in that way. But even if the other adults in students' lives cannot help directly, they affect the tutoring relationship in the ways that they interact with their children and in the attitudes they impart to them.

In the next example, the parent did not have the resources to help her children very much academically. But she did everything in her power to encourage her children to get good educations and to follow their dreams:

> Ms. Trey drove Brent and Tanisha to UCLA every Saturday so the kids could participate in the Saturday Outreach Program. She was a single mother, living in the projects, working hard to support her kids. Despite her limited resources, she managed to bring her children to UCLA campus. After a while, when her work schedule made it impossible for her to bring the kids to school, she started a car-pool program in the neighborhood with the help of the tutors.
>
> I developed the deepest level of respect and admiration for her caring and intelligent ways. She motivated me to do a better job every Saturday I went out there.

This parent's involvement in her children's lives affected the tutoring directly and indirectly. Not only did she provide this great opportunity for her children; her positive attitude further motivated her kids' tutor. She accomplished this difficult task despite her limited resources and despite her own limited educational background.

Some parents who support their children in their schoolwork and other areas of life are still not eager to form close relationships with their tutors. Generally, we emphasize being friendly and trying to form good relationships with students and their parents. But activities that seem very normal to you can make a parent very uncomfortable. In the following case, a tutor who had formed a really close relationship with his student had planned to take him to visit the UCLA campus, the student's dream school. Both tutor and student were excited, but when the tutor called his student's parents to ask permission, they postponed and discouraged the trip:

> I stopped talking to wait for her response. I felt that I made a pretty good point, but I did not feel that great about the situation. After all, if I had a twelve-year-old son, I would be scared

to let him go off with somebody I had never met, even if it was his tutor. My feeling was pretty much right on.

"Well, Jack, I think that a tour of UCLA would be something that Ben would really like to do. He has been talking about it to me all the time. It is just that I am not sure if it would work out. Ben is very busy with schoolwork, and his final exams are coming up. Also, as soon as he finishes school, he will be going to work for his father. Why don't I discuss it with Mr. Martinez, and then we can discuss it again at the party on Wednesday."

In these cases, of course, the parents win. But, as a tutor, try to be open to your students and offer the hand of friendship nevertheless, even if they cannot always take it (but, as discussed in Chapter 2, be careful not to make promises that you may not be able to keep). Be understanding about the parents' caution. Although it is wonderful when parents and students can work together, it is not always possible and should not affect your relationships with the students.

Discouragement and Lack of Involvement

In the same way that involvement and encouragement can boost a student's confidence and achievement, neglect and lack of understanding can devastate anyone's self-esteem and motivation. Tutors sometimes feel that teachers and parents are guilty of apathy where their tutees are concerned, a very frustrating situation.

The child in the next example had been hospitalized for about two years because of leukemia, during which he socialized only with adults and his family, and most of the attention that he received focused entirely on his physical condition. As a result, he was unskilled in socializing with children his own age. Because he was not able to socialize at school and had few nonmedical interactions with his parents, Justin started turning to his tutor for help and friendship. One afternoon, he called to ask his tutor to help him with his homework. The tutor learned that he was home alone with a housekeeper who spoke only Spanish: "I do not know how they communicate, but obviously Justin needs attention at home. Unfortunately, he needs this attention from the two people who seems to be too caught up in themselves right now. Hopefully both parents will realize his needs before it is too late."

Apathy from teachers can be just as difficult for tutors to deal with. When students realize that teachers do not care, they do not care, either. When students realize that their teachers will not collect or correct their work, they presume that the teachers "don't care" if they do their work well. These students often live up to those low expectations and do as little as possible. The following tutor, a Latina, did not know what to do about the dishonest attitude that the teacher's behavior had fostered in her tutee. Her student, a fifteen-year-old African American female, found little incentive to study and to prepare for exams honestly:

> After a brief introduction, Summer and I began working on her Spanish homework. "I have a test tomorrow, and I need to know everything in chapter 7 before the test," she said as she handed me her Spanish book. I began to tutor her by asking her what she knew in chapter 7, and she said, "Nada" and stared at me, looking for answers. When I opened the book to chapter 7, I asked her to work on translating the nouns that were listed in Spanish, and instead she began talking about her boyfriend and about how she skipped classes often and how she could get away with lying to her parents without being caught.
>
> Her conversation was irrelevant and distracting to our session, but I listened attentively, waiting for clues that might help me understand enough about her persona to be able to relate her to the material in her book. I reminded her that we needed to study for the exam, and she assured me that studying was not necessary in her class.
>
> She took out a sheet of paper and copied many of the nouns listed in her book and asked me what they meant in English, and I told her. Then she proudly put that sheet of paper underneath many other blank pages and told me how easily she could fool her teacher during the test. She told me that her teacher does not monitor the exams and often reads the newspaper while everyone (including her) pulls out the page with the answers and writes them down on the test paper.

Still other adults not only seem disinterested in their students but go out of their way to be critical, even mean, which is always hard for a tutor to watch. This Asian female tutor was at a loss for words when she heard a substitute teacher criticize the fourth-grade class she was working in:

I was shocked at some of the comments that Mr. James made to the students about their drawings. To one child, he said, "You made the vase too big. You better start all over on the back." He suggested to some of the other children as well that they start all over, because they did it wrong. I was surprised that Mr. James felt it was all right to criticize the children's drawing rather than encourage them.

When he noticed that some of the children had barely drawn anything, he said, "What's the matter, this is supposed to be fun." I felt angry that he could claim that the assignment was supposed to be fun, while at the same time he was demanding and critical.

Because of his critical remarks, I could see that most of the children were critical of themselves. Most of the children were very dissatisfied with their drawings, though, in my opinion, they were fine. They would say things like, "This is hard," or "I don't like mine," or "Forget it."

Although this comment from a substitute teacher probably had only a temporary effect on the children, from this example it is easy to see how fragile the egos of some young children are and how cruel comments can cause them to give up on themselves.

Perhaps even more tragic than a neglected or discouraged student are the students whose influential adults refuse to accept them for who they are. Whether they do not meet their parents' expectations or they have had bad experiences with teachers, it is sad to see students struggle without the help of those who should be there to support them. The devastating effect on students of their parents' ostracism is evident in the example that follows, in which the tutee had to leave home because his style of living was unacceptable to his mother: "The theme of Chris's paper is 'diversity in society,' so he focused on how the gay community treats him and his gay friends: 'I am frustrated, because I believe the community looks at me like I am a "piece of meat" and a "sex toy." I want to be accepted for who I am—a hardworking, smart young male who has many important skills and abilities.'"

Chris felt ignored and worthless. His letter was addressed to his mom, who knew he was gay but did not support his choice. He felt it was important to tell her how different his life was and the troubles he faced living on his own. Although the tutor could do little to affect her student's relationship with his mother, she could give him some of the support and acceptance he so desperately needed.

Assignments and Activities

A teacher's positive involvement with the classroom can also indirectly enhance the tutor-tutee relationship by providing a conducive learning environment and making learning desirable and fun. Many tutors have found that interesting and intriguing activities involve students in school activities and encourage them to work and to learn. Boring classroom activities lead to students' boredom and apathy—for example, students in a previous chapter got excited about reading *Romeo and Juliet* with their tutor but plodded through their social studies reading with no interest. When teacher-assigned activities are dull or rote, tutors have to work a lot harder to keep their students focused and interested.

Sometimes teachers seem to give assignments without considering student interest or time. Tutors are often frustrated with work that seems assigned to keep students busy, not to get them involved in the subject matter. The white female tutor in the following scenario was repeatedly at odds with her sixteen-year-old Latina student's biology homework:

> Today she has biology homework. Remembering how her history class didn't have enough books to go around, I nervously asked if she had a biology book. I knew that I wouldn't be any help unless she had a book to which to refer. She did. For some strange reason, her teacher had assigned all the "Review It" sections of the entire chapter for one night of homework. That kept us busy.
>
> I think that it was poor planning on the teacher's part to pack so much work in one night of homework, because we wound up just reading through the text to find the answers—not reading it for comprehension. The concepts were relatively easy—Darwin, natural selection, artificial insemination, etc. I've learned these concepts many times in science classes. With the brief review I got from reading the chapter, I was fairly confident about my comprehension.
>
> I got the distinct impression, however, that Angela was not getting much out of the assignment. I tried to let her come up with an attempt at the answers before I helped her out, and she

was often wrong. It seemed as though she was just skimming for answers or the key words used in the question. I did try to explain the main concepts in further depth, but she was mostly concerned with getting this massive assignment done before our time was up. She spent the entire hour and a half writing furiously, and she still barely finished.

After seeing the types of assignments Angela is given from her teachers at school, I am disappointed. I feel that the assignments are very superficial and are mostly busywork. When the assignments are productive, I feel as though she has been given no knowledge in class to use in the context of the assignments. The "Review It" questions might have been a review if the teacher had presented the material to the students earlier in a method that was comprehensible to them. Angela said that they had read part of the chapter in class.

 How to Deal with Boring or Silly Homework

Often, a tutor's job is to deal with homework that was assigned in school. Although a lot of homework (even if it is tedious) is good for students (for example, long-division practice is necessary, even if no one likes it), some homework will seem like busywork. How can you turn busywork into something more productive?

• Help students make connections between the busywork and productive work. For instance, sometimes teachers give students word searches with science or history terms. Often, students take forever to solve the puzzles, and a tutor is left feeling like the time would be better spent actually learning the terms. So help with the word search, but, more importantly, make the student talk about the terms as you look for them. By making sure that the student understands the terms while you search for them, *voilà*, the exercise becomes productive.

• Help with the busywork parts so the student can focus more on the important parts. Many assignments contain several components. Typically some components are more useful than others. If a student is making flash cards to study for a test, help cutting out the flash cards and writing out the words so the student can focus on writing definitions and studying. If the student is writing and illustrating a

Some activities make learning not only boring but downright impossible. The white female tutor in the next example was extremely frustrated with the work that her seventh-grade Latina student brought to tutoring and even more frustrated when she found that the problems lay in the teacher's instructions:

> After we were done with the math problems, she pulled out her torn-up dictionary that was falling apart and a vocabulary list. I looked at what was written on the sheet, and some of them were not words. I asked her, "Where did you get these?"
>
> She mumbled, "My neighbor wrote them down in class, and he is stupid." I was so confused.
>
> It took almost fifteen minutes to understand how these supposed "words" came to be in her possession. She wasn't telling me the whole story. I had to keep probing. I was getting really

story, help fill in the huge blue expanses of sky so the student can focus on writing and doing the detailed drawing.

- Help the student prioritize. Do the hard work together. If the student has two coloring assignments and one reading assignment, do the reading first. The student is more likely to need help with reading (help that you can provide). And the student can do the coloring later in the evening, when everyone starts to get tired. Kids often want to do the easy work first, but push them to get the hard work out of the way while you are available to help.
- Help students navigate around impossible problems. Occasionally, a homework assignment contains an impossible problem: It could contain a typo or be poorly written. Help students try their best on the problem. But also help them move on and do other work if it looks like a problem is impossible. Have the students show all the work that they did on the "impossible" problem to prove to the teacher that they tried. But do not let them waste all their time on an impossible problem. Have them ask the teacher about the problem, and ask them to explain the teacher's response to you the next time they see you (they may explain that it was an impossible problem, but they may also come back with an explanation that you hadn't thought of, so leave that possibility open).

Talking with Teachers

When you work with a student individually, you may see aspects of that child that a teacher with a class of thirty does not see. But, because you are a guest in a classroom (and probably not as experienced as most teachers), you should follow some basic guidelines while talking to teachers.

- Be respectful. You may have learned a lot about your student, but respect that the teacher also knows and cares about the student—and may know more than you think.
- Ask questions. Be willing to learn. Asking questions is a great way to get more information about a student and teaching techniques. Questions are also a good way to tell a teacher about a student without seeming "bossy." A simple question, such as, "Does Javier always struggle with multiplication?" can give you information about Javier, *or* it could clue the teacher in to a struggle that she didn't know Javier was having.
- Be specific. When you approach a teacher about a specific issue, try to show evidence of it. Show the teacher a paper that your student did or a book that the student could or could not read. Show specific evidence. Also, ask specific questions: What level book is best for Leila? How do I identify those books? What do you recommend to help Jason tell the difference between short and long vowels?
- Listen. Teachers are not perfect. But they do have experience and expertise. No matter what your impressions, ask questions and listen to the answers. Be open to hearing answers that you don't expect. Remember, every story has two sides. Just because you got one version of the story from your student doesn't mean that another version of the story doesn't exist.
- Be patient. When you work with a student, you and the teacher are working as a team. But it takes a while for team members to trust each other, so don't expect the teacher to trust you right away. Work hard and continue to put your student first, and the teachers you work with will see your commitment.

frustrated, because she knew what happened and she was just not telling me. I finally figured out that the boy next to her copied down the words for her, and she couldn't understand his handwriting, so she just left it. She didn't realize they weren't even real words until I confronted her.

She told me she tried to look them up and they weren't in the dictionary, and she asked me why. I said, "Nancy, it is because they are not words." I then told her that she needs to go and talk to the teacher the next day first thing and tell her what happened. I then told her to write her own words down from the board next time. She said that her teacher tells the students to copy the words from the board, then exchange lists with a neighbor. I thought this was ridiculous.

Labeling

One issue that almost all tutors will experience is labeling. Labels are used as shorthand to give tutors a lot of information about a child in a short amount of time. If you have an hour to learn about a child, a teacher, parent, or tutoring coordinator can show you samples of work, tell you stories about the child, and give you a full background. More commonly, you have a minute or two to learn about a student before you sit down to work with them. Trying to be helpful, the person giving you the information will often give you some labels. Labels can be official, such as learning disabilities or reading-group levels, or just descriptive, such as "brilliant," "lazy," or "has an attitude." Other times, you will be told that a student is "just like" another student. Every label tells you something—although sometimes it tells as much about the person assigning the label as it does about the student.

Take labels as what they are usually meant to be: a quick way of giving you information about a student. When they come from a trusted source or adviser, a label can save you a lot of time. One tutor coordinator we worked with made a point to tell all new tutors that one of their homework-help students was "manipulative." That particular student used all kinds of stories to convince new tutors that he should do craft projects when he was supposed to be doing homework (he would say that the craft was a school assignment, that his grandma was sick and he had to do it for her, or that his mom told him that he had to do it). The tutor coordinator used the label to try to save new tutors from allowing this student to con them into doing crafts with him (which resulted in the tutors' being embarrassed and the student not finishing his homework). Although some new tutors were dismayed to be warned about a student before they even started working, most learned that being prepared helped them be better tutors to this student, because they knew not to let him distract them from helping him with his work.

Although labels can be instructive, they can have other effects as well. They can become self-fulfilling prophesies. For instance, students labeled as "slow" can come to believe that their work is too hard for them—which strips them of the motivation to try to learn. Thus, these students fall further and further behind and come to "fulfill" the prophecy of bring slow. Tutors must also be conscious of how they field labels: Just because someone tells you that a child is slow, do not neglect to challenge that child, or you will also fulfill that "slow" prophecy.

Tutors are usually assigned to work with students who need extra help—the students most likely to be negatively labeled. Try to use the labels that you hear to make your tutoring more appropriate for a student (so if you are told that a child is a struggling reader, do not assign him to read a book that is above grade level). But allow the student to

---

❧ Official Labels and Acronyms: What Do They Mean?

- **ESL:** English as a Second Language. Usually designates a class for people learning English as a second language, often adults.
- **ELL:** English-Language Learner. Usually designates a student who started school speaking a language other than English and is still working on English proficiency. These students often receive two grades on their report cards: one that compares them to other students at the same grade level and one that compares them to other children at the same ELL level. Students are tested regularly, going up levels, until they are determined to be proficient in spoken and written English.
- **EO:** English Only. Designates students who do not speak a language other than English.
- **IEP:** Individualized Education Plan. Students who struggle in school and have diagnosed learning disabilities or challenges receive IEPs, which are special education plans. The IEPs give them specific plans for their educations. The plans include specific academic goals for each semester and school year as well as modifications that teachers are supposed to make to the students' education programs (sitting in the front of the class, large-print books, oral rather than written instructions, and so forth). Most students with IEPs are in regular classrooms with resource help.
- **LRE:** Least-Restrictive Environment. Students with IEPs are supposed to be educated in the least-restrictive environment, which means

prove labels wrong, too. Tutors often find that "slow" students excel when given the proper one-on-one work and encouragement.

In the following example, a teacher introduced a set of students with a label that provided information and exhibited the teacher's disdain for her own students:

> "These kids are way behind; they are at first- and second-grade reading levels. Just humor them, okay?" The teacher went on about how she had to find second-grade reading books for the children and how even those books were very difficult.

Although it was probably helpful for the tutor to know the students' reading levels (and to be forewarned that even really easy books were

---

that they should be "mainstreamed" with regular-education students as much as possible. The LRE requirement is what puts most IEP students in regular classrooms with resource help.

- **Resource:** Pull-out classes for students who have IEPs. Resource students are special-education students but receive most of their educations in regular classrooms. They just leave the class for a certain number of minutes each day to receive extra help from resource teachers.
- **SDC:** Special Day Class. For some students who need special education (and have IEPs), a SDC is considered the LRE. Special day classes contain only students who receive special education.
- **ADD/ADHD:** Attention Deficit Disorder/Attention Deficit Hyperactivity Disorder. This is a learning disability where students struggle to focus or to sit still (or both). Some students with ADD/ADHD take medication. Others have IEPs or modifications (for example, more time on tests, testing without classmates, sitting in the front row). Many ADD/ADHD students work well with tutors who work with them individually and can help keep them oriented to their work.
- **LD:** Learning Disability. LDs cover a wide range of learning challenges, from dyslexia to ADD/ADHD. If you are told a child has an LD, the more important question for you to ask is whether you should use any special accommodations, strategies, or materials with the student. Often, students with learning disabilities just need more help and patience.

going to seem hard for the students), the tutor could also get a sense that the teacher had given up these students and that she did not really expect the tutor to make a difference either. This kind of disparaging attitude can definitely hurt children, who can learn to feel that they are not even worth helping.

In the next case, the teacher tried to help a tutor by explaining her first-grade student's problem. Even though she was somewhat kinder toward the child than the teacher in the previous example was, the tutor had to work to form his own impressions of the child and to not be convinced by her judgments, sight unseen:

> She spoke about the little boy I would be working with: "There's a little boy in the first grade by the name of Manuel. He has a hard time with motor skills, hand coordination . . . and can barely use scissors."
>
> Here, I thought, "Okay, how'd he get to first grade?" The teacher answered my thoughts when she proceeded to say, "He never went to kindergarten. . . . He comes from a family of nine children. His mom and dad are illiterate. . . . It's almost as if he's neglected . . . like a baby, just out of diapers. Yet he's extremely polite and sweet, no behavior problems at all. He speaks mostly Spanish, but he can also speak English. . . . Sound like a challenge?"
>
> I was a little stunned at the load of information she had just told me, yet I responded with, "I'd be happy to help him out."
>
> [I met Manuel and noticed that he was shy, but he answered my questions and was willing to work.] "So, Manuel, do you want to work on numbers, letters, or shapes?" I asked.
>
> Manuel replied, "Numbers," and pointed to the chart the teacher gave me. He spoke in a quiet low voice that seemed to match his face—inanimate and indifferent. Then he smiled randomly, "I can count to one hundred."
>
> I responded, "Wow, that's good." For the next few minutes or so, I played a game with him. I recited a number and then asked him to point to it on the chart. He did them all correctly. Then I pointed to a number and asked him to tell me what it was. Again, every response was correct, with only a few moments of hesitation for larger numbers. I thought to myself, "This boy seems to be doing okay. What's all this stuff the first teacher was telling

me about?" I had to ignore my expectation from the description the first teacher gave and just go with the initial feelings I got from working with him. In other words, I felt he was smarter than she made him out to be.

Teachers often work with twenty to forty children in a classroom. They rarely have the opportunity to spend much one-on-one time with their students, so they will not always know everything about a student. Listen to the information that teachers try to provide (and do not assume after one session that you know everything about a student—some students have many sides), but always be open to learning more than a teacher tells you. And if you can find insights that a teacher misses or teach in a way that a teacher has missed, you will make that much more of an impact on your student. Also recognize that even if a child is terribly behaved or very slow in a classroom setting, that same child might perform very well in a one-on-one tutoring situation. Even if everything that a teacher says about a student is true, you may see a very different side to that child—and have the opportunity to make a much greater difference. In the following example, a tutor's individual work with a hesitant student gave her a much greater understanding of the student than the teacher had:

> Veronica looked really engrossed in her assignment. I realized that the teacher had given up on her, because she had told me that Veronica could not speak English at all. Had she pushed a little harder, she would have noticed that Veronica was really scared of making a mistake. However, when you explain to someone that it is okay to mess up, all of a sudden that person will be encouraged to try with the fears and anxieties; this will then help the student learn. This lets the student know that the tutor is really paying attention to what is important to her. . . . When I first worked with Veronica, the teacher made it seem as if there was no hope for her. But I had a completely different experience with the student.

Here, the tutor took the time to understand what prevented Veronica from speaking English. Once he made her comfortable and came to understand her fears, he created a safe environment for her to work in and found that she could speak English and that he could help her improve. Although the teacher had jumped to an incorrect conclusion and provided an incorrect label, the tutor was able to overcome the misinformation and to work well with his student.

Even subtle labels can be hard on students. Favoritism, the practice of praising or actively favoring one student or child to the detriment of another, is a common form of labeling that often does not seem harmful to the people who practice it, because it involves speaking positively of at least one child. In the following example, parents' comparisons of their two children became a source of insecurity for their son. During tutoring, Carlos often mentioned his twin sister and how smart she was:

> She is his twin but different from Carlos. He always mentions how much smarter she is but that he is reluctant to ask her for help. He said he could do it on his own. He also mentions how he tends to care for the house and his family more than her. Carlos's experience in his family seems to have influenced his expression of self. I feel that he feels inadequate in some aspect in his life, which affects his academics. He may not have had enough attention and encouragement to believe in himself, thus putting him in the situation he is in.

Carlos's parents' contrasting expectations for him and his sister at home significantly affected his educational progress. In this example, Carlos's parents held a rather traditional expectation of him: to be the "man of the house" and to support the family.

Favoritism also occurs in the classroom. Sometimes it happens inadvertently, as when teachers try to make examples and role models out of students who excel. Other times, teachers simply prefer some kids over others, and their favoritism can affect a less-preferred student's confidence and effort level:

> While tutoring, Alberto and Bert always tutor close to each other. At times, they would begin their conversations about how their school is. They always talk about their history teacher. They say he hates them. He treats them differently from the other students and always points them out. Their teacher always gets mad at them, but they do not seem to know why and do not really care either. Kelly, Bert's tutor, and I ask them if they know, but they just shrug their shoulders.

This treatment may not matter to them, but it could affect their academic performance and their academic esteem. Alberto has shared with me some stories. One story that sticks to mind and really worries me is a story of one of his test days. Alberto had forgotten to do some parts for the exam—the teacher handed out a list of questions before the exam. "The girl in front of me didn't have her stuff either. We told the teacher, but he didn't care. . . . He let her use her book, but he wouldn't let me," he recalled.

"Oh my gosh! Why do you think that he did that to you?" I asked.

He replied, "He does not like me."

Parents often tell students to listen to their teachers and to take them seriously, because "they know what is best for you." Unfortunately, taking a teacher's bias seriously can undermine students' confidence in their academic potential. The unhappy effect of a teacher's comment is evident in the following example:

The substitute teacher was a man whom I would never wish to be a teacher for anyone's children: "They told me that this was supposed to be a magnet school and that you guys are supposed to be smarter than regular students. . . . You're not smarter. . . . Maybe one or two of you are, but you guys aren't smarter."

I was looking at the students' faces when he said this, and for a split second they had all been shocked by what he said and they stopped what they were doing. After a while, they continued to work. But all the kids were in such low spirits.

If a comment from a substitute, whom the students have not even had a chance to grow to like or to respect, has an effect this obvious, imagine what a respected teacher might do.

Fortunately, most teachers are not overtly disparaging. Most care deeply about their students and would not think of deliberately doing anything to hurt them. But, working within the system, teachers are often forced to label, and time constraints make it easy for teachers to overlook students' potential. So, listen and learn from labels, but do not allow them to define a student or your relationship with your student.

Labels are not always negative, but all unjustified expectations can be harmful. For example, repeatedly calling children "brilliant" or "the smartest in the class" leads them to believe that they must always meet these standards. Students who are constantly labeled as "brilliant" learn to depend on that positive label and become more skilled at pleasing their parents or their teachers than at pursuing their own natural curiosities and interests. Because their self-images are based on the opinions of others, positively labeled children often have the most fragile self-esteem and the most difficulties in learning to work for their own knowledge and pleasure. Positive labels can also prevent a student from getting help. Just because students are "gifted" does not mean that they do not need help sometimes.

When you tutor, you may find yourself coming to grips with some labels of your own. The following tutor was working with a group of "troubled" youths in an alternative high school. Although the tutor disagreed with the stated misconception that the students were "slow," in the beginning he did tend to agree that they were troublemakers and thus less interested in their educations. Fortunately, he was open-minded enough to let them prove him wrong:

> Many students, I learned, were bused in from south central, east L.A., and from all over the valley. Although there were some students that would be considered "slow," many were actually quite intelligent. The problem was that their behavior was not tolerated elsewhere. Those who were bused in had to be on the bus by 5:30 A.M. This was a fact in itself that really impressed me. For students whom I had labeled unruly, the overriding fact is that they do care about education.

Putting people and things into categories is a natural process that we all engage in. We label and categorize to organize and to simplify the world around us. But when working with students who function in a bureaucracy where labeling is an everyday necessity, it is important to try to go beyond labels and the convenient cubbyholes students are often sorted into. All children have special talents and abilities, and one-on-one tutors have the unique opportunity to discover and to develop them.

WHAT CAN I DO AS A TUTOR?

Although the issues vary from case to case, when you are tutoring, you may find your tutees' progress impeded by the adults around them. When this happens, tutors face a core dilemma: What can they do, and

Creating New Labels

As a tutor, you have a unique opportunity to be a new, fresh authority figure in a student's life. How can you make use of that chance?

- Praise. Point out when your student does well. When your student is smart about something, say so. Highlight successes. Also highlight effort and hard work. Don't be a liar and make a student artificially proud. But every student has strengths and insights. Notice them— and make sure that your student knows that you notice them!
- Praise to others. Sometimes the best way to praise a student is to praise that student in front of someone else. When your student does good work, mention it in front of a teacher, other students, or a parent. If your student is an adult, sometimes praising that student in front of the student's own child can be powerful.
- Build on the student's successes. Praise is great, but progress is better. When your student masters a skill, make a point to move on to new skills, and celebrate that progress. Make sure that the student sees the progress, even if it is tiny progress.
- Keep and show proof of progress. Hold on to some of your student's tests and papers. Keep track of test scores. Use these bits of data to "prove" that your student is doing well. Showing your student improving test scores, lengthening essays, or increasingly difficult vocabulary is a great way to force a discouraged student to see that his or her skills can and do improve with hard work.
- Focus on hard work. Students can't always control their progress. Sometimes progress is fast, and other times it's slow. But students can control how hard they work. So, no matter what, when your student works hard, note it. Praise your students' effort, motivation, and attitude. If you can instill a sense of motivation and a strong academic work ethic in your students, it will pay off long after your tutoring relationship ends.

how can they help alleviate their tutees' situations without entering into conflict situations with the significant adults?

You often cannot directly intervene in the interactions between your students and the other adults in their lives, but you can help in a few ways. You can form relationships with their teachers and parents, which will make these adults more receptive to your suggestions. You can look beyond the labels that come attached to your students and form your own opinions based upon how they interact with you. And—the crux of the issue—you can form strong relationships with your students and do your best to motivate them to learn and to succeed in their ambitions. You can try to provide the support they are not getting elsewhere.

Forming Relationships with the Other Adults

The first and the most rudimentary action a tutor should take, beginning on the first day of tutoring, is to open communication with the "other adults." Parents, teachers, and administrators who are familiar with the tutor will give greater consideration to the tutor's concerns. Tutors make these connections most easily by being receptive and respectful to the other adults' presences and influences in their tutees' lives. Fill other adults in on progress that students make during tutoring. Once parents and teachers perceive that the tutors take pride in tutoring and care about the students, they will take the tutors' comments more seriously.

When tutors have good lines of communication with the other adults, they are less likely to find themselves helpless and frustrated by those other adults. Many find that they can talk to the teachers or parents whose behaviors upset them. A tutor may not change a teacher's or parent's mind or actions immediately, but he or she can provide another perspective on a child, as the tutor in the following example did:

> I was also able to talk to Mr. Morrison about Dustin this morning. He told me that Dustin has a big motivational problem. I told him that it was not evident to me on Tuesday. He read to me for over an hour and seemed to enjoy it. Mr. Morrison couldn't believe how much time he spent reading to me. He was pleased with my being in the class. Mr. Morrison said that now "Dustin feels like he has a buddy, and that will be very good for him." He stated that Dustin can be a good kid when he wants to be.

The tutor in the next example had an even more successful response from the teacher she was working with. She found that the teacher appreciated her input as much as the tutor appreciated being allowed to talk freely:

> For the past eight weeks, I have tried to keep Ms. Paul, the teacher, posted on Fernando's progress. Ms. Paul is a good

teacher, but sometimes she tends to ignore the students who are behind in the course. I guess I can understand that she wants to keep the class interesting for the other students. But it finally got to me today, when Fernando raised his hand for the first time in the past eight weeks to answer the question, and Ms. Paul ignored him. I think she should have acknowledged the significance of this occasion and let Fernando answer the question. So I decided to talk to her about what was bothering me so much.

As I went to fill her in on our daily progress, I told her about this situation. She paused for a moment and then slightly hit herself over the head and apologized. Apparently she is very overwhelmed with the class and so used to my help with Fernando that she unconsciously ignored him. She promised that she will encourage him to participate in the future sessions.

Because the tutor had developed smooth lines of communication with Ms. Paul, she could voice her concern without running the risk of the teacher's misconstruing her comments as criticisms.

Try Not to Rely on Labels

Tutors will almost always receive students with some kinds of labels, but they do not need to let those labels define the tutoring relationships. Ideally, tutors treat all their students the same, starting out with a blank slate on each. Tutors give students chances to prove themselves and encourage them when they want to challenge themselves. Sometimes the most important gift you as a tutor have to give is your unconditional support.

In the following example, the tutor was told that her student was a "slow" reader. The tutor chose to set the label aside as she began to work with the student and made her first project simply getting him to read with her so she could see his abilities for herself. She found that his reluctance to read was based more on people's perception of him as slow than on his actual skill level:

At first, he was reluctant to read. I guessed that maybe it was because he didn't feel confident enough to read. I told him we could trade off paragraphs. Although constantly fidgeting and squirming, Manny began to read. He read very fluently and paused only on the most difficult words. The reason he didn't want to read was that he had already read that particular book and found it boring.

I was so impressed with his reading ability, mostly because I anticipated him being a slow reader. He didn't need my help in teaching him how to read. He was a fine reader and able to comprehend the material. So why was he stuck in a slow classroom?

This example shows how a label can lead teachers to have low expectations for their "slow" students. As a result, these students may be given material that does not push their limits. Once this tutor got past Manny's label of "slow" reader, the two moved on to work on spelling, writing poetry, and discussing newspaper articles. Soon Manny's father was frequenting the classroom and offering assistance to help Manny. The teachers were stunned. Simply by having an open mind, that tutor may have changed Manny's academic career.

The examples in this chapter illustrate the ways that other adults may influence your tutee's academic and social life—and your experience tutoring. As a tutor, at times you may feel helpless. You may feel that your students are caught up in a system that you are much too small to change or to challenge. You may have no relationship with your students' parents. You may feel that your relationships with the teachers are too precarious to risk. Direct confrontation is by no means the only way to help tutees who struggle with the other adults involved in their lives. As an adult whom they may look to as a role model and mentor, you affect them, too.

At the very least, you will provide them with attention, encouragement, creative activities, and confidence—all things that the other adults may have taken away or withheld.

RECOMMENDED READING

Although labels can be very handy in the classroom, a great deal of "labeling theory" research has shown that they can also be detrimental to students. In *Pygmalion in the Classroom* (1968), by Robert Rosenthal and Lenore Jacobson, teachers in a school district frequently used the labels "slow learner," "low IQ," "poor background," "troublemaker," and "unmotivated." When teachers were given new "information" and replaced the negative labels with positive labels ("gifted," "high IQ," "talented"), student grades and behavior improved.

In "Student Social Class and Teacher Expectation: The Self-Fulfilling Prophecy in Ghetto Education" (1971), Ray Rist shows how kindergarten teachers categorize their students by the eighth meeting of class. Rist also reports how teachers contribute to the creation of the "slow learners" in their classrooms by making these quick categorizations.

Scholars have done a massive amount of work on labeling in a range of settings. One of the classic works is *Being Mentally Ill* (1984), by Thomas J. Scheff. For an alternative view of labeling theory, see Howard Becker's *Outsiders: Studies in the Sociology of Deviance* (1963). A dramatic and brilliant case study of the power of labels appears in David L. Rosenhan's "On Being Sane in Insane Places" (1973), which documents an experiment where "normal people" faked psychiatric symptoms to gain entrance to a mental hospital. After being admitted, they could not get out, even when they acted normal and gave up their "symptoms." Rosenhan concludes that once a person is labeled "abnormal," others see all their other behaviors and qualities through that lens. Similarly, "K Is Mentally Ill" (1978), by Dorothy Smith, illustrates how easy it is to be labeled "ill" just by doing things differently than others and how difficult it is to shake the label once it becomes a socially accepted truth.

6 ▶ Good-Byes

Ending the Tutoring Relationship

FORMING A STRONG, successful tutoring relationship and overcoming the various obstacles along the way are among the most difficult tasks a tutor faces. Equally critical, and perhaps equally as difficult, is ending that partnership. Saying good-bye, which signifies the end of the tutor-tutee relationship, is a milestone for both people involved. Throughout the tutoring experience, tutors strive to help their tutees master different ways to learn, adopt values that push them to reach beyond what they previously strived for, and become self-motivated and self-sufficient. The close tutor-tutee relationship creates a safe space where the tutee can learn new skills and try new things while relying on the tutor for help. The ending stage of the relationship marks the tutee's transition to independence from the tutor: a time to implement these new skills and attitudes without the tutor's help.

Saying good-bye is a common occurrence in life and is inherently emotional. Tutors therefore need to realize the difficulties involved in saying good-bye and must end the tutoring relationship in a way that is constructive and does not damage the student's memories of the experience. No matter how meaningful and successful the tutoring relationship, ending it carelessly may leave the tutee hurt. Hurt tutees may regret having gotten involved with tutoring in the first place, which may affect their willingness to form relationships in the future and trivialize everything they learned from their tutors. When tutors leave without talking with their students and thinking about what the parting may mean to the tutees, tutors risk becoming just more examples of uncaring or unreliable adults in students' lives. Even when tutors cannot say good-bye in person due to outside circumstances, it is still critical that they create some kind of closure with their tutees.

Although children are young, they do remember people whom they care about. And even if a student (or tutor) is absent on the tutor's last day, it is important for the tutor to make contact or to leave some kind of "good-bye" so the child does not feel abandoned. Some tutors leave a note or card for tutees whom they cannot talk to before they finish tutoring. Others who have contact information for their students call and say good-bye. The tutor in the next case was able to convey a positive good-bye to her Latino fifth-grade student over the phone after she chose not to say good-bye in person, because she had thought that she would be returning to the site:

> [I called, and he answered the phone.] "So, when does tutoring start?"
>
> "Well . . . that's what I called about. I thought maybe Thursdays would work for me, but the scheduling didn't work out, so I don't think I'll be able to tutor you this time. I'm so sorry."
>
> "Really? Aw man, that sucks. Aw, what are we gonna do? Are you sure?"
>
> "Yeah, I'm sure."
>
> There was a long awkward silence. I wasn't sure if he was mad, sad, or just disappointed. I was all three. While faking a sniffle, he sarcastically said, "Oh, my, this is such a moment."
>
> And then he started laughing. I was so relieved. "You little brat! You don't even care, do you?" I said sarcastically, laughing with him. "Did you even want me to come back?" By now we were both hysterical, because we knew this wasn't the case. We knew that we'd really miss each other.
>
> "Yeah, I'm gonna miss you. So, who's tutoring then?"
>
> "I'm not sure, but I'll make sure you get somebody who'll give you a hard time and chase you around the school like I did, okay?"
>
> After some small talk about school, soccer practice, summer, and work, we said good-bye.

No matter how it comes about (although preferably in person), tutors and tutees need time together to mark the final steps in their relationships and to celebrate the progress that the tutees have made with the tutors—and will now continue without the tutors. This final step in the tutoring process can either cement or unglue many of the benefits of the tutoring relationship.

In approaching the issues of ending the tutoring relationship, we hope to guide tutors away from harmful ways of saying good-bye and to help them understand and deal with the difficulties of this process. No one approach is best. As a tutor, knowing your tutee and understanding the tutoring relationship itself are your best guides. Nevertheless, one underlying principle holds for all instances: The best good-byes end the relationship honestly and cleanly.

DIFFICULTIES IN SAYING GOOD-BYE

For many tutors, saying good-bye is the most difficult aspect of tutoring. Whether tutors work with individual students, small groups of tutees, or entire classes, bonds develop between students and tutors that prompt a sense of loss at the end of the tutoring period. Saying good-bye offers a host of challenges for tutors who want to separate from their tutees in a manner that honors their relationships.

Feelings of guilt and shame sometimes overcome tutors, as they realize that their tutees do not understand that they will not be there forever. Tutors have trouble breaking the dependence that their students have formed on them. As a tutor, for example, you may wonder how you can leave your tutees without your guidance. You may feel you are abandoning your students, and you may dread answering questions about why you are leaving.

The following tutor was working with two Latinas at an inner-city family center—Bertha, a seven-year-old, and Lila, a six-year-old—when she decided to stop tutoring because of other obligations. As she said good-bye, she felt guilty and worried that her tutees would feel abandoned. She questioned herself and wondered how her students would manage and succeed without her help:

> As the end of the quarter draws nearer, so does the end of my tutoring experience, for now. I found it extremely difficult to tell the girls that I would not be coming back. I really want to return, and I feel bad that I cannot, especially now that we are finally progressing. I keep thinking how they are going to have

to start over again with a new tutor and how great it would be if I could just continue, because they already know me, but I simply cannot. I truly will miss seeing them, and I will wonder how they are doing and if their new tutor is doing okay with them. I hate good-byes.

To make saying good-bye even more difficult, tutees are often reluctant to let their tutors go. Some feel that they are being left behind or that their tutor is leaving because they misbehaved or did not learn fast enough. Others are just sad to see their friend and teacher leave. Tutors should try to address all these issues in their good-byes.

No matter how carefully tutors plan, however, they may still be unprepared for their tutees' reactions to their saying good-bye, as was the tutor in the next example. She had been working in a classroom, and on the day she said good-bye, after the bell rang, the kids came flooding out of the classroom toward her. She hugged each of them, telling them to "have a great summer" and to take care of themselves. She was unprepared for how unwilling they were to let her go:

> We gradually made our way outside, and I stood with eight or ten of them as they told me stories, grabbed my arm or hand, or tugged on my jacket. They told me how nice I looked and how much they loved the treat bags I had brought them. After a while, five of them and I walked out toward my car. They kept me there for another forty-five minutes and surrounded the car so I couldn't leave. They sat on the hood or stood on the back bumper so I wouldn't drive away. I stayed until about 3:30 and then insisted that they get home. They groaned and asked for the millionth time why I couldn't stay.
>
> As I pulled away, I honked my horn, and they all stood next to the curb waving. About halfway down the street, I looked in my rearview mirror, and they were all running behind my car. I couldn't believe how hard this was. I turned the corner and waved my arm out the window.

Other less-dramatic reactions can be just as heart wrenching for a tutor who is already having trouble saying good-bye. The following tutor describes the reaction she received from her tutee: "When I told him I would not be coming back for tutoring, he actually looked at me and put his head down, saying, 'Man, you're the only tutor I really liked—you're the only one I really learned from.'"

Such reactions from tutees can be hard for tutors to deal with. These responses cannot be soothed by kind words or comforting sentiments about the student's getting a new tutor next year. They are individual and poignant reactions to one tutor's departure, and they can make a tutor feel personally responsible for the tutee's future progress.

HARMFUL WAYS OF SAYING GOOD-BYE

After seeing how difficult it can be to say good-bye to a tutee, it is easy to understand why good-byes do not always go perfectly. Tutors confronted with crying or disappointed students often feel helpless. In these moments, tutors conjure up many ways to elude the hurtfulness of saying good-bye. Some decide to leave without saying good-bye or leave tutees with empty promises or false expectations. In most cases, these options avoid the short-term hurt but harm the tutee more in the long run.

In the following scenario, a tutor was confronted with the negative consequences of a prior tutor's failure to say good-bye. Upon meeting her new tutor, Charmien, a nine-year-old African American student, said, "So, you're here for ten weeks like Megan, my old tutor, right? Are you taking the same class? Because I know you will be leaving after the class is over, aren't you?" Because Charmien did not receive satisfactory closure from her former tutor, she assumed that tutors were only motivated by obligation, not caring. She had been left leery and suspicious.

Knowing how to say good-bye, then, becomes vital for any tutor. A "good" good-bye must convey to the student that the relationship was valuable—for both parties. It must also emphatically express that the tutor's leaving does not reflect any negative quality of the tutee or the relationship. A good parting can leave a tutee with great memories of tutoring; a bad parting can leave a nine-year-old as jaded and cynical as Charmien.

Not Saying Good-Bye

Many tutors fall into the trap of thinking that not saying good-bye will hurt their tutees less. They think that it will be easier for the students if they do not make a big deal out of leaving. Some tutors honestly believe that ending the relationship is a completely negative experience and

❖ How to Say Good-Bye

Do:

- Make sure that you say good-bye. Although it may seem easier to just disappear, don't leave your students to wonder what happened and why you're gone.
- Give a week or two of warning if possible. Let the students know that you'll be wrapping up your time together. Some kids need time to process change, and letting them know at the very last session is a little cruel.
- Leave them with specific encouragement. Think about the ways that the students have improved while working with you, and give specific words of praise. Let your students know what goals seem closer because of the work that the students did with you.
- Share praise, goals, and thoughts for the future with parents, teachers, and coordinators. You now know a lot about your students, so share that knowledge with the other adults who will continue to work with the them.
- Let your students know what working with them has meant to you. Let them know that you learned from them and that you will miss them.
- Give them some token of your time together. Cards and notes are very sweet (and show a nice example: no gift necessary, just sincere thoughts and words). But small tokens are fine, too: a pencil from your college, a book that you think the students will enjoy, a notebook for them to use for their stories, and so forth.
- Feel free to give some work for the students to continue with. If students have been working on times tables and just need to complete 8s and 9s, hand off some worksheets that cover 8s and 9s. If you've been working on writing, give the students notebooks with some writing prompts included. Let the students know that you expect them to continue to make academic progress.

therefore better taken lightly or avoided altogether. Others avoid the encounter because of their own anxiety. As one tutor explained, "Juanita looked indifferent when I told her that our sessions were going to come to an end next week. She seemed as if she didn't care. I figured that she didn't want to make a big deal out of it. So I decided not to talk about it any longer, and we moved on with our activities."

Don't:

- Don't just disappear. If you think you might be leaving, let the students know. It's rotten to have someone just fall out of your life.
- Don't push the children to have a particular kind of reaction. Some kids are emotional, and some are not. Some are more stoic than others. Say your good-byes and be honest, but don't expect or push for any specific reaction from your students.
- Don't be hurt if your students don't react the way that you expect. Remember, students have a wide range of experiences (with other adults and with other people leaving). Sometimes they are hard to read. Be yourself and be honest, but don't take it too seriously if your students don't seem to care. You may not be getting the whole picture.
- Don't make promises that you can't keep. Don't promise that you'll be back or that you'll call or visit unless you are *absolutely* certain that you will.
- Don't exchange contact information if you don't intend to use it. Kids tend to call if you give them your phone number. Are you going to call back? Even when you're busy? If you think that the answer may be "no," then don't give the students your number. It will be hard to say no when they ask, but it is much worse when you find yourself avoiding them when they call.
- Don't give an elaborate gift. Don't make your students feel indebted to you—and don't overshadow your time together with a gift. The bigger the gift, the more it should be tied to your work together.
- Don't give a gift until the very last day. You don't want the students to feel obligated to reciprocate.

In this example, even though the tutor notified the tutee ahead of time of his leaving, he avoided a discussion about the end of their relationship. Leaving the relationship with such an incomplete good-bye was a cop-out, even though it seemed easier not to make a big deal of it. It may seem easy to just avoid the subject of good-bye and to walk away—but just disappearing does not respect the student or the time that you spent together. Most people would never consider not saying good-bye to their friends if they moved away. Most people would not even walk away from a group of people they had lunch with without saying good-bye. Your students, with whom you have worked hard to build a trusting relationship, at least deserve a good-bye, and a chance to say their own good-byes.

Other tutors do not avoid saying good-bye but instead attempt to handle good-byes casually. They do not want to make an issue of leaving and consequently make ending the relationship harder for the student, especially if the student is dealing with the situation privately. The following example poignantly illustrates how a tutee's silence may indicate that you, as a tutor, need to work especially hard to discuss your leaving and how you both feel about it. This white female had formed a close relationship with Dustin, a Latino fifth grader who was considered a troublemaker. However, by waiting for Dustin to make the first move in saying good-bye, she put a huge burden on him and almost missed out on saying good-bye and wrapping up what had been a good relationship:

> I usually leave the classroom at 10 A.M., but today I thought I would stay until recess at 10:15. About ten minutes after ten, Dustin said, "Samantha, look at the time!"
>
> I said, "I know, but I don't have class today, and since it's my last day here, I thought I would stay until recess."
>
> The two girls in the group moaned and said, "Today's your last day? How sad."
>
> Dustin didn't really respond at first, but after a few minutes passed, he said, "Can't you just stay until lunch?"
>
> I told him that I just couldn't, because I had a paper to write and I had to finish it. I also said, "I am coming to your graduation, though." Dustin got a big smile on his face and started cheering with his hands, saying, "Yeah!"
>
> Mr. Morrison next dismissed the students out to recess. I asked Mr. Morrison if I could put some candy and a pencil on each of the students' desks. He told me that I could. The students came in from recess and were happy to see the candy and pencils on their desks. They started eating and sharpening their pencils right away.
>
> Mr. Morrison then told the students that I would be leaving in a few minutes and if any of them wanted to talk to me, they could do that right now. Just as he said that, about twenty of the twenty-seven students in the class ran over to me at the back table. They all gave me a hug, thanked me, and asked if I was coming to their graduation. I could not help but notice that Dustin was sitting alone in the middle of classroom at his desk

when all the students were gathered around me. I did not feel bad. Dustin did not have to come over and thank me or tell me he appreciates me and that I have influenced his life—I know I have—but I would have liked to give him a hug.

As I was getting ready to leave, Sean came up to me with a sad face: "Are you leaving right now?"

"In a few minutes," I said, "but we can read your book if you want."

"Okay," he said, as he ran to get his book.

As he was retrieving his book from his desk, Dustin walked over to me. He did not say anything or have his arms outstretched for his hug. He walked over very slowly, had his hands in his pockets, and was looking down. I knew this was his way of saying good-bye. I reached out, gave him a hug, and told him that he made my time in Room 29 a lot of fun. He did not say anything but did give me a small smile and went back to his desk. That was all I needed to make my time in Room 29 complete.

Dustin's tutor waited for Dustin to come to her. Fortunately, Dustin found the strength to make his own personal good-bye, but if he had not, his tutor might have walked out without hugging him at all. The tutor was thinking about herself rather than Dustin. She rationalized that Dustin did not have to make the effort for her, because she understood that he cared; she did not realize that *she* had an obligation to make an effort toward *him*. No child should have to be the one to gather up the courage to say a proper good-bye: That is the tutor's job.

As a tutor saying good-bye, your feelings or comfort are less important than those of your tutees. Sometimes you have to go through an emotional good-bye that is difficult for you to explore their feelings and to make sure that they understand what they meant to you and why you have to leave.

Making Empty Promises

When tutors do say good-bye, they often find themselves making empty promises to their students to alleviate the pain of parting. But empty promises can be as devastating as not saying good-bye at all. Promising to call, to write, or to visit or giving students your phone number or address and permission to continue the relationship can ease the situation in the moment but cause problems in the long run. In these situations, tutees are left with the hope that their tutor will be back or that the relationships will continue. When neither happens, or happens but does not fulfill their expectations, tutees can be left as confused about what their relationships meant as if no good-bye had taken place at all.

Empty promises come easily. The following tutor struggled to contain his emotions after informing his tutee that they would not be working together any longer and found an empty promise a convenient way to alleviate guilt and sadness:

> He gave me a long, soft look and then whispered, "I'm gonna miss you."
>
> I was fighting back the emotions and tried to keep my composure: "Yeah, me too." My voiced cracked, and I knew I had to say something to liven up the conversation: "But, you know, you have my phone number and address—you can come visit or call anytime you want, and if we ever get our transportation together, then we'll be able to see each other."

Such promises, however sincere at the time, are generally hard to keep. We all have busy lives full of obligations. Is the tutor really prepared for his tutee's call "anytime"? No matter how great the temptation, tutors must resist making these empty promises. They create false expectations for the students and, typically, also leave the tutors feeling even guiltier (as the unreturned phone calls pile up).

Not only are false expectations disheartening; they may prevent tutees from progressing to the next step in the relationship: autonomy. Constantly hoping for a reunion or a phone call, tutees may refuse to put their old tutor-tutee relationship behind them. How deeply these expectations affect tutees is evident in the following tutor's experience: "I hate sharing Gilberto with his old tutor, Oton. Especially today, he was extremely sad, and when I asked him what was wrong, he said that Oton promised to call him yesterday, but he never returned his call. I explained to Gilberto that maybe some accident might have occurred and that I am sure that he will call, but nothing seemed to matter. It was hard to connect with him as long as he was so preoccupied by his old tutor."

False expectations can be disheartening for a student. The best policy is to avoid situations that can lead to disappointment for the tutee. Do not make promises that you cannot live up to. Being honest is one of the best gifts that you can give your students.

HOW TO SAY GOOD-BYE: THE CLEAN-BREAK PRINCIPLE

Following the clean-break principle is as simple as it sounds. As a tutor, end the relationship once and for all when you say good-bye. Be kind, constructive, and enthusiastic about your students' accomplishments and their futures. But avoid making promises to your tutees that you cannot keep—that you will visit or call, for example, or that you will tutor them again next year. It is better to be direct with your students than to leave them with lingering doubts or questions.

Even when there is a possibility that you might return to tutor, do not mention it unless you are certain. As one tutor explained, "I wasn't going to say I would see her next quarter, because I didn't want to promise her anything I didn't know I could keep." If you come back, your tutees will be happily surprised; if you do not, you avoid setting them up to start the next school year with disappointment.

All tutors struggle with the pain of separation. In the following example, a tutor described how, as hard as it was, he wanted to say good-bye the "right" way:

> It was as if he could sense our time together was growing short. He reached over and grabbed my hand and, looking at me solemnly, asked, "Are you going to be around next year?"
>
> I tried to recall how I was taught to say good-bye in lecture, and I began hesitantly, "Hiseo, I've had a great time working with you this quarter, but I'm afraid that I won't be able to come back next quarter."
>
> He asked, "Why not?"
>
> "I have too many classes to fit into my schedule, and, along with other activities I am doing, I cannot find a free block of time to come out here, like I did this quarter." I felt a little better knowing that I was being honest with him.

In the following example, a female tutor found it very difficult to say good-bye to her female tutee. Nonetheless, she made the effort to stay honest and to end the relationship positively:

> I had warned her before that our tutoring session was coming to a close. I reminded her on Wednesday, when I first saw her. She couldn't believe me when I told her again. She kept asking

me, "So you're never coming back? But why?" These questions definitely made it harder for me to say goodbye! I explained to her that I was moving up north, to a city near San Francisco that was six hours away from here. I wished I could continue to volunteer there, but I won't be in the area in July.

Being straightforward, sincere, and honest with a tutee is the best way to end the relationship. No tutors want to hurt their tutees' feelings, but by being genuine (even if it hurts), they help students understand and become more independent. Saying good-bye can be painful for tutor and tutee. But the beauty of the clean-break principle is that the tutor remains true to the values the relationship was built upon: respect and honesty.

At the beginning of the tutoring relationship, tutees become dependent on the acceptance of their tutors, and tutors become dependent on their tutees' feedback and reactions, which allow them to do the best job possible. Mutual trust and dependence make the relationships work. With good-bye, that dependence must end. But the ending should not leave the tutees feeling helpless and alone. The tutees should end the relationships knowing that tutors and tutees have grown and learned and are ready to move on to the next challenges life has to offer.

GIFTS

When saying good-bye, the tutor should aim to start the tutee on the road to autonomy, which is no easy task. Tutors spend a long time building trust and often leave the good-byes to the very end. You may have only a few moments to end your relationship positively so your student can continue to draw on the lessons that you have learned together. As they try to find ways to end tutoring relationships and to symbolize the growth they have experienced with their students, some tutors find that bringing small gifts helps. Gifts can either symbolize an accomplishment that the tutor and tutee have achieved together or the tutor's faith in what the student can accomplish in the future. Such gifts should not be expensive or extravagant, but rather small and meaningful. In the next example, the tutor brought gifts that captured the relationship: "At the potluck, I brought my tutees little framed pictures of us with a note telling them each how special they were to me."

Other tutors bring presents more representative of the work that the two did together while tutoring, such as the following tutor who gave

> ### ❖ Good Ways to Wrap Up a Tutoring Relationship
>
> How do you make sure to end things on a positive note? Many possibilities exist, and many will come naturally out of the tutoring relationship. But some ideas include:
>
> - Make an award. Kids love awards, and, as a tutor, you have the opportunity to make a very personal award. Use your computer to make a certificate that highlights one (or several) of the accomplishments that you have made. Make it personal, even funny, but the effort will show that you thought the student made valuable progress.
> - Use a photo. Sometime before the last tutoring session, have someone take a picture of you with your student. A photo together, with a nice note, will make a nice memory for your student.
> - Make a list of the accomplishments you achieved and the activities you worked on together. This can be a decorated list, a silly poem, or even a little children's book. Again, just do something personal that highlights the fact that you cared enough about your time together to do something special.
> - Plan a group celebration. Tutoring relationships often end at the end of the school year. If you are tutoring with a group of other tutors, you may be able to arrange a small celebration for the departing tutors and tutees. Even a very simple recess-time celebration would give everyone a chance to say good-bye and to talk in a happy setting. Obviously, talk with the teacher or site coordinator before organizing any kind of celebration.

her tutees artistic evidence of what they had accomplished: "I had gotten little notebooks of index cards and with colored pens had written all the words they had learned. I also wrote each one a personal note." Similarly, another tutor kept and compiled her tutee's work throughout their time together and made a portfolio for them to look at while discussing their relationship:

> We had finished with arts and crafts, and so I pulled out the portfolio I had made. The first thing Vicky saw was the pictures of SpongeBob and Yoshi. I could see her eyes widen a little with curiosity as to what I was about to give her. I gave her the portfolio, and we went through it together. She seemed happy to see some of the work she had done and forgotten about. I showed her the words she had written in the beginning of our tutoring

and compared them to the words she had most recently learned, and she was proud to see that she improved. It wasn't a huge portfolio, since we had only met for a few weeks, but she seemed to like it. She gave me a hug and thanked me.

Another tutor brought her student M&Ms to symbolize the most significant feat of their relationship—conquering the letter "M." By giving tutees gifts, tutors give tutees something with which to remember their tutoring experiences. The gifts serve to finalize the relationships, while keeping their memories and significance alive.

Gifts can also serve as visions of the future. Some UCLA tutors brought UCLA pencils or T-shirts to encourage their students' hopes of attending the university. The following tutor gave her tutees presents to provide continuity over the winter break, so she brought them mechanical pencils like the one she used:

> I decided to get them good-bye presents. I got each student the lead pencils, the ones they had asked for during my first tutoring session. Mando [a Latino nine-year-old] said, "I finally have a lead pencil, thank you so much! Can I kiss you? No one has ever treated me so nicely!"
>
> I responded, "With this pencil, you will be able to solve every math problem. From now on, math will never be a problem." As he smiled, I hugged him, and we quickly went to the other students to compare his new pencil. They were so proud of their new pencils, they continued thanking me and showing them off to other students. I was going to miss them so much.

The simple gift of the pencil made the children focus their attention on the positive aspect of the good-bye: what they had accomplished and what they might accomplish in the future. Other gifts are even more explicit:

> Over the past ten weeks, my tutee has been telling me how difficult it has been for her to motivate herself to come to school. She told me stories about how she had no support at home, school was boring, and teachers didn't care. Throughout our tutoring process, my tutee has spoken with all of her teachers about getting a little extra help with her class work—she has

even begun to build a new relationship with her counselor, and her personal relationships are beginning to look good. Therefore, I wanted to give her a gift that had meaning.

As a farewell gift, I gave her a UCLA sweatshirt. I didn't want her to think that the sweatshirt was about making it to UCLA as her goal or that UCLA in itself should inspire her to do well, because I could have just as easily bought her a smaller (much cheaper) piece of UCLA memorabilia, such as a pennant. So I told her that I know that it has been hard for her to get as far as she has gotten already and that I know she may sometimes feel like she is in it alone. I told her that I wished I could be there with her during her senior year to make it a little less stressful and provide motivation and inspiration for her to finish with her head held high. I then told her that she does not need me to do any of that, because she is fully equipped to succeed on her own; with all of that said, I gave her the sweatshirt and told her whenever she feels down about her personal or academic lives, needs that little boost of encouragement, or feels like she has no one in her corner, to put on the sweatshirt and remember that she has someone rooting for her.

I told her that I wanted to let her know that for as long as she has that sweatshirt in her life, that she has me in her life. I wanted all of the hard work she has put into her life the past ten weeks to be symbolized in that gift and to remember if she could accomplish all that she has accomplished in such a short amount of time, try to imagine what she can do with her life. By the end of my short speech, we were both crying! It was sad to be leaving her, but I also felt like I was transferring a piece of my strength onto her. I believe that she has discovered a sense of empowerment. She saw what she needed to do, and she went for it. While, yes, I was helping her along the way, she definitely took the lead and is responsible for all of her successes. I have a good reason to believe that she will be just fine without me.

TALKING ABOUT THE EXPERIENCE

An effective good-bye require does not require gifts but does require talking about the relationship and the separation process, focusing on the positive aspects of the tutoring and showing tutees that, no matter what, they will always carry a piece of their tutor. Tutors can show tutees that the tutoring relationship was a unique experience. The conversation might start with remembering the first day of tutoring and go on to summarize and to highlight the student's experiences and achievements. As a tutor, you can talk about the good times you had together or bring up the special talents your tutees possess. No matter what path you take, ending on a positive note works best. Show your tutees what they can take from the relationship to help them pursue their dreams and ambitions. You can leave them with an air of confidence, letting them know they are fully capable, on their own, of carrying on what you did together.

It is also important to talk about the end of the relationship before the last day. Sometimes students have difficulty expressing themselves. Some need time to adjust to the fact that their tutor is leaving. A tutor can mention, a week ahead, that the last session is coming up. This gives tutees time to digest the information. It also gives them time to think about what they might want to say or whether they want to do something special for their tutor on the last day of tutoring. Although it is often easy to push aside the idea of "the last session," it is kinder to give notice than to surprise your students by saying good-bye out of the blue.

The following almost perfect good-bye, between a Latina university student and a male African American fourth grader, was marred by the student's suspension, just minutes before his tutor arrived. Although the tutor was somewhat cut off when her tutee had to leave early, and the mood was anything but joyous, this well-executed good-bye proves that even under the worst of circumstances, a tutee can leave a relationship with nothing but good memories and positive feelings:

> Today was my last day going to tutoring. I had told Terrence before, so he knew. When I arrived, I told him, "I have something for you." I took out the candy and said, "Here is something sweet for a sweet guy."
>
> Terrence reacted by smiling and opening his arms, walking toward me, and giving me a hug. As he hugged me, he told me, "Thank you." He looked at the candy, which was Hershey's Kisses, and said, "Mmmmm! I'm going to put them in my backpack."
>
> I told him, "Wait, here are some pencils I brought for you, too." He took them, said, "Thanks," and went into the other room. When he returned, he had a seashell. He gave it to me

and said, "Here is a little something to remember me by." I reacted like he did, because I did not expect it. I said, "Thanks, it's beautiful," and I gave him a hug.

The class had not returned from lunch. Sara and I were talking in the hallway. Terrence returned from putting away his candy and told us, "I have something to tell you."

I said, "Go ahead, what is it?"

He answered, "I got suspended today."

Sara and I were shocked; we asked him, "Why?" I was surprised, because he was always very well behaved.

"I got into a fight. There is this boy named James in my class that is always teasing me because I'm darker than the other kids. I went up to him today during lunch and asked him, 'Why are you always calling me names?' James said, 'Get out of my face.' I was about to move when he pushed me, so I pushed him back. I just got back from the office, and they suspended both of us."

Sara and I looked at each other and did not know what to say. He was always so calm and polite. Sara asked him, "Did you tell anybody that he was teasing you?" Terrence said, "No."

I then asked him, "Did Mr. Grace know? Did your mom know?" He just shook his head from side to side. I told him the next time, he should tell someone if he is being teased by someone else. I said, "If you do not feel comfortable with a teacher, then tell your mom. She should know." He responded with a whisper, "Okay."

I could tell that his suspension greatly affected him. He was always attentive during the tutoring, but today he kept looking at the floor and did not smile as usual. The candy had brought him some joy, but it had ended when he told me what happened. I tried to cheer him up by asking him, "What do you want to do today?"

He said, "I don't know." The fact is that he did not care.

I then said to him, "As you know, today is my last day. I want to ask you a few questions. Is that okay?" He said, "Yes." I asked him, "What do you think is good about the tutoring? What could you improve?"

He answered, "Everything was good. I know how to divide." I asked him to elaborate, and he said, "I know the steps without

looking at the sheet." I felt good about his statement. It con-
firmed to me that I had made an impact.

I told him, "I enjoyed working with you. You're a very good
person. I especially like the poems you made about your race.
You have a poetic instinct."

I was about to continue when an aide from the office came
and said, "Terrence, your mom is waiting in the office."

Terrence told me he had to go. I told him, "Take care,
thanks, and good-bye." He replied the same, smiled, and left.

LEARNING EXPERIENCES

Tutoring is a wonderful experience. Through their tutoring experiences,
many tutors learn a lot about themselves, the environments in which
they live, and the education system. Tutoring often opens their eyes to
how much some communities need their help and inspires many to continue their work. One tutor wrote:

> Throughout this experience, I have gained insight into myself
> and others' lives. The tutoring has further encouraged me to
> work for the youth community and in education. Our students
> are thrown into a world they may not fully understand but
> experience every moment. All I know is that these students
> need love and encouragement, which they are not getting a lot
> of the time at school. Thus, the role of me, as a tutor, was to
> provide them with the encouragement and love they may have
> lacked in an academic environment.

This tutor has grown and learned from his experience and has realized
that all it really takes to be a successful tutor is acceptance of tutees and
the willingness to give them the care, attention, and understanding they
need.

Another tutor had a change of heart after spending several weeks
with his tutee. You may recall the following quote, used earlier in this
manual, to demonstrate the attitude not to have when entering a tutoring situation:

> I really wasn't happy with the school I was chosen to tutor at, and
> I was even less happy when I arrived at the school. I thought, "Is

this some kind of joke?" I wondered, as I stood outside of the dilapidated school, "Am I even safe here?" . . . I expected to be teaching highly motivated white students who were not just college bound but Harvard bound. I never even considered teaching students who were minorities who might not even be interested in learning. . . . I had to ask myself, "What the hell am I doing here?"

As this tutor recapped his tutoring experience with a young Asian student named Hiseo, he showed that tutoring can touch the hearts of even the most reluctant converts: "When I initially began the tutoring project, I was skeptical about my chances of touching someone and affecting his life, but as I leave the program just a quarter later, I can honestly say that I have made a difference in Hiseo's life, and he has made even more of a difference in mine."

This tutor also wrote about how his tutoring experience opened his eyes to his long-held stereotypes of underprivileged children as lazy, stupid, and unmotivated. He ended his tutoring feeling confident that he would one day teach in a community like the one he had tutored in, where students lack access to resources but are nonetheless hungry to learn.

Many tutors also discover part of themselves as they work with students. The following tutor rediscovered a childhood passion through working with an inspiring young student:

The decision to become a physician was not made until later, at age twenty-one, when I relearned from my six-year-old tutee, Collin, what it really means to do what I love—something that I had lost in the process of growing up! I started tutoring with the intention of giving back some of the opportunities society had given me. Never did I entertain the idea that I would benefit from this experience as well, by learning more about myself, my ambitions, and desires.

I underestimated the emotional, moral, and intellectual power that the interaction with my tutee could bestow upon me. Until then, the idea of tutoring seemed a unidirectional act of giving. Little did I know that it was also about receiving.

Many tutors find so much personal satisfaction in tutoring that they cannot say enough good things about it, even if the experience is sometimes a difficult one. The following tutor captured just a few of the moments that make tutoring so fulfilling:

> If I were to have just a few "words of wisdom" unto you, it would be my suggestion that at one time or another in your life, you experience the wonderful joys of teaching a child. Because it is you who will learn more and get the most out of the experience. The child will learn, but it will be you who will have the greatest sense of satisfaction and overwhelming pride. Especially at that point in time when she is struggling, but you encourage her to keep trying, and she does and gets the answer to the subtraction or addition problem right (without using her fingers), or she comes across that one word she continually cannot get and reads it naturally and without hesitation. You catch a glimmer of excitement and interest, and her face glows when she answers correctly, and for a brief moment there's a spark, and that is what makes it all worth it.

Through teaching, this tutor clearly grew as well. She has discovered the profound truth that some of the greatest gifts in life come through giving. Another tutor, despite her hesitation in the beginning of the tutoring experience, learned that she could truly impact the life of another person and change her ideas of how working with inner-city children would be:

> Though I dreaded this assignment at the beginning of the quarter, I learned and gained a lot from this experience. I didn't think I could influence and bring so much happiness to someone whom I thought I would have so little in common with. I didn't think I could accomplish any significant improvement in academia for someone from an urban, inner-city background in just one quarter. I didn't think I would enjoy going to Watts to teach someone. However, Ian has proved this wrong at so many levels. Not only has his company brought me great pleasure, but he has taught me that I can make a positive influence on people's lives.

To realize the significance of the good-bye process and appreciate its intricate nature, you should view the development of the tutoring relationship as a journey. As we move through life, encountering new and unfamiliar situations and obstacles, we follow a path of progress. We start out heavily dependent on another, one who knows the ropes, to guide us through. Ultimately, learning to navigate on our own, we arrive at autonomy.

Like other life paths, the tutoring relationship initially requires the tutee to rely heavily on the tutor. And, as in other successful journeys, the termination of this relationship marks the beginning of the tutee's independence from the tutor and movement forward. So good-byes are best regarded not as the end of a relationship but as progress—for the tutee.

Progress is one of the best things that any tutor could wish for a tutee, even though most of the relationship is dedicated to building a dependence based on trust. As you, the tutor, move through the relationship—teaching, supporting, motivating your students—you will be passing on the tools your tutees need to succeed on their own. Ultimately, you would like your tutees to make so much progress that they do not need you anymore. When we are lucky, by the time we say good-bye to tutees, they no longer need our help. Other times, they still need a lot of help, but you should see progress. At the end of a good tutoring relationship, you should find yourself looking at a student with better academic skills, more confidence, more motivation, and more willingness to trust a helper like you. So, by the time you get to good-bye, you should have plenty of moments to remember and plenty of ways to encourage your students to keep moving forward. Tutors, cherish this chance and make your impact while you can, because missing the chance to say the right good-bye can undermine your entire relationship.

Your tutees can handle the truth. The pain and difficulty of saying good-bye are inevitable. When you respect each other and allow yourselves to feel this pain, however, you both grow. It only hurts because you created a relationship, trusted, and impacted one another. It only hurts because you succeeded, together. Good-byes are not unnatural and should not be avoided. Your good-bye is, instead, your last opportunity to share your thoughts, feelings, and encouragement with your tutees—and then let them go to seek their own paths.

RECOMMENDED READING

Robert Coles's *The Call of Service* (1993), a moving tribute to service work of all kinds, is an inspiring and thought-provoking book for anyone embarking on, or already entrenched in, volunteer work. Through the decades-long introspection of volunteers of all stripes, Coles offers many accounts of exciting and innovative tutors, teachers, and mentors that are sure to help tutors improve their work. In talking to volunteers ranging from civil-rights workers in the segregated South to soup-kitchen workers and tutors in Boston, Coles and the people he interviews dare to ask the big questions: Why am I doing this? What does it mean—to me and to them? What are my ideals, and what do they mean? Invoking a wide range of fiction and nonfiction and drawing on the personal stories of many volunteers, Coles captures the emotions, conflicts, and dilemmas of volunteer work. It is a book that anyone hearing the "call to service" should enjoy and learn from.

Twenty-five Final Pointers for Tutors

- Tutees, whether children or adults, are capable people deserving of respect: Treat them as such.
- Listen to what your tutees want to learn, what they care about, and how they learn best. They can teach you how to teach them.
- Don't worry about mistakes—they provide the best opportunities for teaching and learning. Apologize, reteach, and move on.
- Recognize differences between you and your tutee, a vital step to building a tutoring relationship.
- Recognize the commonalties you share with your tutee—they are also a vital part of the tutoring relationship.
- Be supportive of tutees' efforts as well as of their accomplishments.
- Be hopeful. Be optimistic about your students' abilities to improve and your own abilities to teach.
- Make learning active, fun, visual, and hands-on.
- Do not use bribes or gifts to motivate your tutees.
- Be willing to share your experiences when you think it is appropriate.
- Don't make empty promises.
- Show up and be on time: Your tutee depends on you.
- Be open-minded.
- Challenge your students. Most of us need encouragement to work hard enough to reach our potential.
- Challenge yourself. Tutoring will push you in new directions. Don't be afraid to say, to do, or to try something that seems difficult.

- Be empathetic toward your students and their experiences.
- Be observant and pay attention to what your tutees enjoy and how they learn.
- Incorporate tutees' interests into your activities and assignments.
- Be creative.
- Be forgiving of your tutees and of yourself.
- Set educated goals and strive for them.
- Involve the other adults in your students' lives. You will make more progress as a team.
- Don't rely on labels to tell you about your students. All students are more than the labels we assign them. Talk, listen, and observe to learn who your students are.
- Judge slowly, carefully, and generously. You do not know everything about a student, parent, or teacher. Try to understand before you judge.
- Remember that your students have much to teach you.

 **To the Reader**

W E HOPE that you have found this manual useful and that you enjoy your own tutoring relationship. If you are looking for more "fly-on-the-wall" experiences, Brady Matoian (one of the tutors whose field notes informed this book) has prepared a video on the tutoring process. This twelve-minute video is available for $9.95 (including shipping and handling) from Professor J. Rabow, 10350 Santa Monica Boulevard, Suite 310, Los Angeles, CA 90025 (California residents must add sales tax of 8.25 percent, for $10.77 total).

Thank you.

Bibliography

Ashton-Warner, Sylvia. 1963. *Teacher.* New York: Simon and Schuster.

Becker, Howard. 1963. *Outsiders: Studies in the Sociology of Deviance.* New York: Free Press.

Becker, Howard, Blanche Geer, and Everett C. Hughes. 1968. *Making the Grade: The Academic Side of College.* New York: Wiley.

Codell, Esmé Raji. 2001. *Educating Esmé: Diary of a Teacher's First Year.* Chapel Hill, NC: Algonquin Books.

———. 2003. *How to Get Your Child to Love Reading: For Ravenous and Reluctant Readers Alike.* Chapel Hill, NC: Algonquin Books.

Cohn, Peter A., James A. Kulick, and Chen-Lin Kulick. 1982. "Educational Outcomes of Tutoring: A Meta-analysis of Findings." *American Educational Research Journal* 19, no. 2: 237–248.

Coles, Robert. 1993. *The Call of Service.* Boston: Houghton Mifflin.

Conley, Terri D., Joshua L. Rabinowitz, and Jerome Rabow. 2010. "Gordon Gekkos, Frat Boys and Nice Guys: The Content, Dimensions, and Structural Determinants of Multiple Ethnic Minority Groups' Stereotypes about White Men." *Analyses of Social Issues and Public Policy* 10, no. 1: 69–96.

Delpit, Lisa. 1995. *Other People's Children.* New York: New Press.

Dennison, George. 1969. *The Lives of Children.* New York: Random House.

Emerson, Robert M., Rachel I. Fretz, and Linda L. Shaw. 1995. *Writing Ethnographic Field Notes.* Chicago: University of Chicago Press.

Esquith, Rafe. 2007. *Teach Like Your Hair's on Fire: The Methods and Madness inside Room 56.* New York: Viking Penguin.

Freire, Paulo. 1989. *Pedagogy of the Oppressed.* New York: Continuum.

Goodlad, John. 1984. *A Place Called School.* New York: McGraw-Hill.

Green, Ann E. 2001. "But You Aren't White: Racial Perceptions and Service-Learning." *Michigan Journal of Community Service Learning* 8, no. 1: 18–26.

Hayden, Torey. 1980. *One Child*. New York: Avon.

———. 1981. *Somebody Else's Kids*. New York: Avon.

———. 1988. *Just Another Kid*. New York: Avon.

———. 2003. *Beautiful Child*. New York: Avon.

Heath, Shirley Brice. 1982. "Questioning at Home and in School: A Comparative Study." In *Doing the Ethnography of Schooling*, ed. George Spindler, 102–131. Prospect Heights, IL: Waveland.

———. 1983. *Ways with Words*. Cambridge, UK: Cambridge University Press.

Herman, Rebecca, and Sam Stringfield. 1997. *Ten Promising Programs for Educating All Children: Evidence of Impact*. Arlington, VA: Educational Resource Service.

Howard, Gary R. 2006. *We Can't Teach What We Don't Know: White Teachers, Multiracial Schools*. 2nd ed. New York: Teachers' College Press.

Kohl, Herbert. 1967. *36 Children*. New York: Plume.

Kohn, Alfie. 1993. *Punished by Rewards: The Trouble with Gold Stars, Incentive Plans, A's, Praise, and Other Bribes*. Boston: Houghton Mifflin.

Kozol, Jonathan. 1968. *Death at an Early Age: The Destruction of Hearts and Minds of Negro Children in the Boston Public Schools*. New York: Bantam.

———. 1991. *Savage Inequalities: Children in American Schools*. New York: Crown.

———. 2005. *Shame of a Nation: The Restoration of Apartheid Schooling in America*. New York: Three Rivers Press.

Langer, Ellen. 1998. *The Power of Mindful Learning*. Cambridge, MA: Perseus Books.

Lareau, Annette. 1989. *Home Advantage: Social Class and Parental Intervention in Elementary Education*. London, UK: Falmer.

Lewis, Catherine. 1995. *Educating Hearts and Minds: Reflections on Japanese Preschool and Elementary Education*. Cambridge, UK: Cambridge University Press.

Miller, Alice. 1997. *The Drama of the Gifted Child: The Search for the True Self*. New York: Basic Books.

Milman, Noriko, and Jerome Rabow. 2006. "Identifying with the Role of 'Other': 'The Pink Triangle Experiment' Revisited." *Qualitative Sociology Review* 2, no. 2: 61–74.

Natriello, Gary, Edward L. McDill, and Aaron M. Pallas. 1990. *Schooling Disadvantaged Children: Racing against Catastrophe*. New York: Teachers College Press, Columbia University.

Nieto, Sonia. 1996. *Affirming Diversity*. White Plains, NY: Longman.

Obama, Barack. 2006. *The Audacity of Hope: Thoughts on Reclaiming the American Dream*. New York: Crown Publishers.

Paley, Vivian. 1993. *You Can't Say You Can't Play*. Cambridge, MA: Harvard University Press.

Rabow, Jerome, Hee-Jin Choi, and Darcy Purdy. 1998. "The GPA Perspective: Influences, Significance, and Sacrifices of Students." *Youth and Society* 29, no. 4: 451–470.

Rabow, Jerome, and Laura Saunders. 1992. "The Legacy of Jonathan Kozol." *Educational Policy* 6, no. 3: 335–345.

Rabow, Jerome, Jill M. Stein, and Terri D. Conley. 1999. "Teaching Social Justice and Encountering Society: The Pink Triangle Experiment." *Youth and Society* 30, no. 4: 483–514.

Rabow, Jerome, and Pauline Yeghnazar. 2009. "Transformative Teaching in the University: Uncovering and Confronting Racism, Sexism and Homophobia." In *Teaching Race and Ethnicity in Higher Education: Perspectives from North America*. Birmingham, UK: The Center for the Study of Sociology, Anthropology, and Politics—The Higher Education Academy Network, University of Birmingham.

Rist, Ray. 1971. "Student Social Class and Teacher Expectation: The Self-Fulfilling Prophecy in Ghetto Education." In *Challenging the Myths: The Schools, the Blacks, and the Poor,* ed. Susan Stodolsky, 411–451. Reprint series no. 5. Cambridge, MA: Harvard Educational Review.

Robischon, Thomas G., Jerome Rabow, and Janet Schmidt. 1975. *Cracks in the Classroom Wall.* Pacific Palisades, CA: Goodyear.

Roemer, Joan. 1992. "Stars and Bribes Forever." *Parenting* 58 (October): 61.

Rose, Mike. 1995. *Possible Lives.* New York: Houghton Mifflin.

Rosenhan, David L. 1973. "On Being Sane in Insane Places." *Science* 179 (January): 250–258.

Rosenthal, Robert, and Lenore Jacobson. 1968. *Pygmalion in the Classroom: Teacher Expectation and Pupils' Intellectual Development.* New York: Holt, Rinehart and Winston.

Scheff, Thomas J. 1984. *Being Mentally Ill.* Rev. ed. Chicago: Aldine.

Smith, Dorothy. 1978. "K Is Mentally Ill: The Anatomy of a Factual Account." *Sociology* 12 (January): 23–53.

Snow, Catherine E., Wendy S. Barnes, Jean Chandler, Irene F. Goodman, and Lowry Hemphill. 1991. *Unfulfilled Expectation: Home and School Influences on Literacy.* Cambridge, MA: Harvard University Press.

Tatum, Beverly. 2003. *"Why Are All the Black Kids Sitting Together in the Cafeteria?" A Psychologist Explains the Development of Racial Identity.* New York: Basic Books.

Wolfinger, Nicholas H., Jerome Rabow, and Michael D. Newcomb. 1999. "The Different Voices of Helping: Gender Differences in Recounting Dilemmas." *Gender Issues* 17, no. 3: 70–86.

Zemelman, Steven, Harvey Daniels, and Arthur Hyde. 1995. *Best Practices: New Standards for Teaching and Learning in America's Schools.* Portsmouth, NH: Heineman.

TIFFANI CHIN is the Executive Director of EdBoost, a nonprofit that includes a learning center serving K–12 students in Los Angeles. She is the author of *School Sense: How to Help Your Child Succeed in Elementary School,* and she has been tutoring for twenty years.

JEROME RABOW, the recipient of numerous distinguished teaching awards, is Professor Emeritus of Sociology at the University of California, Los Angeles, and a Lecturer at California State University, Northridge. He is the author of *Voices of Pain and Voices of Hope: Students Speak about Racism.* Rabow is the Director and Co-founder of CCODE (Center for the Celebration of Diversity Education).

JEIMEE ESTRADA is a K–12 Education Policy Analyst with the California Legislative Analyst's Office and a Master of Public Policy graduate from the University of Southern California.